Enjoy The
It looks like a good
one —
    Love,
      Glenn, Patti & Cody

The Texas Sheriff

The Texas Sheriff

Lord of the County Line

By Thad Sitton

University of Oklahoma Press : Norman

ALSO BY THAD SITTON

The Loblolly Book (Austin, 1983)

(with G. L. Mehaffy and O. L. Davis, Jr.) *Oral History: A Guide for Teachers (and Others)* (Austin, 1985)

(with Jim Conrad) *Every Sun That Rises: Wyatt Moore of Caddo Lake* (Austin, 1985)

(with Lincoln King) *Loblolly II: Moonshining, Basketmaking, Hog Killing, Catfishing, and Other Affairs of Plain Texas Living* (Austin, 1986)

(with Milam Rowold) *Ringing the Children In: Texas Country Schools* (College Station, Texas, 1987)

Texas High Sheriffs (Austin, 1988)

(with Sarah Sitton) *Austin's Hyde Park: The First Fifty Years, 1891–1941* (Austin, 1991)

Backwoodsmen: Stockmen and Hunters along a Big Thicket River Valley (Norman, 1995)

(with Dan K. Utley) *From Can See to Can't: Texas Cotton Farmers on the Southern Prairies* (Austin, 1997)

(with Jim Conrad) *Nameless Towns: Texas Sawmill Communities, 1880–1942* (Austin, 1998)

Library of Congress Cataloging-in-Publication Data

Sitton, Thad, 1941–
   The Texas sheriff : lord of the county line / by Thad Sitton.
      p.   cm.
   Includes bibliographical references and index.
   ISBN 0–8061–3216–7 (hardcover : alk. paper)
   1. Sheriffs—Texas—History.   I. Title.
HV8145.T4 S57 2000
363.28'2'09764—dc21   99–055159
                                                                CIP

The paper in this book meets the guidelines for permanence and durability of the Committee on Production Guidelines for Book Longevity of the Council on Library Resources, Inc. ∞

1 2 3 4 5 6 7 8 9 10

For my father, Thad "Bubba" Sitton,
1912–1985

CONTENTS

List of Illustrations ix

Preface xi

Introduction: Shire Reeves and Feudists 3

1. Politics, First Terms, and More Politics 20

2. Life in the Jail and Trade Craft 76

3. Whiskey and Blood 138

4. A Friend at the Courthouse 173

Epilogue: Last Days of the High Sheriff 197

Notes 215

Bibliography 235

Index 245

ILLUSTRATIONS

Coleman County sheriff H. F. Fenton examines a murder
    weapon, ca. 1950   17

Long-term sheriff Truman Maddox of Austin County, ca. 1980   18

Sheriff Jess Sweeten of Henderson County, ca. 1932   30

Sheriff Corbett Akins of Panola County and father, ca. 1948   40

Sheriff T. W. "Buckshot" Lane of Wharton County dressed
    like an FBI agent, ca. 1949   72

Sheriff H. F. Fenton of Coleman County and wife, Loretta, ca. 1950   78

Sheriff Frank Brunt and captured drugstore burglars in
    the Cherokee County jail   86

Terrell County sheriff Lee A. Cook and woman accused
    of murder, 1931   106

Confessed ax murderer Ernest Herwig with Sheriff J. S. Carpis   109

A Bexar County deputy questions a witness to a tavern
    homicide, 1938   110

Sheriff Andrew Jackson Spradley with his favorite trailing hound   114

A Bexar County deputy surveys the work of safecrackers, 1935   118

Jasper County officers displaying captured whiskey-making
    equipment, ca. 1920   151

Bexar County sheriff Jim Stevens and shoeshine boy, 1925   177

Kleberg County sheriff J. S. Scarborough III   190

Kleberg County sheriff J. S. Scarborough II   195

Chief Deputy Tom Brown of Caldwell County, ca. 1930   212

PREFACE

For twenty years, I have researched and written histories about the lost world of the Texas countryside during the first decades of the twentieth century. Like unpredictable minor gods, county sheriffs often wandered through my data for these social histories of country schools, Pineywoods stockmen, cotton farmers, and sawmill towns. This piqued my interest in rural sheriffs and resulted in my first book about them, a collection of eleven oral autobiographies of Texas sheriffs published in 1988.

My struggles with devising an adequate introduction for those colorful, complicated, and often very "politically incorrect" accounts spurred me on to additional interviews with sheriffs and to another decade of intermittent research about the practice of rural law enforcement during an era when, as one man told me, "the sheriff was really the sheriff." This social history of the rural sheriff at mid-century is the result.

Perhaps the most basic conclusion of this book is that rural and small-town Texas around 1950 was a strange, often violent, complicated place, where nineteenth-century life-styles persisted, blood ties held, racial apartheid remained rigidly enforced, and sheriffs played the key role in keeping a lid on things. The rural sheriff operated as his county's "Mr. Fixit," its resident "good old boy," and the turf-master of a rural society more complicated than at present—a place where, as an elderly farmer once told me, "fifteen miles down the road was like another land."

"The past is another country," an old saying asserts, and this book describes an obsolete mode of law enforcement practiced by an elected county official in a society very different from that of the present. Inevitably, readers will join the historian in struggling to decide what they think about the rural sheriff. Light and dark, good and bad, political correctness and extreme political incorrectness are closely juxtaposed in this book and in the historical reality the book attempts to describe. The same sheriff who gave farm families several days' notice of foreclosure writs so they could raise money and save their farms also forced "hip-pocket bootleggers" to down life-threatening pints of whisky at gunpoint and harassed sleeping tramps by setting their feet on fire.

Sheriffs possessed a social and political power beyond formal definitions of office, and their actions often seemed larger than life. They often "interpreted" the law in search of a more perfect justice than the law provided. "Taking care of my people" was the goal of most sheriffs, but slippery slopes of illegality stretched away from their exercises of informal power, and—even in their world—they sometimes got into trouble. A few sheriffs slid away into excesses of violence and corruption, while others toiled selflessly for the public good, like dedicated social workers carrying pistols, until they died in office.

To make historical judgments even more difficult, in many strong sheriffs the "light and dark" were functional aspects of the same individual. To do his job, the rural sheriff needed to be Janus-faced, two-sided: well known as a "mean sheriff" to outside outlaws, so they would avoid his county, but still regarded as an approachable "friend at the courthouse" by all law-abiding citizens.

In small-town East Texas when I was growing up back in the 1950s, my sheriff was such a man. At that time the sheriff was still the "high sheriff"—master of the county courthouse, feudal lord of the county territory, manhunter, and keeper of bloodhounds—the person you least wanted to see while on teenage beer-drinking excursions down remote county roads. The western movie-star good looks of my sheriff were nonetheless associated with a nature both combative and controversial. I heard my father talk of the sheriff's latest public confrontations with jail bondsmen, county attorneys, and various "courthouse lawyers." Many voters, including my father, liked our handsome sheriff's style, but others found him too feisty, abrasive, and proud for their tastes. He was a high-visibility, old-style sheriff in a new day of federal judges and civil rights, and he still did things in the old way. He was kind to little children and old ladies but was reputed to be very rough on the criminal element. He kept a friendly old bloodhound around his office for kids to pet, and on occasion to help locate lost children and old people who had wandered away from home, but he kenneled his real pack on the edge of town. A mix of Bluetick and Walker hounds from the "Walls" pack at Huntsville prison, they meant business. Like the sheriff himself, they had a taste for manhunting, and before they got to you, you had better climb a tree. Law enforcement in my county had teeth in it.

The historiography of Texas law enforcement runs strongly to studies of Texas Rangers, though popularly elected sheriffs are to my mind far more variable and interesting. Rangers are appointed officers, professional agents since 1935 of the state's major law enforcement bureaucracy, the Texas Department of Public Safety. Texas Rangers' memoirs and biographies often contained accounts of officers' earlier experiences as deputy sheriffs, and they sometimes proved useful for this study. Much data about sheriffs resides in local newspaper files, and I have sought it out by hook, crook, and random sampling. By the early 1950s a few sheriffs wrote weekly columns for their local papers; some of these proved useful, and the wonderful column of Sheriff T. W. Lane of Wharton County (which grew to a full page in the paper) helped enormously. Future historians of the Texas sheriff are advised to survey all extant newspaper archives, though they will need good health and long lifetimes to accomplish this. The *Sheriffs' Association of Texas Magazine* (later renamed *Texas Lawman*) also proved a fertile source of data for my social history of Texas sheriffs, although entire monthly issues at the Center for American History in Austin still had their pages stuck together from the printer a half-century after publication. The sheriffs' association editor typically stated news stories factually with little comment or elaboration, but he excluded little. If a sheriff ran away with county money or accidentally shot himself in the leg by carelessly sitting down in his office chair, the editor reported the disgrace.

More than anything else, however, this interpretation of the Texas sheriff is based on oral history interviews with Texas sheriffs conducted by myself and by political scientist James Dickson. Sheriffs, even incumbents who had to watch what they said, proved very forthright about the old way of the Texas sheriff, and I learned much of what I know by carefully studying what they told me, what they hinted at, and what they did not say.

In truth, they said a lot. Sheriffs were politicians as well as lawmen, and once the game was over, they dispassionately analyzed their wins and losses. Historian T. Harry Williams wrote in the preface to his Pulitzer Prize–winning biography of Louisiana politician Huey Long:

As I continued with the research, I became increasingly convinced of the validity of oral history. Not only was it a necessary tool in compiling the history of the recent past, but it also provided an unusually intimate look into that past. I found that the politicians were astonishingly frank in detailing their dealings and often completely realistic in viewing themselves. But they had not trusted a record of these dealings to paper, and it would not have occurred to them to transcribe their experiences at a later time. Anybody who heard them would have to conclude that the full and inside story of politics is not in *any* age committed to the documents.

Furthermore, I might add, neither is the "full and inside story" of law enforcement.

THAD SITTON

Austin, Texas

The Texas Sheriff

INTRODUCTION

Shire Reeves and Feudists

An aura of ancient power persisted about the person of the Texas county sheriff, even into recent times, and troubled citizens often felt they needed an audience with the man himself. Cherokee County sheriff Frank Brunt recalled one such occasion during the 1940s: "I had an old lady come in the office one day, said she wanted to see the high sheriff. Deputies wanted to know if they couldn't handle it. Says, 'Naw, y'all too light. I want the high sheriff.'"[1]

Even urban Texans felt this same way. By 1965, Sheriff Bill Decker of Dallas County had a staff of two hundred and over one thousand prisoners in his jail, but every morning people still lined up to see the high sheriff with their problems. Working sixteen-hour days, answering hundreds of telephone calls a shift, Decker held court in his glass-walled office, listening to people's troubles and communicating with his private network of informants.[2] Decker had a squinty eye, believed in some quarters to be a sign of evil, and Deputy Charles Player said, "I'm not entirely convinced he didn't have an evil eye."[3] Decker ran his urban sheriff's office in a one-man, rural-sheriff style, the last big-city sheriff to do so, and he had great power in Dallas County. There was something called a "Decker hold." Once it was noted beside a prisoner's name by High Sheriff Decker, it meant that "no bond, no writ—virtually no power on earth—could open that prisoner's cell door until the hold was lifted."[4]

"High sheriff" was an archaic term of reference to a political office already ancient at the time of the European settling of the New World. The origins of the sheriff go back more than a thousand years to a time of increasing royal power in Saxon England. Seventh-century England was organized first for war, then later for administrative purposes. Ten families residing together in a *tun* (town) comprised a *tithing*. Each tithing chose a *tithingman* to lead them, and ten tithings made up a *hundred*, which came to be led by a *gerefa*, or chief. Over the centuries, the word *gerefa* evolved in the Saxon language into that of *reeve*, although the previous title was retained as well. The gerefa and the reeve became elected officials of the hundred, with both police and judicial powers.[5]

King Alfred the Great (A.D. 871–899) revised and extended this system of local government in order to promote greater centralization of royal power. The existing hundreds were now gathered into *shires*, the direct ancestor of the county. Over each shire was placed a headman called the *shire-reeve*, the principal judicial and administrative official of the shire. He played a multiple role as royal tax collector, law enforcement officer, judge, and the shire's military commander in time of war. This jack-of-all-trades and master of everything in the ancestral county became the *sheriff* (or, to distinguish him from his underlings, the "high sheriff").[6]

The coming of Duke William and the Norman kings to the throne of England after 1066 only served to enhance and extend the powers of the sheriff. Thereafter, the local sheriffs were even more the "king's men," playing a critical role in royal tax collection and the extension of kingly authority into every remote district of medieval England. The jobs paid for themselves for the great noblemen who usually held them. The king sold the offices to the highest bidders, who were free to pocket all tax revenues collected above the king's quotas. Later, the legal reforms of Henry I greatly strengthened the sheriff's police powers by codifying major crimes into a penal code centralizing criminal justice in the king's hands.[7]

As dynasties and centuries passed, the sheriff's role changed and evolved, but he remained the chief administrative and judicial official of the county. Laws reduced the sheriff's function as tax collector, and other local officials took away some of his multipurpose power. His fiscal and judicial powers gradually declined, but the sheriff remained important, the main link between central and local government and the chief law enforcement official of the shire.

With the settling of the North American colonies, the office easily adapted to its New World context. Sheriffs were at first appointed, instead of being elected, and some symbolic and ceremonial trappings dropped away, but people still thought of the office holder as high sheriff, the central figure of county government. When colonial settlers moved west, the sheriff went with them. As in England, the American sheriff could make use of the *posse comitatus*, the "sheriff's posse," the ancient right to enlist the aid of any able-bodied persons in the county, their weapons, boats, and horses, in times of public danger. A constitutional historian wrote of both the English and American sheriff: "He is also to defend his county against any of its enemies, when they come into the land. And for this purpose, as well as keeping the peace or pursuing felons, he may command all the people of his county to attend him, which is called the posse comitatus, or the power of the county."[8]

In colonial Texas, at the time of the Anglo *empresarios*, the ancient office of sheriff met with a not incompatible Spanish equivalent, the *alguacil*, whose duties of patrol, arrest, custody, and execution of executive and judicial writs were very like those of the sheriff. After national independence in 1836, the constitution of the Texas Republic provided for sheriffs in each county, elected for two-year terms. Dave Rusk, San Jacinto veteran and later ferryboat operator, served as the first Texas sheriff, commissioned for office in 1837. Not much is known about the activities of Texas sheriffs under the Republic (1836–45), but they clearly assumed their ancient duties of tax collection as part of the new government's efforts to exert its proper national authority upon an unruly citizenry. Disorderly Harrison County in the "Texas Badlands" had no less than ten sheriffs during the Texas Republic, including one murdered by a mob that then burned his tax book. Later in the nineteenth century, Harrison County sheriffs resumed their proper authority and ran the county for decades at a time. In 1876, despite recent unpleasant experiences with Republican authority, the resurgent Texas Democrats wrote a strong traditional sheriff into their constitution of that year. According to Article 5, Section 23, "There shall be elected by the qualified voters of each county a Sheriff, who shall hold his office for the term of two years, whose duties and prerequisites, and fees of office, shall be prescribed by the Legislature, and vacancies in whose office shall be filled by the Commissioners Court until the next general election."[9]

The nineteenth-century Texas sheriff had much the same formal duties as the American sheriff of a century before and after.[10] As the principal law enforcement official of the county, the sheriff was charged to protect citizens' lives and property, to keep public order, to prevent crime, and to arrest lawbreakers. He also took care of the county courthouse and administered the county jail, which might have behind its bars, at any given time, persons apprehended and waiting trial, persons convicted of state crimes and waiting transfer to the state penitentiary, and persons sentenced to short jail terms by county courts. Beyond these major duties lay another, less well known to the public, perhaps, but equally demanding. The sheriff functioned as executive officer for the district and county courts, serving all their writs, subpoenas, summonses, and processes, in both civil and criminal matters, a job requiring long hours in the saddle every week for sheriff or deputy.[11]

Sometimes when a lone sheriff arrived at someone's home in the remote countryside with his court papers, he found himself up against an individual so formidable that he "could not make his writ run," one of the matters leading to the rapid turnover of Texas sheriffs during the nineteenth century. Dallas County, for example, had fourteen sheriffs in the first twenty-two years after its founding in 1846.[12] Many Texas counties, or parts of counties, were in an unsettled condition into the 1890s, troubled with local traditions of outlawry, vigilante justice, and feudism. In Navarro County about 1850, for example, the sheriff resigned after failing to enforce court writs on a man named William Ladd and some other badmen. The county commissioners persuaded Buck Barry to serve as sheriff, because they knew he had faced Ladd down the year before. On that occasion, Ladd's threat to Barry to "dance over his liver" had provoked a measured counterthreat from the frontiersman and Indian fighter: "I told him in a good-humored tone that if he did, not to have any friends help him dance but that it was all right with me for him [to try] to dance." After that stand-off, Sheriff Barry had no problem with Ladd during his terms as sheriff, though in the primitive circumstances of frontier Navarro County the sheriff had no jail and "had to chain the prisoners like so many pet bears inside a log cabin," had on several occasions to defend his courts from armed men attempting to overawe the juries, and in 1855 suffered the embarrassment of having his courthouse burned, "supposedly by the murderer of one Wells, in order to destroy the indictment."[13] Defending the courthouse was one of the sheriff's primary responsibilities, but many Texas courthouses went the way of Barry's, and for similar reasons.

Outlaw families sometimes troubled and intimidated neighbors and county law enforcement officials during the nineteenth century and afterward. In this, as in so many things, parts of rural Texas remained strangely unchanged for almost a hundred years. For example, about 1890 a rustler family terrorized Chambers County ranchers in an area remote from the county seat, with the distant sheriff powerless to stop them. Besides stealing cattle, this family's ten sons rode through the countryside by night, pistol-whipping any enemies they chanced upon and amusing themselves by shooting into people's homes, trying to hit the kerosene lanterns. Soon, at the first sound of horses after dark, people extinguished their lanterns and took cover on their floors. Texas Rangers banished this family from Chambers County just before their desperate neighbors launched a collective war of extermination.[14] A half-century later, in 1935, another outlaw family so intimidated the Alto community and the Cherokee County sheriff that Alto officials hired a formidable native son, Bill Brunt, as city marshal and then helped elect him sheriff. "This bunch in Alto, people was actually scared to serve on a jury against em," younger brother Frank Brunt explained in 1986, still careful not to mention any names. "They figured if they did and they convicted 'em, they might slip around and burn their barn or their house up, shoot 'em in the dark, or something else. They would jump on people and whup 'em and beat 'em nearly to death right in the middle of town, and nothing done about it."[15]

The Brunt brothers changed all this, although they paid a price. Bill Brunt killed the outlaw family's leader in a shootout, died himself in a night battle with one of the family's bootlegger allies, then was succeeded as sheriff by Frank Brunt, who finished what his brother had begun.[16]

At many places and times between 1840 and 1910, local outlaws became so numerous and brazen that they provoked vigilante responses. Total breakdown in local law enforcement and the courts drove vigilantes to take this drastic action. In such situations, as in Lee County during the 1880s, local law enforcement officials feared to arrest, grand juries to indite, and trial juries to convict.[17] Virtually all murders, even those perpetrated with a shotgun from behind in the presence of witnesses, were ruled self-defense and thus unpunishable killings, and the killers walked free.[18] Despairing of official justice, vigilantes rose in rightful vengeance to lynch and assassinate, and, if things went on long enough, the ferocity of their actions often triggered counterreactions. This happened in Shelby County at the time of the Texas Republic, when the Regulators organized to regulate bands of outlaws, and the Moderators organized to moderate the Regulators. A period of arson, assassination, and lynching gradually moved towards full-scale armed combat, with citizen armies roaming the countryside.

Sam Houston ended the Shelby County War by sending in state troops. Typically, state militia, Texas Rangers, or other outside lawmen were needed to stop local feuds, often after considerable blood having been spilled. Sheriffs, elected officials in communities where political consensus had broken down, usually failed to stop the violence. At feud time, the county sheriff's options became very limited. He could get out of the way of the feudists and let matters take their course, join one side in the conflict, or appeal to the governor to send in help. Even politically neutral sheriffs, elected by both sides as compromise candidates, often became involved in feuds against their will. Feuds had great "social suction," often pulling in would-be neutrals, referees, and peacemakers.[19]

Sometimes frustrated sheriffs covertly or publicly supported vigilante violence as the only way to reestablish control. Sheriff Jim Brown of Lee County made little effort to solve the fourteen or so lynchings of rustlers, highwaymen, and feudists during the late 1870s and early 1880s—even the lynchings of prisoners "mobbed" from his own Giddings jail.[20] Far from decrying the lynchings, a Giddings newspaper editorialized for more of them. "We must have hanging," the editor wrote. "There is no crime in this part of the country that is so exempt from punishment as murder."[21] During the Trinity County disorders following the Civil War, J. F. "Redbone" Moore served as chairman of a "vigilance committee" that quickly hung seven men. Moore remarked about his illegal actions, "The rope is a severe remedy, but the only effective one."[22]

Feuds broke out during (and immediately after) Reconstruction, during the Populist challenge to Democratic political control in the 1890s, and in association with local battles over Prohibition after 1900. Historian C. L. Sonnichsen judged Texas feuds to have been "more numerous and bitter" than the better-known conflicts in nineteenth-century Appalachia and to have numbered in excess of one hundred. Only a few feuds reached the epic proportions of the Regulator-Moderator conflict, but there were scores of others, smaller but just as deadly.[23]

Typically, feuds began with vigilantism—clandestine hangings, burnings, ambushings, and property crimes—and moved toward pitched combats between large groups. Also typically, as the conflicts deepened and spread, they drew in relatives, friends, and sympathizers to each side from many miles around. Bell, Fannin, Grayson, Collin, and Hunt Counties saw major feuds after the Civil War. Typically, returned Confederates feuded with former union sympathizers now empowered by Union occupation forces. Disrespect for official authority under Reconstruction caused outlawry to blossom during the 1870s and early 1880s, and vigilante responses triggered feuds in De Witt, Lampasas, Hood, Bastrop, Lee, Young, and San Saba Counties. The aftermath of Reconstruction, and the sometimes violent reassertion of Democratic political control about 1880 ignited feuds at various places, including the famous Jaybird-Woodpecker War at Richmond, Fort Bend County, in 1889. Attempted takeovers of local politics by the newcomer Populist party and struggles for control of the black vote sparked feuds in San Augustine and Colorado Counties and elsewhere during the 1890s. Bitter local conflicts over Prohibition reached feud proportions at a few places, including Trinity County and Waller County in 1905.[24]

Local vigilantism, long-smouldering family animosities, political conflicts, and economic competitions mixed and merged in complex ways to cause these affairs. Feuds might begin over trivial incidents, but such things only lit the spark. Matters of honor, property, or life itself were always at stake. And once begun, feuds took on their own momentums, making them hard to stop and encouraging the "regulator-moderator" phenomenon in which new factions emerged to oppose older ones. Feud historian Sonnichsen generalized:

> Any code is certainly better than none, popular justice is an improve-ment over no justice, but there is one major objection to the revival of feud law: the fact that all forms of self-redress, but especially hanging and ambushing, are both catching and habit-forming. Vigi-lantes, mobsters, and feudists are all alike in the inability to stop of their own accord. Once men take the law into their own custody, they seem unable to lay it down. Pride or fear keeps them going until they commit "outrageous acts under the excuse of enforcing folk law." Then, another party rises in righteous wrath, and only a higher authority or mutual extermination can stop the proceedings. A feud has no brakes.[25]

Nor were Texas feuds usually conflicts among the illiterate "white trash" of county brush country and backwoods. Sonnichsen noted: "There is a tendency for feuds to move out of the hills or the mesquite pastures and come to town. The final battle is often fought around the courthouse; and before the last shot is fired, doctors, lawyers, and the sheriff—members of old families, and the products of education and culture—are likely to be mixed up in it."[26]

When the feud came to town at Groveton, Trinity County, in 1905, and a Prohibitionist mob of 205 men led by Methodist minister Jesse Lee methodically went door-to-door in the courthouse town—smashing every liquor bottle and barrel, nailing up doors of liquor establishments, and roughing up their proprietors—Sheriff John Stanley chose one of his several unpleasant options and simply stayed out of their way. Stanley ignored the mob just as he had previously ignored the illegal whiskey dives they attacked. Pro-lynching sheriff "Redbone" Moore aside, Trinity County had a tradition of electing inactive sheriffs who often lurked in their homes or offices and looked the other way.[27]

Circumstances had been entirely different when the Democratic "Jaybirds" came to town to cleanse the courthouse of Republican "Woodpeckers" at Richmond, Fort Bend County, on the morning of August 16, 1889. Known as the "King of the Woodpeckers," Sheriff James Garvey chose to defend his courthouse to the death. No votes against succession had been formally recorded in Fort Bend County, and over 90 percent of the adult males had signed up to fight for the Confederate States of America. By 1889, federal troops were long gone, freedmen had been intimidated from further voting, and a Democratic takeover of county government loomed on the horizon. Many Republicans and unionist sympathizers, Anglo and African American alike, discreetly left the county (or were murdered), but county officers led by Sheriff Garvey still held the courthouse. A "quasi-military branch of the local Democratic Party," termed "Jaybirds" by their Republican enemies, the "Woodpeckers," vowed to "clean out the courthouse," but Garvey and other diehard Unionists swore to hold their ground, although they knew they were certain to be voted out of office in the coming election.[28]

State officials recognized the gravity of the situation. Governor Sul Ross visited Richmond to plead for peace with leaders on both sides, and after the governor left, a four-man contingent of Texas Rangers under Ira Aten remained in the town. The Rangers patrolled the Richmond streets for two weeks, but on the morning of August 16 a military line of Democratic Jaybirds slowly marched across the courthouse square toward an advancing line of Republican Woodpeckers, led by Sheriff Garvey. Aten's Rangers got between the combatants to try to stop the battle, but to no avail. Shooting broke out, a Ranger fell in the crossfire, and Sheriff Garvey, the Jaybird leader Frost, and two other men died. A number of combatants were wounded, some severely. Both sides withdrew to lick their wounds, and by daylight the next day Richmond had been placed under martial law by Governor Ross, all local officials relieved of their duties, and Ranger Ira Aten appointed as acting sheriff. Aten did his duty, a friend of nobody in this bitterly divided town, until the end of dead sheriff Garvey's term of office. At that time the Democrats swept all local offices, and Aten gratefully moved far away from the scene of his distasteful experiences in Fort Bend County.[29]

In San Augustine County, just after 1900, a sheriff and a former sheriff died in a bloody feud that also witnessed an armed assault on the courthouse, and the succession of events at San Augustine well exemplified the breakdown of law and order at feud time and the impossible situation of the local sheriff.

Bad blood had existed between the Walls and Border families of San Augustine County from Civil War times. "Buck" Walls and George Border were the patriarchs of large, powerful, politically active landowning families. Each family had intermarried with other important families, and each patriarch had several sons. Potential combat troops abounded, including each family's legion of tenant cotton farmers. George Walls and "Curg" Border, the oldest sons on each side, especially disliked each other.[30]

George Walls and his father and brothers successfully organized a grassroots Populist party to oppose the Democrats in the 1894 election, and with the aid of black votes they swept all San Augustine County offices. George Walls became sheriff as the bitter and disbelieving Democrats brooded and licked their political wounds.

Walls proved an abrasive and domineering sheriff, the Border faction believed, and as time passed relations between Sheriff Walls and the irascible, unstable Curg Border worsened. Border often got drunk and stalked the streets around the courthouse square, making threats, intimidating passers-by, and daring the sheriff to accost him. Finally, Walls accepted the challenge, physically overpowered Border, put him in jail for public drunkenness, and listened to his blood threats upon release the next day. Curg was a big talker, but this time he meant it. Soon thereafter, on April 21, 1900, Border came to town with a shotgun, not his usual weapon, picked an argument with Sheriff Walls, walked away from Walls to get his shoulder weapon from his wagon, then returned to shoot the unsuspecting sheriff from behind.

The usual round of house burnings, shots from the dark, and cattle killings, the normal precursors of feud, had preceded this event, but the real Walls-Border conflict began with George Walls's assassination. Curg Border temporarily left the county seat, while George's younger brother, Eugene Walls, began to patrol the San Augustine streets, daring Curg to come out and fight. Meanwhile, the dead sheriff's chief deputy, his young nephew Noel Roberts, had been appointed acting sheriff by the commissioners court. The Border faction pressured the new sheriff to do something about Eugene Walls's flagrant daily street patrols of San Augustine during the month of May 1900, but Roberts took no action. Caught between the two warring parties, the new sheriff tried to remain neutral, although he knew the Borders believed him to be entirely a Walls man.

Losing patience with waiting for Curg Border to come out and fight, Eugene Walls soon made do with another enemy. He shot Ben Broocks, a Border family ally, from behind, then fled to the Walls family home. Some two hundred armed men, Wallses and Walls inlaws and friends, swiftly rallied to the family compound, while the Border and Broocks families gathered their troops at San Augustine. The Border-Broocks faction forced Sheriff Roberts to visit the Walls encampment to ask for Eugene's surrender, but this was refused. Eugene Walls told Roberts he feared being mobbed and lynched while helpless in jail. Under the right circumstances he would surrender, but he would not be jailed in San Augustine. Walls leaders did, however, authorize Sheriff Roberts to tell the Border-Broocks warriors that Eugene considered himself under house arrest and would not leave the county.

That message was not acceptable to the Border-Broocks faction, who prepared to vent their rage on the sheriff and courthouse as a safer target than the heavily armed Walls encampment in the countryside. Sheriff Roberts now feared for his life. On Sunday, the day after Broocks's killing by Eugene Walls and his unsuccessful visit to the Walls home place, Roberts telegraphed Governor Sayers to ask for Texas Rangers and a company of state militia, and the alarmed governor swiftly wired back that these were on their way.

They arrived too late by about two hours, however. Early on Monday, June 4, 1900, Curg Border and the dead Broocks's brothers returned to San Augustine, and later that morning their troops launched an attack on the courthouse. Only Sheriff Noel Roberts's brother and uncle stood beside him in the courthouse when the Borders and Broockses opened fire from a saloon across the square, and they both quickly died in a hail of bullets. Wounded several times himself, Sheriff Roberts took refuge in a doctor's home long enough for the Texas Rangers and militia to arrive later that day, restore order, and arrest Curg Border and several other men. Eugene Walls now surrendered to authorities. By June 28, 1900, Noel Roberts had recovered enough to come before the San Augustine County Commissioners Court and resign his office; he told them he wanted nothing more to do with law enforcement in their county.

Although the lid had been forced on the pot by Texas Rangers, Texas militia, and a newly appointed temporary sheriff, the feud simmered on, and—as so often was the case in feud time—local courts failed to do their duty. No-billed by grand juries or acquitted by trial juries, everyone went free—Curg Border for the killing of Sheriff George Walls, Eugene Walls for the murder of Ben Broocks, and two riflemen from the courthouse square saloon for the shooting of Sheriff Roberts's relatives. Only blood-feud vengeance ground on, and as time passed, the body count increasingly favored the Border-Broocks faction. Lopez Walls, Eugene's younger brother, then Eugene Walls himself both died in assassinations by party or parties unknown, and most surviving members of the Walls family left the county.

The Border-Broocks faction now dominated San Augustine County, and in 1902, with the help of low Anglo voter turnout and a captive black vote, it elected George Walls's killer, Curg Border, as sheriff. This was too much for many citizens, and a law-and-order faction, previously unaffiliated with either side in the feud, began to come to the fore. Led by a man named W. S. "Sneed" Noble, the law-and-order faction organized to take control of county government. Prohibitionists as well as political reformers, the law-and-order group voted the county dry in 1903, harassed local saloons and gambling joints (which, as usual, had continued operating), and began to shadow Sheriff Curg Border around, watching for the commission of misdemeanors or felonies. Soon indicted for gambling, Border began to spend much of his time on personal business in adjoining Nacogdoches County, neglecting his official duties, and in 1904 the county judge removed Border from office and appointed Sneed Noble in his place.

That set the stage for the last major event in the San Augustine County feud. Curg Border returned to San Augustine, armed himself, got drunk, swaggered about the courthouse square, and made threats on the life of the sheriff, much as he had done before his killing of Sheriff George Walls. This ended when Sneed Noble confronted Border on May 7, 1904, attempted to disarm and arrest him, and then, when Border reached for his pistol, shot him through the head.[31]

The events at San Augustine County between 1900 and 1904 typified the breakdown of social order, law enforcement, and justice at feud time. Legal order was based on social consensus, and when that disappeared, a county's official apparatus of law enforcement—sheriffs, grand juries, and courts—became almost useless. Isolated in the courthouse town, a sheriff and his deputy could do little to stop the rise of arson and assassination in the remote countryside or to dampen the escalating scale of violence as family ties drew more and more persons into the conflict. The more powerful the landowning families involved, the stronger the social suction into the feud, and in this case both sides pulled relatives, poor white cotton tenants, and (as captive voters) sharecropping blacks into their camps, whether they wished to be there or not. After trouble began, pressures mounted on neutrals to align themselves with one side or the other, and the centrist law-and-order faction—an endangered group—shrank accordingly. As in San Augustine County, the office of sheriff often became the captive of one side even before the real battle began. During the San Augustine troubles, a Border-Broocks–faction sheriff succeeded a Walls-faction sheriff, with a hapless neutral trapped in between. And when the assault on the courthouse began on June 4, 1900, only blood ties held, and only Sheriff Noel Roberts's doomed family members stood by his side.

After World War II, young Nathan Tindall returned to San Augustine County, ran for sheriff, and—along with many like him—was elected to office on the votes of other returning veterans. In some ways, not much had changed in San Augustine County since the Robertses made their stand in the courthouse. The automobile had replaced the horse, and electricity, coal oil, but the sheriff and his deputy were still on their own in a diverse, multiracial county—keeping order, enforcing the law, running the jail, and serving the local courts. Sometimes, during spring "mudtime," delivering court papers or answering a trouble call in the remote countryside, even the horse came back into use. When Sheriff Tindall told a fighter to stop fighting or a drunk to come with him to jail, or repossessed a man's pickup, it was still a one-on-one situation, with no backup, as it had been in Buck Barry's day, a century before. The deputy had business elsewhere, and there was no radio with which to call for help. In 1950, the lone officer still had to face up to the "William Ladds" of his time and place and to "make his writ run." Nor were the feud events of the turn of the century (or those of the local whiskey wars of the 1930s) really forgotten; history haunted the present and blood relationships mattered. Descendants of the old feud families still occupied social and economic high ground in San Augustine County, some of them still not attending the same churches, socializing with each other, or supporting the same candidate in the sheriff's race.[32]

History haunted the present in every Texas county in 1950, and new officers needed to recall the past as a practical matter, part of that intricate knowledge of place and circumstance that was local officers' greatest law enforcement resource. Other resources might be scarce to nonexistent. Many a new sheriff came down to inspect his office on January 1 and found very little with which to do his job: jumbled records, a couple of Winchester .30-30 carbines, a few pairs of handcuffs, a telephone, and not much else. At Lockhart, Caldwell County, in 1956, new sheriff Desmond Reed found he didn't even have pots and pans for the jail kitchen and would have to furnish them himself.[33]

At San Saba, San Saba County, in 1950, fledgling sheriff Brantley Barker inherited a politically unfireable seventy-two-year-old deputy (inherited in turn from the sheriff before Barker's predecessor), two old cars that he ran until they dropped, and two "girls" who worked as clerks in the tax office. (Like many rural sheriffs, Barker also wore the hat of county tax assessor-collector.) The cars had no radios, and when a call for the sheriff came in to the San Saba operator at a time when Barker was out of the office, she turned on a red light at the top of a downtown building to alert him to call in.[34] At Lockhart in Caldwell County, Sealy in Austin County, and various other places, a "police alarm" outside of jail or courthouse began a thunderous ring to accomplish the same thing.

Young war-hero sheriff H. F. Fenton entered the Coleman County Sheriff's Office in January 1947. Fenton hired one deputy, another young man who had fought beside him in the bloody Italian campaign,

> and we had the whole shebang, the whole county. I moved my deputy into the jail, we didn't have a jailer, and we didn't have nothing but two old wore-out automobiles. We didn't have no two-way radios. They didn't have no police department here in Coleman, only a night watchman and a chief. We had to take calls from every-thing—city, county, everywhere. That was a different ball game back then, you'd take off in a car and wouldn't know what was happening anywhere, cause you didn't have a radio. Lots of times my deputy would take the south part of the county and I'd take the north part,

we'd split it down through the middle. We'd just take off and patrol here, there, and yonder. We'd check in by telephone every once and awhile with each other. If we needed any help, we'd have to get to a telephone.[35]

In other rural counties about 1950, new sheriffs and deputies split their counties into north and south or east and west and set out to enforce the law. Marcus Steck of Austin County defeated the incumbent sheriff in 1948, then hired young veteran Truman Maddox from Sealy as his only full-time deputy. Maddox had returned from the service, opened a meat market and barbecue in Sealy, and quickly made friends in southern Austin County. Prominent local citizens approached Maddox on the sheriff's behalf with an offer of a deputy's position, and after some doubts (Maddox had no law enforcement experience), he agreed to serve, though he continued to run his barbecue place in downtown Sealy. Sheriff Steck stayed at Bellville, the county seat, at the north end of Austin County. Maddox explained:

It was kind of thought of as "the law south of Mill Creek" and "the law north of Mill Creek." We didn't see each other but maybe every two weeks. We didn't have no radio and couldn't even call much, cause it cost ten or fifteen cents to call from Sealy to Bellville, and that ran into money and the commissioners didn't like that. The commissioners didn't allow us to do any patrolling, either. We furnished our own cars and was paid so much for mileage, up to $25 a month. When that $25 was up, the rest was on you. I stayed there except on court days, and Marcus would usually stay up here [Bellville].[36]

At Sealy, as in San Augustine and everywhere else, feud memories still festered across the generations, and county law officers could not afford to forget about such things as the old "feud family" relationship between Austin County's Wards and Hibbolts. Maddox recalled: "Just a few months after I went in as deputy, I was back at the barbecue pit when I heard a gunshot. Then I heard another one. I ran to the front and looked, and laying in the front door of my market was this gentleman, Dallas Hibbolt. He lay face down, with the screen door open, blood running off his back. He says, 'Forrest Ward shot me, go get him!'"[37]

Twenty seconds after leaving his barbecue pit, ripping off his apron, and stepping outside, young Deputy Sheriff Maddox found himself in a high-

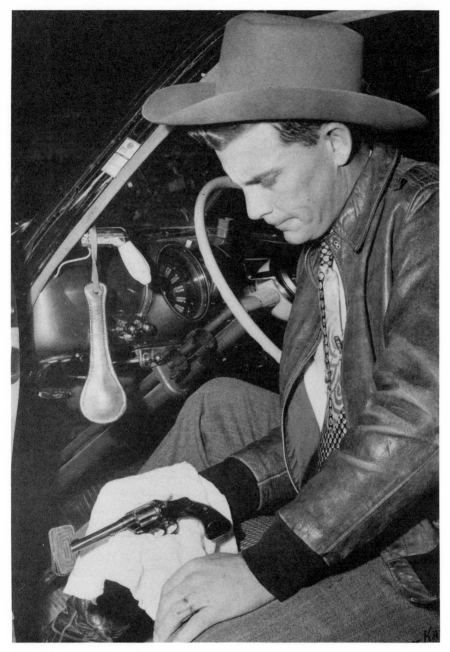

Coleman County sheriff H. F. Fenton examines a murder weapon, about 1950. The object hanging from the spotlight control is a lead shot–filled bag called a "slapper." (H. F. Fenton famiy, Coleman, Texas)

Long-term sheriff Truman Maddox of Austin County during his last years in office, early 1980s. (Author's collection)

noon pistol battle down the crowded Sealy street. Sealy citizens ran for cover, while Ward and Maddox leapfrogged along a line of parked cars, firing through the car windows at each other. Finally, his eyes full of bullet-shattered glass, Forrest Ward gave up, and Maddox faced his next problems. Forrest Ward's dangerous father was also on the scene, and did he have a pistol under his customary long black coat? And how could Maddox get Forrest Ward safely out of town before Hibbolt's game warden brother drove up to exact blood revenge? Maddox had no proper jail in Sealy, only a small, one-room, wooden "hoosegow" with an open window convenient for executing any prisoner inside.

Maddox quickly proved himself potential high-sheriff material to a milling crowd of Austin County citizens (though they may not have been much impressed with his pistol marksmanship). Maddox faced down old man Ward, commandeered a private car to take Ward's handcuffed son to the Bellville jail, then began a long process of cooling down Hibbolt's brother, who had roared up, tires squealing, lusting for vengeance. One year later, Austin County voters elected Truman Maddox sheriff.[38]

CHAPTER ONE

POLITICS, FIRST TERMS, AND MORE POLITICS

Young Truman Maddox had anticipated long years of faithful service to Sheriff Marcus Steck as his chief deputy and the "law south of Mill Creek," but that was not to be. Steck quickly discovered that he did not enjoy being sheriff. Phone calls from Austin County citizens demanding service came in to Sheriff Steck's Bellville office at all hours of the day and night, the responsibilities of the job proved worrisome, and Steck had done something no sheriff could afford to do: he had lost a fistfight. As Maddox tactfully explained: "Marcus had one little occasion at a dance hall one night where three guys jumped on him and overpowered him, didn't hurt him, but they shook him up quite a bit. That kind of discouraged him. And he just didn't like the responsibility, he got nervous about it."[1]

By the midpoint of Marcus Steck's first two-year term, he knew he did not wish to run again, so he encouraged his young chief deputy to make the race for Austin County sheriff. While Steck's reputation had been going downhill after losing the fight with three big German farmers, Maddox's had been moving in the opposite direction. His high-noon gun battle with Forrest Ward had gotten everyone's attention, and the local papers subsequently carried a series of stories about Maddox's spectacular one-hundred-miles-per-hour car chases after drunks and outlaws in his high-powered 1949 Oldsmobile 88. Maddox was not a native son—a mark against him—but he had married an Austin County girl and had made himself known to everyone in the south part of the county by operation of his popular meat market and barbecue restaurant in Sealy. He looked like sheriff material to most county residents.

Truman Maddox found himself with limited options: to run for sheriff or to retire from law enforcement. Marcus Steck's successor would be very unlikely to retain the popular Maddox as his chief deputy. Every sheriff knew that this term's chief deputy often turned into next term's electoral opponent. Backed by Steck and his former supporters, Truman Maddox announced for the sheriff's race and began to make the customary political rounds, visiting the various "kingpins" in the scattered farming communities of this mixed-race, multilingual, German, Anglo, Czech, and African American county. Then he set out to meet every Austin county voter, shake his hand, and ask for his vote. Maddox explained:

> Campaigning then was much different than what it is now. At that particular time, one man could command a lot of votes. Most all communities would have a kingpin in them. You mostly went out to them, and if they gave you encouragement you were in pretty good shape. You still needed to go around and meet all these people, all that stuff. If the man in a community was for you, you kind of did like he said to do as far as meeting the public. We made all the dance halls, we made all the public gatherings, and Austin County has been known for good-time goers, always. It had eighteen country dance halls, and all eighteen tried to have one dance a month. Think how many you got! One Saturday night before the election, I went all over handing out cards and buying beer. That night, a lot of my friends were in the old Club Rendezvous, a cafe and little dancing place in Sealy, and I come in there about one o'clock. I told em, "I believe I just finished my campaign, I've just made five dance halls and one colored rodeo."[2]

Although it might have been politically unwise to have admitted this, some men running for sheriff about 1950 had been waiting to do it all of their lives. Such ambitions were not supposed to be the norm. As did Truman Maddox, sheriff candidates commonly presented themselves as reluctant recruits to the nasty political fray—good citizens going about their respective businesses until the fateful days that other good citizens persuaded them to save their counties from incompetents and outlaws. Sometimes this image of "Cincinnatus," peaceful Roman farmer recruited from behind his oxen and plow to save the Republic, was the literal truth, but often it was not. "Big Ed" Darnell admitted that he had yearned to become sheriff since childhood days, when his grandfather, a one-armed Civil War veteran, took him into Canton, Van Zandt County, on horse-trading weekends. Grandfather and grandson commonly spent the night in the wagon yard, then on "First Monday" trade day the elder Darnell swapped horses and mules while seven-year-old Ed accompanied his grandfather's friend, the sheriff, on horse- and-buggy excursions serving court papers. Something about that experience set the boy's course in life. Ed Darnell's grandfather knew his grandson planned to run for sheriff someday, but he made him swear that he would wait until age thirty-five to do so, since "no man has any sense till age thirty-five and damn few afterward," and Darnell did as he had promised.[3]

At Angelina County, Leon Jones's father, Enoch, at first objected to his son's ambitions regarding the office of sheriff, first expressed at age four-teen in 1924, the year that Enoch Jones himself ran for sheriff and narrowly lost. Leon greatly respected his game warden father, and as an older teenager he had often driven his father's car on back-country patrols "so he could have both hands free." More than one man had sworn to take revenge on Enoch Jones, one of the combative first generation of East Texas game wardens, so a person to drive the car and a person to watch out for assassins and handle the weapons made good sense. Enoch Jones gave his son mixed messages about getting into politics and law enforcement. Never go after a man to arrest him unless you are certain you are legally right, but then "arrest him or die," the elder Jones advised. It would be best if Leon stayed out of politics in later life, Enoch thought, but if he insisted on planning to run for office, he should "start speaking to people right now—some of 'em will be here to vote when you get old enough to run, and they'll remember that kid that used to speak to 'em." Leon Jones heeded his father's advice and found that he had told the truth, though Jones waited to run for office until 1950, after a law enforcement career with the Texas Liquor Control Board, Sanitary Livestock Commission, and Parks and Wildlife Department.[4]

Although only a few individuals admitted to being obsessed with becoming sheriff from childhood years, the office had a mystique and a power that—should the time seem ripe and the incumbent vulnerable—attracted many candidates. Some counties had two-term or three-term traditions of office holding, and, at the end of these customary lengths of service, chief deputies, former sheriffs, and rank newcomers tended to challenge incumbents. Traditions of term length aside, over several years in office sheriffs of average political abilities gradually eroded their political bases by arresting voters, rubbing people the wrong way, and just trying to do their jobs. Two or three terms in, many sheriffs became politically vulnerable. Every drunk jailed, every traffic ticket or civil citation issued, potentially cost the sheriff a vote, and arresting the clan patriarch on a minor bootlegging charge might lose a man all of a large family's votes. Sometimes the incumbent had a clear view of the coming electoral disaster, but often he did not. At such times chief deputies tended to resign and run against their former bosses in self-defense, and perennial sheriff candidates lined up to try again. In Coleman County, war hero H. F. Fenton served as sheriff for several terms, lost an election, worked as Special Texas Ranger for the Texas Sheep and Goat Raisers' Association for some years, then returned to Coleman County to serve the incumbent sheriff as chief deputy. Former sheriff Fenton did not mind working as another man's chief deputy (or so he said), but as public discontent with the sheriff's office grew and as the incumbent readied himself for one campaign too many, Fenton resigned, ran against him, and won "in self defense."[5]

Occasionally, incumbents saw the writing on the wall and recruited their chief deputies to run as designated successors. This was something of the tradition in Jasper County and other places, as former sheriff Aubrey Cole affirmed.[6] Sometimes, however, as filing deadlines neared, the long-term sheriffs found they could not bear to step down and entered the races one last time, whatever their electoral chances. Sheriff L. R. Johnson of Brazoria County had recruited young Jack Marshall to be his deputy in 1938, despite the fact that all Marshall had done before that time was "run wild cattle and build fence" and that he "didn't know the difference between a warrant and a citation."[7] Eight years later, Sheriff Johnson faced electoral defeat, recognized this, and told Marshall, "I want you to have this sheriff's office." However, as Marshall recalled, "Lo and behold, when the time came, that old stinker filed. That made me so confounded mad, I said, 'I'm going to soak my shoes and run against him.'" Sheriff Johnson's political star had not fallen as far as he had feared, but his young chief deputy still defeated him by 240 votes in the 1946 election. Admitting defeat, but not his attempted political double-cross, Johnson remarked, "Mmmm, that boy must have stomped down lots of briar patches out there."[8] Eighteen years later, the situation essentially repeated itself between Sheriff Jack Marshall and his chief patrol deputy, Bob Gladney.[9]

Sometimes state or national events placed many incumbent sheriffs in jeopardy all at once and drew many challengers to the fray. Just before 1900, with the aid of the black vote, grassroots Populist candidates challenged Democratic sheriffs all across Texas, and a good many of them won. During the middle 1920s, at the time of Governor "Ma" Ferguson's war on the Ku Klux Klan, anti-Klan candidates opposed incumbents tarred with the brush of Klan affiliation or political support. During the election of 1940, with war clouds on the horizon, incumbent sheriffs with foreign surnames came under political fire. At Wharton County, hyperactive constable T. W. "Buckshot" Lane had a long-standing deal with the incumbent sheriff allowing Lane to collect most of the fees for law enforcement duties in the county seat of Wharton—this to keep the popular Lane from running against the sheriff, Lane claimed. However, as Lane explained:

> Finally, I did run, I knew he was gonna get beat. His deputy was a drunk and had turned his car over several times. The sheriff was a German and the war was coming on, too, and the people was against Germany as a rule. We'd have county meetings, and he'd say, "What you gonna talk about tonight?" I'd say, "I ain't gonna say much." He'd say, "If you don't say nothing, I wouldn't either."
>
> He was a nice old fellow, he and I were friends all the way through. But I knew he was gonna get beat and I think he knew it too.[10]

No twentieth-century event so impacted the office of sheriff as did the return of veterans and war industry workers after World War II. Especially during the elections of 1946 and 1948, veterans voted as a bloc to place one of their own in sheriffs' offices throughout rural Texas. During the peak turnover year of 1946, 110 of 254 incumbents retired or were defeated, almost always by returning veterans.

H. F. Fenton's experience typified those of many of the new war-veteran sheriffs. A much-decorated combat veteran of the 36th Infantry Division, Fenton returned to Texas, took a job on the Pampa police force, then—responding to many public requests (or so he said)—returned to Coleman County to run for sheriff in 1946. After receiving the blessing of a powerful county judge, the boyish-looking, twenty-three-year-old Fenton stumped the county handing out cards and asking for votes. Here, as elsewhere, the opposition argued that the war-hero candidate would be too young, unstable, and accustomed to blood and violence to make a good sheriff, but veterans voted for Fenton, and he was elected.[11] At nearby Comanche County, fellow army veteran Gaston Boykin returned to the farming life, tried plowing behind a horse for a time to soothe his war-jangled nerves, swiftly became bored, and ran for sheriff. Veterans supported candidate Boykin as they did Fenton, but with occasionally bad effects. During one rural community's graveyard cleaning, a standard Comanche County political event, five veteran brothers with bad local reputations followed the veteran candidate wherever he went. "Where I hoed in the cemetery, they hoed too," Boykin said. "I couldn't get away from them to visit anyone else, and I lost the box. I only lost two boxes in the county, and that was one of them. The sheriff had to keep clean company, you know."[12]

Although world events occasionally impacted sheriffs' races across Texas, purely local issues dominated most campaigns. Many challengers for the office of sheriff cast themselves in the role of reform candidates, although the reform issues might be nothing more than achieving greater frugality in department operations, improving cooperation with the county commissioners court, or getting the rats out of the jail. More significant reform issues often lurked unstated just below the surface of candidates' public rhetoric but were well understood by most voters, who in rural counties usually knew their would-be sheriffs very well. Improved social control of "dangerous" minorities or a stricter interpretation of state laws and local customs regarding the consumption of alcohol often were advanced as reform issues, though the sheriff candidates might not elaborate on these things during their brief speeches at rural "school closings" and graveyard cleanings.

Fairly often the underlying reform issue was the incumbent's personality and the growing public perception that he had become too prideful and overbearing to continue as the voter's friend at the courthouse. In Angelina County in 1950, Sheriff J. D. "Red" Conditt was Worshipful Master at the Masonic Lodge, the approved candidate of organized labor, and a two-term incumbent. Conditt felt so confident about his political situation that he went out of his way to goad game warden Leon Jones into running for sheriff several years before Jones had planned, remarking to one of Jones's businessman supporters, "What happened to your little game warden, did his guts go down on him?" Stung into action by this insult, Jones retired from enforcing the unpopular game laws and launched his campaign, subtly trying to out-humble the too-cocky Sheriff Conditt in order to impress the voters. Jones explained: "In any kind of public office you're running for, you couldn't have any hairs on you at all, you had to be just humble and down to earth. And especially sheriff, because they looked to him to be just a little cocky anyhow." Humble, down to earth, and smiling, Leon Jones went everywhere in the county asking each voter for his or her vote in the approved manner; "I knew how to smile," he said. When Leon Jones and Red Conditt attended political pie suppers, Leon distanced himself from the incumbent by circulating through the crowd shaking everyone's hand while Conditt "backed up to a car and expected everybody to come to him," exposing his fatal flaw of pride to the sensitive voters. Jones beat Conditt by five hundred votes in 1950 and by several thousand in 1952, and after that, Conditt never ran again.[13] Several years as high sheriff raised a man's self-esteem, but he had better hide this from the public.

Another often unstated reform issue involved the place of origin of the sheriff candidate. In many counties, voters in the county seat dominated election after election, usually electing a native son to the most important county-wide office and leaving rival communities and rural hinterlands feeling underrepresented. Bastrop County, for example, normally elected sheriffs from Bastrop, so when Red Rock native I. R. "Nig" Hoskins began to run for sheriff in 1948, it took him three campaigns to get elected, and during a forty-year, in-and-out-of-office career, the Bastrop town vote ousted Hoskins from office on four occasions. Hoskins usually carried the southern part of the county, away from the county seat; Bastrop's rival town of Smithville; smaller outlying communities, such as Red Rock; and the countryside, but county seat voters often cast ballots for one of their own. Nig Hoskins tried to combat the Bastrop vote by zealously building political support everywhere else. He gave half of his small sheriff's salary back to rural volunteer fire departments and frequented the small-community fund-raiser circuit, once bidding $750 for a McDade FFA watermelon and $2,000 for a Smithville FFA chicken.[14]

In Jasper County about 1970, sheriff candidate Aubrey Cole faced the same problems. Jasper so dominated sheriffs' elections that the "south-county" communities of Buna, Evadale, and Kirbyville had not placed a native son in the sheriff's office during the twentieth century. Running as the "south-county candidate" while campaigning in the south of the county and choosing other needed reforms to talk about when campaigning at Jasper, Cole and his supporters stumped the county door-to-door.

On election day, zealous south-county voters turned out in droves while many Jasper citizens went fishing or stayed home, anticipating yet another country boy's certain defeat. Aubrey Cole beat the incumbent by twenty-five votes, then so ingratiated himself with the Jasper voters that he remained in office until retirement.[15]

Such sheriffs as Aubrey Cole and Nig Hoskins typified the normal, peaceful, and relatively noncontentious counties of rural Texas. At various other places and times, from the 1870s to the 1950s, oil booms, nearby military bases, and local traditions of outlaw behavior so dominated county economic and political life that either true reform sheriffs came to the fore or the governor sent in Texas Rangers. The reform candidate vowing to "clean up the county" or die in the attempt was a timeless political story, whether at Lee County in the 1880s or Galveston County in the 1950s.

In outlaw-ridden Lee County in the 1880s and again during the 1890s, as at other places and times, county voters elected violent sheriffs to fight fire with fire. In Sheriff Jim Brown's case, Lee County voters perhaps got more than they bargained for. Brown killed some stock thieves and highwaymen in the line of duty (and perhaps assisted in the illegal lynchings of others), but he also murdered several local men for purely personal reasons and so intimidated citizens that they dared not defeat him for sheriff for four terms. A shotgun attack by an assassin took Brown out of action only for a time, and after he left Lee County for Fort Worth and Chicago, he continued his violent ways. Shot to death by Chicago municipal police during the 1890s, he took two of "Chicago's finest" with him to the grave.[16]

A few years after Jim Brown, Lee County still had its outlaws, especially the dreaded Yegua Knobbs Gang, and voters elected another shootist sheriff, Jim Scarborough I, to fight fire with fire. Scarborough killed several men in the line of duty, though he proved far more discriminating in this regard than the irascible Brown. A showboat sheriff who backed it up, Scarborough once pursued an outlaw on the train all the way to Chicago, shot him to death in a gunfight at the railroad station, then posed for the big-city photographers with gun drawn. On another occasion, this time in Houston, he had himself photographed beside the bullet-punctured corpse of his most recent would-be assassin.[17]

Voters elected Brown and Scarborough partly because of their reputations for effective violence at a place and time that seemed to call for such a man. Sometimes county seat towns hired special city marshals to do what the sheriffs could not, or would not, do; shootists themselves, they intimidated other shootists. Ben Thompson, who had no less than fifteen homicide warrants brought against him during his lifetime, served as city marshal of Austin for several years during the 1880s—presumably because the sheriff could not stand up to the local badmen.[18] In 1908 a law-and-order faction on the Navasota city council hired twenty-four-year-old Frank Hamer, a former Texas Ranger, as city marshal to help control the traditionally "wide open" county-seat town. Rudely informed on his day of arrival that he should concentrate his law enforcement efforts on "niggers and outsiders" and leave leading white citizens alone, since "we don't allow our kind to be arrested," Hamer ignored the threats, subdued challengers by a unique combat style of slaps and kicks ("My feet were always loaded," he said later), threw people into city jail, and proceeded to run bootleggers, gamblers, and whores out of Navasota. He also had the audacity to protect African Americans from gratuitous assaults while on legitimate business at the county seat—something especially offensive to racist whites, who regarded such harassment as traditional recreation.[19] After a few momentous months spent taming wicked Navasota, Frank Hamer returned to service with the Texas Rangers.

In the out-of-control community, whatever the time or place, it was the Buck Barry–William Ladd confrontation once again, and someone had to be found who could protect citizens and enforce court orders. Hired to fight fire with fire and intimidate local badmen, Constable Jess Sweeten of the oil-boom town of Trinidad, Henderson County, and City Marshal Bill Brunt of Alto, Cherokee County, went on to serve their counties as sheriffs. In 1929, city officials at oil-boom Trinidad observed a confrontation between Jess Sweeten and local toughs and thought Sweeten might be able to stand up to them as constable. Still in his early twenties, at six feet five and 230 pounds, Sweeten proved to be everything the city fathers hoped. Nobody successfully opposed him in customary "stomp and gouge," no-holds-barred, hand-to-hand combat. Sweeten explained: "It was a knock-down-and-drag-out. The ordinary person just couldn't have competed with them, because he just wasn't man enough physically. They didn't want to kill you, they just wanted to beat you to death, they just wanted to whip the officers."

Challenged by a drunk, the previous constable had failed to subdue the man even by using his pistol as a club. Sweeten described: "Directly, the constable rapped him up aside the head with the pistol and blood was flying. Then the old boy said, 'Now, hit me right there!' He whammed down on him again. 'Now, hit me over here!' Well, he hit him again but he still didn't go down, and that old constable just walked over and resigned. He couldn't even bring him down with his pistol."[20] Sweeten, however, had no such trouble felling Trinidad's drunken and combative oil workers, and he rarely used his pistol.

Having established an awesome reputation, Sweeten extended his reform efforts county-wide, winning the 1932 election for Henderson County sheriff. Sometimes, however, at other places, things had become so bad that no reform candidate for sheriff dared to make the race, and pro-outlaw voters elected one do-nothing or look-the-other-way sheriff after another. Often for rational economic reasons, a majority of voters some-times preferred their counties to remain "open" for illegal booze, gambling, and prostitution, and they tended to elect inactive or corrupt sheriffs to help perpetuate the prosperous status quo.[21] Even the Texas Rangers often failed to reform such places. Just after 1900, Ranger captain Bill McDonald tried and failed to intimidate the whiskey outlaws and gamblers of Groveton and Trinity County, and the local sheriff was part of the problem. After withdrawing his Rangers from Groveton, McDonald wrote in his formal report that he had found Trinity County entirely hopeless as a field of reform: "If a whole community has no use for law and order, it's not worth while to try to enforce such things. You've got to stand over a place like that with a gun to make it behave, and when you catch a man, no matter what the evidence against him, they'll turn him loose. In Groveton, for instance, when I was there they had only two law respecting officers—the district court and the county attorney, and the county attorney they killed. Good citizens were so completely in the minority that they were helpless."[22]

Not much had changed at Trinity County by 1928, when a new contin-gent of Texas Rangers moved in to renew warfare with local whiskey outlaws, this time during national prohibition. Young Ranger Carl Busch described: "Those were the bootleg days, and it was a terribly bad bootleg-whiskey-making county. Everybody was related from river to river—first, second, or third cousins. They had thirteen speakeasies in the city of Trinity that were all paying off the deputy sheriff, and he was first cousin to the sheriff! But that was the 'Free State of Trinity' at that time."[23] In 1936, having married a local girl and retired from the Rangers, Busch took office as Trinity County's first twentieth-century reform sheriff, but he lasted

Sheriff Jess Sweeten of Henderson County during his first term in office, 1932–34.
(Author's collection)

only one harrowing two-year term and failed to reform much of anything. National prohibition had ended, and the county had gone wet, the better to make money as "the only wet county, legally wet, anywhere in East Texas, between Beaumont and Dallas or between Shreveport and Houston. So many of the crooks in the state come in there to take advantage and set up honky tonk joints and get rich overnight. I had all that to contend with, and I enforced the law as best I could."[24]

Busch regarded his unsuccessful 1938 reelection campaign for sheriff as "a blessing in disguise, cause they would have killed me a little later, anyway," and perhaps he was correct.[25] Certainly, at least one person already had tried to kill him. As often was the case at such places, Busch's opposition had included not just carpetbagger outlaws, down from the big cities to make a quick profit, but some of the oldest, wealthiest, and most politically influential families in the county. After a locale had been "wide open" for illegal alcohol and gambling for a few years, professional outlaws became entrenched, law enforcement became intimidated or corrupt, and many legitimate businessmen were drawn into the illicit economy. Grocery store owners became accustomed to their huge sugar sales to moonshiners and café operators to their profits from slot machines in back rooms. Local entrepreneurs often moved behind the scenes to sponsor bootleggers, whiskey makers, gamblers, and prostitutes. Vice was, as always, very good business.

In such a situation, a would-be reform candidate, however well supported he might be from the "dry" side of the community, took certain risks. Too much was at stake for too many people attached to the status quo. In 1912, at Grayson County, after the demand for reform of county-wide bootlegging and gambling "became almost an uprising," Lee Simmons ran as reform candidate and defeated the incumbent sheriff—an almost unheard-of feat, since Grayson County sheriffs customarily received at least two terms in office. As Simmons waited to assume office, "open violation of the law" continued, and one Saturday someone called him to the front door of his home after dark and shot him three times "through-and-through" as he began to push open the screen. Simmons recovered to apprehend his attempted assassins, but not the people involved with the "old regime" he believed had hired them.[26]

In 1956, sheriff candidate Paul Hopkins took on formidable twelve-term incumbent Frank L. Biaggne in an avowed attempt to reform the "Free State of Galveston County." Hopkins told reporters that he had "plans to bring the law to Galveston," where "there hadn't been adequate law enforcement in a hundred years." Hopkins won, although he endured numerous death threats during the campaign and learned to look his car over very closely each morning before attempting to drive to work. One day during the campaign, Hopkins discovered that someone had loosened all the lug nuts on one wheel. Potentially, his problems were more explosive than lug nuts. Hopkins's neighbors watched apprehensively to see when the candidate emerged every morning to start his car, then discreetly moved to the far side of their houses. "My neighbors are always worrying about my car blowing up," Hopkins told a reporter, "so I check it every day."[27]

Flagrant local violations of national prohibition during the 1920s and early 1930s, and lax wartime enforcement of liquor and vice laws around military bases during the 1940s, launched waves of would-be reform sheriffs into local cleanup campaigns. Certain rural Texas counties with plentiful water sources, ready market access to big cities, and good hiding places for stills became centers for illegal liquor production during Prohibition. Harrison, Trinity, Somervell, and Freestone Counties, as well as some others, fell into this category. At Somervell County, in particular, the limestone spring water was of high quality, the landscapes were wooded and remote, and the local officials were in collusion with the whiskey outlaws, at least according to Ranger Captain William W. Sterling. At one point the state senator for Somervell County (county seat, Glen Rose) asked Sterling to remove the local Ranger before irate locals had him assassinated for conduct bad for business. Instead, Sterling sent in other Ranger investigators, who discovered a situation in which moonshiners, merchants, and local officials all worked in harmony, with large loads of illegal whisky regularly rolling out to Dallas, Fort Worth, and San Antonio.[28] Even the sheriff at Glen Rose had joined the whiskey manufacturers, as neighboring Sheriff Gaston Boykin of Comanche County explained: "It was pretty well open over there and the sheriff was making it, too. I knew the old sheriff pretty well. He went to the pen. He sold a bunch of his moonshine on credit, and the fellow didn't pay him, so he went over and got enough of his cows to sell to make up for it, and they got him for stealing cattle. He served his hitch and come back and was elected again as sheriff."[29]

At Freestone County in 1930, law-and-order voters from the agricultural western half of the county narrowly elected J. R. Sessions as reform sheriff to clean up the wooded, hilly, and moonshine-ridden eastern half of the county, where Sessions had few supporters. According to Sessions's son, moonshining had been the "most prevalent occupation in the county" since the Mexia oil boom of the early 1920s. By 1930, the local oil booms had busted, and the Great Depression had arrived to blight the cotton-raising western part of the county, but whiskey production did not slacken. Big money from Houston and Dallas backed the local whiskey business, in which small-scale moonshiners combined their products under the direction of local middlemen, and a few large-scale operations reached the size of small sawmills. As at Somervell County at about the same time, daily trucks filled with illegal whiskey rolled out bound for Dallas and Houston— so many that a major hijacking trade developed, with outlaws stealing from outlaws. A man named Roger Young even labeled his product "Roger's Red" and shipped it out by the railroad boxcar load to Dallas and Chicago.

Voters elected the intrepid J. R. Sessions to end all of this and clean up Freestone County, and he set about his business in a characteristic way for a rural sheriff. During the months between election and taking office, Sessions went about the eastern Freestone County sand hills shaking hands and politely warning whiskey men that they had better stop making their product, or he would have to arrest them.[30]

Fifteen years later, just after World War II, reform sheriffs H. F. Fenton, Gaston Boykin, and others sought to rein in the bootleggers and gamblers that had flourished servicing nearly military bases, and they often used the same initial tactic: they personally asked the bootleggers to cease their wicked ways.[31] Firmly supported by the "United Drys," teetotaler Boykin ran for Comanche County sheriff in 1946. Boykin's predecessor had contented himself with catching a few whiskey outlaws for show and looking the other way at all the rest, but not so Gaston Boykin. He planned to honor his campaign promises. Boykin had a list of seventy-three local bootleggers, and he went around warning each man to leave his illegal profession, or else. He told a bootlegger friend of his during the campaign: "I said, 'I have a list of all of em, there's seventy-three, and I may let seventy-two go and center on you. You'll be the one that won't sell, cause you're my friend.' He said he was still gonna vote for me, but I said, 'Now, don't forget.'"[32]

Reform candidates' serious conversations with their resident bootleggers and moonshiners usually occurred in the normal course of campaigning, since voters in rural counties expected candidates for sheriff to meet them personally to ask for their votes. Saturday afternoon at the county seat was a good time to walk the streets, shake people's hands,

distribute campaign cards, and ask for votes, but new candidates like
Gaston Boykin had to go far beyond that. "Whenever three people gather,
you got to be there, just like Jesus and his disciples," a sheriff's wife
advised her candidate son,[33] and Gaston Boykin and other would-be sheriffs followed this dictum at public speakings, pie suppers, fish fries, dances,
graveyard cleanings, school closings, rabbit drives, and other social occasions of the early-twentieth-century countryside. Affairs such as the ubiq-
uitous school closings, pie suppers, and graveyard cleanings repeated
themselves from county to county, but others were less common. Social
life in counties with heavy German and Czech populations focused on
Saturday night dances at the large, barnlike, public dance halls sponsored
by the dancing, singing, shooting, athletic, and insurance societies, and
candidates who wanted to win elections had better put on their dancing
shoes. Rabbit drives were a West Texas specialty in which voters marched
toward each other in two long lines, then shot the panicked rabbits trapped
in between. After the last shot had been fired, the dead rabbits were piled
and counted, and the participating candidates laid down their shotguns
and made short speeches.[34]

Some candidates brought greater entertainment resources than others
to such affairs. If the candidate had a special talent, this was the time to use
it; voters appreciated humble sheriffs, but they also liked to be amused.
Jess Sweeten demonstrated his crack pistol marksmanship at Henderson
County political affairs, shooting marbles from the air and cigarettes—bit
by bit—from assistants' lips, sometimes firing backwards between his legs
to accomplish this. At Panola County, Corbett Akins dazzled rural voters
with electric light displays powered by his portable Delco generator. Akins
also "made many votes by taking off warts, that's a gift to me," and by
amusing and rabble-raising speeches about his plans for removing the new
parking meters from around the courthouse square. "I've got a voice like
a bugle and a mouth like a dishpan," Akins told his listeners, "but I get the
job done."[35] Meanwhile, at Comanche County, candidate Gaston Boykin
staged trained animal shows with his saddle horse and Great Dane, Pretty
Boy Floyd. An avowed Christian reform candidate, affiliated with the
county's United Drys, Boykin nonetheless admitted that "my horse and
dog elected me sheriff."[36]

As at the dances and rabbit drives, candidates earned their speech-
making time by active participation in the affairs at hand, thus giving
people a chance to interact with them and observe how well and how

cheerfully they participated. Pie suppers and graveyard cleanings often proved especially troublesome for would-be sheriffs, since at most counties tradition required candidates to compete with each other in bidding exorbitant amounts for the pies, and the graveyard cleanings sometimes lasted all day. At Angelina and Coleman Counties in 1946, traditional pie-bidding competitions had so escalated that candidates for sheriff met informally before the campaigns to agree on maximum prices to be bid for individual pies at pie-supper fundraisers.[37] Most rural candidates felt happy enough cleaning rural graveyards with hoes in their hands, but more than one would-be sheriff accused local cemetery associations of waiting for election years to get the underbrush out. According to one candidate: "When I was running for sheriff in Trinity County, they had sixteen cemeteries, and the natives there would never work them or take care of the loved ones' graves. They would always invite the candidates, and we had to do it! In a nice shirt and all, and all we got was dinner on the ground. And if you didn't come out there the old sisters wouldn't vote for you. It was terrible. That was the style of the time.[38]

The "old sisters" often evaluated sheriff candidates in terms of how well, cheerfully, and humbly they performed the public service aspect of their role, and the graveyard cleaning or home visit allowed a candidate to be tested and observed. About 1902, for example, a West Texas candidate went around his sparsely settled county asking for votes and—at voters' requests—fixing windmills, vaccinating calves, and dipping sheep.[39] The Trinity County sheriff quoted above lasted only one term, but Sheriff Wallace Riddell of Burnet County remained in office forty years, and one reason is clear: as did Jim Scarborough II of Kleberg County, Riddell prided himself in serving the people as a "personal sheriff," everyone's friend at the courthouse.[40] Candidate Riddell not only cheerfully cleaned country graveyards, but he also performed other neighborly services. While going door-to-door during his first race for sheriff in 1938, accompanied by a friend who was running for county commissioner: "I asked one woman if she had anything we could do. She said she had some firewood that needed splitting. I went to the shed and chopped the wood. When I finished, I went back to the house. I walked into the kitchen and old Tom [the county commission candidate] was sitting on a stool churning butter."[41]

Although a politically secure incumbent might get by with handing out cards on Saturdays and making a few speeches at political meetings and social affairs, local traditions usually required candidates to go door-to-door and farm-to-farm throughout their counties, asking in person for citizens' votes. Nig Hoskins of Bastrop County explained: "You just went and seen everybody that you could and give 'em a card—you had to see a whole lot of 'em or you wouldn't get no votes."[42] In 1946, H. F. Fenton of Coleman County attempted to give every person not one card but two or three after encountering them at different times and places during the campaign.[43] That same year, candidate Roy Herrington drove Anderson County back roads with horse and trailer, and if a man toiled in his field or pasture on the day that Herrington drove up to visit, no matter. The candidate unloaded his saddle horse, rode down to see the voter, and gave him his card. Candidate Herrington made no grand promises to the farmer in the field, only telling the man that if elected he would do his best. He handed out a campaign card with his name and political slogan, "Do unto others as you would have them do unto you," and informed the voter, "I might have to arrest you, but if you deserve it and I can, I'll help you."[44] Humble and disarming approaches often worked best with rural voters wary about whom they elevated to high sheriff. At Haskell County, Garth "Tangle Eye" Garrett used the same pitch every time: "Lady (or mister), I don't want to bother you, but just let me leave you a card and remind you that you'll probably never have another chance to vote for a cross-eyed sheriff."[45]

By the late 1940s, when candidates like Garth Garrett and Roy Herrington passed the rural home places of African Americans, they sometimes turned aside to their doors and asked them for their support. Blacks had not voted in most rural counties since the demise of Populism and the coming of the "white primary" a half-century before, but after World War II, with little or no fanfare, here and there and at first cautiously and a few at a time, they once again began to vote. No longer were blacks political nonpersons in quite the same way, and shrewder candidates quickly took notice of this fact. Young Nathan Tindall now greeted black people on the streets of San Augustine, shook their hands, and asked them for their votes—something East Texas sheriff candidates had not done since the 1890s, and then only a few scattered Populists, such as candidate A. J. Spradley of Nacogdoches County. At Wharton County, constable and then sheriff T. W. Lane discerned the shape of the future and paid some attention to African Americans' political concerns. Elected to the sheriff's office in 1940, he listened to leaders in the county seat's black quarter, "Oxblood," and tried to help them with their most vexing problems, one of which was the tradition of Anglo sexual excursions into the black community. Houston newsman Wesley Stout chronicled Buckshot Lane's reward when, "voting in the 1950 primary for the first time since Reconstruction, the Negroes gave Buck an overwhelming endorsement."[46]

A candidate demonstrated his humility and personal respect by visiting every voter's home, no matter how poor or remote. When Dan Saunders first campaigned to be sheriff of Martin County in 1952, he called at "every house, every shack and every business and office at least twice during my campaign." Rural voters often were unprepared for the visitor. As Saunders noted, "You hated to go to a house and cause people to open the door, but you knew if you didn't go by they wouldn't vote for you." Once, Saunders walked up on a buxom lady in bra and panties cooling herself on her back porch, and he faced off with many a threatening farm dog. "The worse thing about electioneering is the dogs," he wrote. "I am afraid of dogs and of course they can sense it. Well, if you are running for Sheriff you can't kick a dog and you can't run. Either way you will lose a vote."[47]

However, in this face-to-face rural society, the personal visit worked; the candidate had to do it. Once, on a very hot day, Dan Saunders walked far into a plowed field to talk to a farmer on his tractor and give him a card. Without dismounting from his tractor, the farmer studied the card in silence for some time, then looked down at the candidate standing ankle deep in the soft dirt and said, "Well, I wasn't going to vote for you, but if you want that damned job this bad I'm going to vote for you."[48]

The incumbent sheriff had stepped down at Martin County in 1952, and Dan Saunders and his four fellow candidates for sheriff were "all good friends," running "clean campaigns" and speaking no ill of each other. Other first-time candidates were less fortunate and soon found out what Nig Hoskins meant when he said, "politics is dirty, it's as dirty as dirty can be."[49] Bastrop County had traditions of contentious campaigning, and Hoskins's opponents in his first two unsuccessful bids for office charged that the retired man hunter and "dog captain" from the Texas Department of Corrections penal farm would make "too rough" a sheriff for Bastrop County. That accusation had been expected, but to further emphasize Hopkins's roughness, the opposition soon delved into painful details of the Hoskins family's history. Hoskins explained: "If you ever done anything in your life, you can bet it'll come out on you if you get in politics. They'll do anything in any way to try to beat you. My grandaddy was killed in Red Rock in 1916. They brought that out on me, about my grandaddy getting killed in 1916, about how rough I was and all such as that."[50]

The war-veteran candidates of 1946 and 1948, just returned from battlefields in Europe and the Pacific, often endured opponents' accusations that they would make unsuitably rough sheriffs, and in Coleman County, H. F. Fenton had to combat these claims. It was not always easy. Fenton was young and somewhat hot-tempered, and the local paper had been full of stories about the hundreds of Germans and Italians the war-hero candidate had slain in patriotic duty. One day during the campaign, Fenton ventured into a Coleman barber shop to put up a political poster, then passed by later to see his face still in the window but now marked upon and cut to shreds. Fenton became furious but quickly gained control of himself. The barber shop was enemy political territory, and barbers and customers closely observed him from inside the window. Without mentioning the mutilated poster, Fenton marched inside the shop, gave every man inside a card, and asked him for his vote. He explained: "It was a set-up deal, cause them three old barbers in there were all George Robey men. They had set that deal up hoping I would come in there and kick the snot out of 'em, and that really would have hurt me cause I was supposed to be hot-tempered."[51]

Most commonly, the would-be sheriffs endured trial by anonymous political rumor, with party or parties unknown "putting smut on them" with accusations of things they could not easily disprove or even afford to talk about publicly.[52] Only a risk-taker such as Corbett Akins would dare to have his father and mother stand up at a political gathering and say, "What my son is telling you folks is true, he did not accept any money from the bootleggers and gamblers!"[53] Rather often, as during Gaston Boykin's first campaign, the negative rumors attributed the "putting smut" to the candidate himself, an ancient political trick. Boykin told, "They'd make up stories about my opponent and tell 'em that I told 'em—say, that I said this about his wife, that I said he didn't have a restroom in his house, and so on."[54]

Candidates often faced accusations that they ran as front men for behind-the-scenes economic or political interests, and sometimes such things were difficult to rebut. Accused of being in the pay of whiskey outlaws, Corbett Akins of Panola County publicly denied this, then counter-assaulted with the accusation that his opponent served as political front man for the parking meter company that had erected the hated devices around the Carthage courthouse square and now lobbied to keep them in place. As many sheriffs before him had done, Akins vowed to support local customs (in this case, free parking) over the letter of the law, telling voters: "If I'm elected sheriff, I want y'all to bring your tractors, mules, and grubbing hoes, and everything you got, and come up here and help Corbett Akins dig up them damn parking meters."[55]

Sometimes the accusations of political and economic powers lurking behind the candidate were the simple truth, and many voters recognized this. At various places and times, liquor and gambling interests did sponsor a particular candidate, and—influenced by such interests—a majority of voters favoring an "open county" knowingly voted for the status-quo or "antireform" candidate. Sometimes, for his own good reasons, one very rich man placed his sheriff in power and strove to keep him there. This was the situation in 1944 in Montgomery County, where young Clint Peoples knew he faced not only one-term incumbent sheriff Hershal Suratt but also his formidable oilman brother-in-law. The oilman poured money into Suratt's campaign, secretly attempted to bribe Peoples's wife with a fur coat if she talked her husband into withdrawing, and pressured the Montgomery County Draft Board into sending the thirty-three-year-old candidate a draft notice. Peoples's wife refused the coat, and the candidate proved physically unfit for active service, but the oilman's money still helped win a narrow victory for Sheriff Suratt.[56]

In some counties, early and late, one major economic interest so dominated affairs that only its candidate could be elected sheriff. With twelve sawmill towns scattered across four southeastern Texas counties, the Kirby Lumber Company dominated local politics for three decades after 1900. Kirby not only had its own resident deputies in each sawmill town, but would-be sheriffs also needed company approval to mount successful campaigns. Kirby employees often voted as a bloc for the company candidate, and there were a great many such employees during the heyday of East Texas bonanza lumbering. Occasionally, Kirby Lumber Company compelled local sheriffs to do their duty, as defined by the big company. During the Brotherhood of Timber Workers challenge of 1912, for example, John Henry Kirby ordered a company executive to order the Newton County sheriff into action. "Have Hooker get in touch with the sheriff of Newton County and see that a suitable number of deputies are detailed," the lumberman wrote.[57]

Sheriff Corbett Akins of Panola County and his father, about 1948. (Author's collection)

At other places and times, big ranches dominated the politics of the office of sheriff. The 6666 Ranch backed successful candidate George Humphreys for King County sheriff in 1928, and after 1932, Humphreys served as both county sheriff and 6666 Ranch manager.[58] F. L. Barber played a similar role in sparsely settled Dickens County just after World War I. If cowboys got into trouble on their rare trips into town, "All I had to do was tell his ranch boss, the different spreads took care of their own personnel problems, I didn't even wear a badge."[59] During 1942, off-duty Texas highway patrolman Clint Peoples accompanied a latter-day "company sheriff" as he went about his political duties. Sheriff Jim Scarborough II entered Mexican Town in Kingsville to tactfully request that a political leader withdraw his support from a certain mayoral candidate, lately displeasing to the King Ranch. Sheriff Scarborough did his job; the Mexican leader readily agreed, and no wonder. The King Ranch was not, properly speaking, in Kleberg County; Kleberg County was in the King Ranch. Not only did the ranch call the shots in local sheriffs' elections from the origin of the county in 1913 into the 1980s, but, with the exception of a single one-term anomaly, all Kleberg County sheriffs had the same name— father, son, and grandson—Jim Scarborough. Over the years, special traditions had developed between ranch and sheriff; for example, if Bob Kleberg accidentally ran over one of the ranch's pet peafowl at ranch head- quarters, someone promptly delivered the delicacy road kill to Sheriff Scarborough.[60] During the early 1970s, no sooner had Jim Scarborough III retired from a twenty-eight-year career in the Air Force than his father, Jim Scarborough II, began trying to recruit him to run for sheriff. In office since 1935, a thirty-eight-year incumbent, the last three decades without a serious political opponent, the elder Scarborough much wished to step down. "Bob [Kleberg] doesn't want me to retire," he told his son, "but he'll consider it if you take my place."[61]

Election years sometimes passed almost unnoticed for politically domi- nant sheriffs such as Jim Scarborough II, Wallace Riddel, Dan Saunders, and others, but at many places this was not the case. Hotly contested races for sheriff commonly occurred, with public interest and political combat peaking just before the Democratic primaries of July and August. In a one- party state, the official November election normally only rubber-stamped the winner of the late-summer Democratic wars.

Rather often, in hot-election years, large numbers of citizens cast their ballots, then came down to the courthouse on primary Saturdays to be close to the action while the votes were counted and to observe the candidates during their thrills of victory and agonies of defeat. Now, the new men with uncertain political futures found out the results of all their gladhanding around the county and knocking on people's doors for votes. Rural citizens might care deeply about who won the county judge's race or the race for county commissioner in their precinct, but nothing so preoccupied most voters as the election for sheriff. Sometimes when the office of high sheriff seemed likely to change hands, the crowds on the courthouse squares became almost as nervous as the candidates. A journalist at a San Augustine County sheriff's election found the crowd around the courthouse willing to discuss every race except the race for sheriff, though "that was all they cared about." Citizens were too tense to talk about their greatest preoccupation. A change in the sheriff's office potentially affected everybody, voters thought, and their anxiety was obvious. "More than once, I overheard residents in their cups declaring that their lives would be utterly different if only So-and-So were sheriff," the journalist wrote. "They dream about him, turn to him in every sort of extremity, blame him for every sort of distress. The sheriff is held accountable not just for law enforcement but for the community's moral and economic health. He sets a tone, he defines an era. Presidents are marginal figures by comparison."[62]

Hotly fought sheriff's elections galvanized rural voters like nothing else. On primary day of Frank Brunt's first election for Cherokee County sheriff in 1940, a friend encountered an elderly one-legged man stumping painfully down the dirt road on his wooden leg two miles into Maydelle to vote. As Brunt recounted, the friend asked: "'Where are you going, Mr. Roach?' Says, 'Going up here to vote for Frank Brunt and W. Lee O'Daniel.' That was all he was interested in. Wasn't no use anybody running for anything else."[63]

When newly sworn in sheriff Frank Brunt walked through the door of his Rusk office on January 1, 1941, he already knew what he would find there. Brunt had served as chief deputy and de facto sheriff since the county commissioners appointed Sheriff Bill Brunt's widow to the office of sheriff immediately after Bill's violent death in 1939 and hired younger brother Frank to actually do the job. Commissioners often followed this courtesy, which allowed widows financial support for the remainder of their dead husbands' terms of office. Almost always the widow sheriffs were sheriffs in name only, and a deputy ran the department until the next election.

New sheriffs taking office on January 1 varied enormously in law enforcement experience. Brunt had been a railroad detective and a deputy, but other men had never strapped on a pistol or pinned on a badge, and they had much to learn. The honor of having been elected as high sheriff must have paled for many, even on the first day, when they walked into unfamiliar offices to find jumbled records, scanty equipment, unfamiliar legal documents piled high on desks, and phones that immediately began to ring.

The range of citizens' requests that came over the telephone startled the uninitiated. H. F. Fenton's first call required him to drive thirty miles into a Coleman County ice storm to expel dogs from under a voter's house. Fenton explained:

> His house was built up off the ground, and there was an old bitch dog under there with a bunch of dogs that had followed her in, and he wanted me to get them dogs out from under his house! I laid down on one side of this house at a hole with a flashlight, and every one of them run out the other side. I got back in the car and drove home. Boy, it was cold, and I didn't have no defrosters on that thing, you know. I didn't realize the sheriff got those kind of calls.[64]

In San Saba County, Brantley Barker had no law enforcement experience when he took office in 1951, though he had worked in the county tax office and had "visited quite a bit" with the sheriff in an adjoining room and had become somewhat familiar with what he did.[65] In Angelina County in 1947, new sheriff J. T. "Red" Conditt, who had a background in construction work but no law enforcement experience, told a reporter that the Department of Public Safety's two-week school for new officers had saved the day for him. Just back from Austin full of this new knowledge, Conditt announced a crash program to modernize and reorganize what he described as the outmoded and disorderly Angelina County Sheriff's Department.[66] What former sheriffs and other experienced local lawmen thought of the pronouncements of this two-week sheriff can only be surmised.

Jail reforms often got the new sheriffs' immediate attention, especially since many of them moved their families into jail apartments as one of their first official acts. Reform of the jail had commonly been a political plank of the candidates for sheriff, but now such matters took on a new urgency.

As the new sheriffs soon discovered, the county commissioners, who controlled the departments' purse strings, loathed spending money for jails. Something approaching the "black hole of Calcutta"—too hot, too cold, and with rats and vermin abounding—served prisoners right, many commissioners believed. Unfortunately, the sheriff and his wife and children also usually lived in the jail in a special apartment set aside for them.

When the Wallace Riddell family first moved from the deep countryside into the Burnet County jail in 1939, Mrs. Riddell found her circumstances more primitive than at her abandoned backwoods home. The jail cookstove was out back, in a dirt-floored lean-to open to the air, and she was expected to feed family and prisoners with this device. Moreover, the Riddells quickly discovered that the antique Burnet jail harbored "rats as long as your arm."[67] After taking a close look at the sheriff's apartment in the Coleman County jail in 1947, Sheriff H. F. Fenton ordered his deputy's family to live in it. However, after a short time, fearful of rat attacks on her baby, the deputy's wife compelled a change, and the Fentons reluctantly moved into the Coleman jail, where they would dwell, off and on, for thirty years. The Coleman jail not only had the usual rats and roaches, but it had snakes and bats as well. Fear of snakes (and escaped prisoners) haunted sheriff's wife Loretta Fenton during her trips to the distant toilet after dark, and she made her husband shout at intervals during her absence; as long as she could hear H. F.'s voice, Loretta felt reassured. Bats often invaded Loretta's kitchen, where she fought them with a broom.[68]

Living with jail inmates also came as a shock to the new sheriff and his family. When sheriff's daughter Leona Bannister first stepped through the door of the Coleman jail apartment in 1915, expecting her father, John Banister, to be there to meet her, she heard instead the loud sobs and cries of a deranged young man in a cell upstairs. The man awaited transfer to the Texas State Lunatic Asylum in Austin, but other jail inmates were destined for the "Walls" prison at Huntsville, and they were desperate to escape. On Lorena Bannister's first night in the Coleman County jail, as she recalled, "the sheriff and his family heard the steady grating sound of hacksaws on the steel bars."[69]

No wonder, then, that jail reforms were much on new sheriffs' minds. John Bannister launched daily searches for prisoners' hacksaw blades and had the partially severed bars welded closed. Sheriff Tiemann Dibbel of Washington County announced to the Brenham newspaper that his jail had been cleaned, freshly painted, sanitized, and eradicated of several species of vermin. Washington County jail inmates now had new bedding and had been deloused, and new prisoners would be disinfected before being allowed in. Furthermore, inmates had just as well give up all hopes of escape, since Sheriff Dibbel had just installed a pack of six bloodhounds to run down any escapees.[70] Soon after taking over as Dallas County sheriff in 1948, J. E. "Bill" Decker announced a massive cleanup and shakedown of jail cells and prisoners. Prisoners had been "dehorned" of many improvised weapons, and the long-term inmate with the well-equipped woodwork shop on the eighth floor had been shut down.[71] New sheriff Lon Evans staged a similar crackdown at the Tarrant County jail in 1960 and told the media about it. Jailers searched cells and prisoners' bodies with great care, and illegal weapons and "kites," long strings let down from open cell windows after dark to bring contraband up from friends on the ground below, became things of the old regime. Furthermore, as Evans said, "all ties were severed between county jail prisoners and their guards and between suspected criminals and sheriff's deputies." No longer did Tarrant County jail guards play dominoes with inmates along jail corridors or Tarrant County deputies pat the backs of suspected felons at court arraignments. Finally, for the prisoners' own good, the diabetic sheriff told a reporter, he had "discontinued the sweets in their diets."[72]

Reform of sheriff department staffs often went hand-in-hand with early reforms of the jail—actions of the new man's first days in office. Immediately after his 1965 swearing in, Brazoria County sheriff Bob Gladney called a meeting of jailers and deputies, and so certain were department employees that the meeting would prove short and terminal that their wives waited for them outside in cars, some with their engines running. Gladney, however, retained all hands, only telling them to expect to go to work. And by this he meant "Work!—off of their ass and on their feet and in them cars and on the county roads, and taking care of the citizens' business."[73]

The appointment of deputies to help run the jail and help answer the ever-ringing telephone was high on the new sheriff's agenda, but sometimes no deputies had been authorized by the county commissioners court. Sheriff Wallace Riddell had no deputies to assist him from the time he entered office in 1939 until the early 1950s. Normally, however, by about 1950, reluctant commissioners had authorized one or two deputies for the overworked rural sheriffs, and immediately after winning the fall election, a new man set about recruiting someone to assist him.

Sheriffs usually chose deputies they knew personally, thought they could get along with, and believed they could trust to back them up. Previous law enforcement experience usually was not their main priority. In 1947, H. F. Fenton chose as his lone deputy Raymond Greaves, a man he had grown up with and served beside during World War II. "He was a good officer, a good solid boy," Fenton said. "We knew each other for a long many years, and back then we could more or less read each other's minds for what the other one was gonna do."[74] Of his first deputies, Bastrop County sheriff Nig Hoskins remarked: "The deputy was just a man that you knowed was a pretty good feller, and had been all his life. There wasn't no training, we never even thought about it. But we knew every house in the county, every road."[75] Leon Jones of Angelina County explained of his choice of deputies: "I knew most of 'em from family backgrounds. I never did publicize the fact that I needed a deputy. I hired a clean-living man, cause he doesn't mind dying as bad as one that's not living right."[76]

Jones trained his deputies as did many other sheriffs. He let them ride around with him for a couple of months while he went about his official duties, then he cut them loose. Other sheriffs, with smaller staffs, had no time to train deputies and left them on their own to learn on the job almost from the first day. The common opinion that good officers were born and not made facilitated this drastic, sink-or-swim approach. "You can send a man to school till doomsday and not make an officer out of him," Jack Marshall believed. "I can spot the makings of a good officer a mile away." Consequently, Marshall just told a new deputy, "Enforce the law!"—the same thing his sheriff had told him. Then came certain implied political cautionings: "When I broke an officer in, I'd tell him one time, 'As long as you're right, I'm going to stay with you until hell freezes over, and when you get wrong, I'll quit you like a dirty shirt.'"[77] Asked by new deputy Clint Peoples how he should do his job at Montgomery County in 1930, Sheriff Ben Hicks said, "Enforce the law!," then offered a few conventional words of wisdom about misuse of his new authority. "Son, you can take this pistol that you have the authority to wear and you can make a great man out of yourself, or you can make the biggest fool out of yourself that ever was. Don't ever get to where you feel this pistol on your hip."[78] Rather often, sheriffs knew exactly what formidable challenges faced their new deputies and offered words of warning as stark as those spoken to young Tom Brown by Caldwell County sheriff Walter Ellison in 1933: "Now, they're gonna try to run over you. If you give one inch, you might as well quit. Whatever you do, I'm behind you."[79]

Sometimes deputies needed no training and were hired to offer behind-the-scenes instruction to the newcomer sheriffs, who had no previous background in law enforcement. After his election, Aubrey Cole swiftly hired two former Jasper County chief deputies to perform this function.[80] Furthermore, if a wise old deputy specializing in serving civil papers was on the scene when the new sheriff moved in, the sheriff was likely to try to retain him, even if this meant personally subduing twice as many drunks in roadhouses. New men often feared writs and summonses more than fistfights.[81]

Especially when a new sheriff's staff was small, political considerations, often those of a geographical nature, influenced their choice of deputies. Walter Ellison chose his single deputy, Tom Brown, from Luling, the railroad town in southern Caldwell County that stood in bitter traditional rivalry with the county seat of Lockhart to the north. Having been taught since childhood to "love God and hate Lockhart," Brown for a time hesitated to take the job.[82] Sheriff Marcus Steck of Bellville chose Truman Maddox of Sealy for much the same reason; Sealy and Bellville, the county seat, were the largest towns in Austin County and natural rivals.[83]

Nor was geography the only political consideration involved in choice of a deputy. Deputies from large, well-known, and well-respected families helped to bring in needed votes, as did Hispanic deputies and black deputies (once such groups began to return to the polls). Furthermore, since deputies were political extensions of the sheriff himself, they needed to be men of tact and discretion, able to arrest voters without insulting them or making them mad. For the sheriff's department, as Gaston Boykin asserted, every arrest was "political."[84] Fine judgments about ethnicity, socioeconomic class, family affiliation, and other things also guided a good deputy's actions as he accosted a man on the street or approached a car pulled over on the shoulder of the road. In the latter case, the careful deputy always took a quick look at the license plate to tell if the car belonged to a resident voter or to an outsider and nonvoter—the greatest of all social and political distinctions to the elected official he served. Deputies were potentially bulls in the china shop of the sheriff's delicate political affairs, and rudely arresting the bank president for driving while intoxicated or pistol-whipping the county attorney simply would not do. But like everybody else, deputies sometimes ran amok. On September 2, 1963, Sheriff Dan Saunders wrote in his daily log: "Bad day. My deputy and his wife are getting a divorce. He went downtown by the barber shop and shot all four tires on her car. Had to put him in jail."[85]

Despite the delicacy of the law enforcement job the deputies performed, and how easily they could get their sheriffs in political trouble, rural sheriffs often could not hire or long retain competent deputies at the low salaries mandated by county commissioners. During the late 1950s, after county commissioners allowed Sheriff Wallace Riddell to hire deputies, he found hiring and firing them a great pain. Asked by his children about a familiar face no longer seen, Riddell commonly replied, "Aw, he wasn't nothing but a dadgummed pistol packer."[86] The *Sheriffs' Association of Texas Magazine*, professional news organ since 1932 for Texas sheriff departments, every month recorded numerous terse notes about deputies dismissed for reasons unspecified.

By the years after the end of World War II, sheriffs' staffs in the more populous rural counties commonly resembled that of new sheriff Jim Flournoy of Fayette County. In 1947, Flournoy had a chief deputy and a town deputy stationed with him at the county seat of La Grange, resident—doubtless part-time—deputies at Schulenberg, Round Top, Hammondsville, and Flatonia, and a few unpaid "special deputies."[87] Nobody spent much time in patrolling in Fayette County or anywhere else in the state's rural counties. Patrol tactics were based on the two-way radio, which few rural departments possessed even in primitive form until the 1950s. A patrolling officer was out of touch, unable to take citizens' calls, and answering calls remained the sheriff's priority. Consequently, sheriff and deputies commonly sat around the phone until a call came in to the sheriff's office, then a lone officer departed to check out the complaint.

Resident community deputies, stationed in the largest subtowns of Fayette County, took calls in their localities. Resident deputies made good political and law enforcement sense for Sheriff Flournoy. Local citizens felt pleased to have native sons in charge of local affairs, and resident deputies cut down on response times in an era of slow cars and dubious "all-weather" roads. Although sheriffs like Flournoy normally chose their own men to serve beside them at the county seat, resident deputies sometimes were political "no-fires" who continued to serve sheriff after sheriff. At nearby Colorado County in the year Jim Flournoy took office, for example, Deputy Otto Strunk had kept the peace in the Oakland community for forty years and would serve several decades more.[88] Sometimes communities traditionally without a resident deputy lobbied new sheriffs to station such a man in the midst. In 1958, for example, Franklin County sheriff John Tittle designated a new officer in Winnsboro to "clean out the back roads outside the city limits of the drinking, and gambling, and cutting up that has been going on."[89]

Most rural sheriffs had a few "special deputies" scattered about in 1950—deputized volunteer officers unpaid by the county. In earlier times, many resident deputies had been volunteers of this sort—"pistol deputies," a Wilson County sheriff's son termed them.[90] Special deputies got involved in law enforcement for the action, the prestige, and the right to wear a pistol in public. Sometimes special deputies physically embodied a symbiotic relationship between the sheriff's office and some local economic power—a sawmill town, industrial plant, or large cotton plantation. As his part of the bargain, the understaffed sheriff got an unpaid, sometimes full-time and professional, deputy, and the company got deputy status for its salaried security guard. At Kleberg County, the King Ranch's large staff of "Kleberg County deputies," all ranch employees, represented an extreme example of this sort of thing.[91]

Special deputies worked football games on Friday nights, stood around keeping order at Saturday night dances, helped police the midways at county fairs, and turned out as the sheriff's posse to find lost children and outlaws on the run. T. W. "Buckshot" Lane of Wharton County and others commonly had one or more "colored special deputies" for decades before the first Texas African Americans attained formal deputy status. Some of these individuals wore badges and pistols in the open, but more worked undercover as "snitches," keeping the sheriff informed about doings in the local black community.

About 1950, many a rural citizen called his or her sheriff's office only to get a busy signal, to have the phone answered by the community operator, or to listen to the phone ring and ring unanswered. A sheriff with one or two deputies had to take calls as they came in, jump in his car to go deal with them, and let the phone take care of itself. Many counties did not feel they could afford a full-time office secretary, and so the local switchboard operator—if anybody—took down the numbers of the sheriff's callers and passed them on. Prisoners left alone in Sheriff Gaston Boykin's Comanche County jail heard the phone ring constantly in the sheriff's absence—104 calls in one afternoon, they reported.[92]

Some new sheriffs had known what they were getting into in terms of hard work and time on the job, but many sheriffs had little or no law enforcement background, and what they now experienced came as a shock. The phones rang and rang with every conceivable sort of report, inquiry, or request for assistance. Civil papers and warrants issued by county or district courts arrived almost daily at the sheriffs' desks, each one requiring an officer to find someone and serve the paper in person. Addresses normally were not included, the new sheriff discovered, so each writ launched a virtual missing-person search. If the sheriff had a deputy, he often drew this duty, which changed little across the decades. About 1910, Deputy Charlie Munson of Lavaca County put in many sixteen-hour days and fifty-mile horseback rides serving papers and summoning jurors, and in 1964 a Deaf Smith County deputy logged 363 hours in his automobile during one month doing much the same thing.[93]

New sheriffs also found that they served the courts by summoning persons for grand jury or trial jury duty, by guarding the deliberations, and by remaining with jury members twenty-four hours a day during trials. Juries in 1950 had to be sequestered, and Sheriff Dan Saunders of Martin County recalled: "Our old jury room in the old courthouse contained only double beds and two of us always had to sleep together. I always stayed with the jury myself. I didn't ask a deputy to. I usually would end up sleeping with some old man who snored all night."[94]

Sheriffs such as Dan Saunders, serving in counties with total populations under ten thousand, also did double duty as county tax assessor/collector, a job that required them to monitor the activities of the county tax office and to sell state license plates to the public. Saunders explained, "We had lots of little country stores back then and I would set up and stay at the little stores one day a week before the deadline as a service to the people."[95] Already sheriff and tax collector, Brantley Barker somehow managed also to wear the official hats of San Saba police chief and San Saba Independent School District truant officer during his long career.[96]

But nothing so insistently intruded on the sheriff's time as the telephone. In this era before effective two-way radio communication, sheriffs almost relaxed when they went out to locate a suspicious abandoned pickup on a back road, quell a family disturbance, or investigate a strange light behind someone's barn; at least now, for a little while, the phone left them alone. In a time before municipal police, Department of Public Safety (DPS) troopers, or emergency medical services, virtually all calls came in to the sheriffs' offices, so the phones rang off the hook. Sheriff Jess Sweeten took charge in Henderson County in 1933 with "one outside deputy and a secretary and a jailer and a population of thirty-eight thousand people to police, including all of Athens." Athens, the county seat, had a city marshal, "but he never attempted to do anything." Sweeten and his deputy answered calls day and night, with no time off. "Very seldom did I ever go to bed that I wasn't called up from one to three or four times," he recalled. "If I hadn't of been young I couldn't have kept up with it. It was a terrible job."[97] In Burnet County in 1939, Wallace Riddell had a smaller county population but no deputy, secretary, or jailer. Riddell's wife and family watched his jail, the Burnet operator took his messages, and Wallace himself endlessly drove county roads answering trouble calls. Normally, Wallace Riddel stayed up all Friday night, came home and changed clothes sometime Saturday (if he got a chance), then stayed up all Saturday night as well. Fourteen years passed before the county commissioners gave Sheriff Riddell a deputy, but even after that most voters who called the office still demanded to speak to the high sheriff. Wallace Riddell took no vacations in nearly four decades in office and rarely left the county. According to his son, when Riddell neared the point of physical collapse, or became so exasperated that he could not stand his job any longer, he sometimes checked in to the Burnet hospital for two or three days' rest with no visitors allowed.[98]

For the first-term sheriff or the thirty-year man, the ringing phone in the sheriff's office held a certain fascination; the officer never knew what he might hear when he picked it up. Sometimes the news was of terrible highway accidents or shotgun suicides, and new men quickly had to adjust to working these bloody scenes. On the still-primitive public roads of 1950, powerful automobiles went faster and faster, and, as Sheriff T. W. Lane of Wharton County noted: "Few men feel they are violating the laws when they violate traffic laws. Think, in our county for 1949, 13 traffic deaths and how many murders? Just one."[99] In his newspaper columns, as cautionary tales for the motoring public, Buckshot Lane described some of the horrors that he saw in line of duty: severed arms, tongues bitten off, brains knocked out, and bodies scrambled beyond recognition. At nearby Austin County, at about the same time, Sheriff Truman Maddox struggled to get used to "people torn all to pieces, arms and legs tore off, insides scattered all over the ground, maybe brains knocked out on the ground," and suicides. Maddox admitted: "I've had lots of wrecks, lots of fists, and lots of cuttings, and shootings with their heads blowed off and all over the ceiling, and wrecks where the body is tore up everywhere. When I first started, it kind of followed me home."[100]

Sometimes, when the new sheriff's phone rang, it was something few who were not officers had ever received: bribe offers or death threats. Every sheriff got death threats or threats on his family; they came with the job. Nig Hoskins of Bastrop County recalled "letters that have a heart drawed on it, then an arrow sticking through it, and then look like blood dropping from it, all such as that, I've had my life threatened many-a-many a time. They call me, daring me to be at such and such a place, saying 'There's a .30-30 waiting for you.' But I've went to em and I never could find a .30-30."[101] In Bell County during the reform era after World War II, the sheriff phoned Deputy Lester Gunn to bring his shotgun loaded with buckshot and join him on a certain remote dirt road east of Temple. A death threat had been made, a gauntlet thrown, and the sheriff planned to call the outlaw's bluff. Gunn got in the sheriff's car, joking, "Well, damn, I wish you could have let me know so I could have told my wife goodbye." However, sheriff and deputy went to the assigned place and "set till daylight and nobody showed up." Later, after Gunn had become sheriff himself, a voice told him on the phone, "One night when you come home, your wife's blood is gonna be all over that house."[102]

Such calls were only harassment, most sheriffs thought, believing that a real assassin would strike without warning. After a bootlegger made repeated death threats in public against Sheriff Gaston Boykin, Boykin walked up to the man's car window in downtown Comanche in front of witnesses and called his bluff, telling him, "If you got any guts, let's see em!" The bootlegger did nothing and—publicly humiliated—soon left the county. Many new sheriffs had given some thought to the dangers of the job and the threat of assassination, and most took a fatalistic attitude towards the possibility. "If I'd gotten killed every time I had a threat made I'd have been dead lots of times," Gaston Boykin remarked. He rarely carried a gun as he went about his job, believing that "if they set out after me, they're gonna get me, cause they're gonna shoot me in the back."[103] Occasionally, as for Caldwell County sheriff J. H. Franks in 1915, the shot-gun assassin proved real enough. Someone waited in the dark across the street from Sheriff Franks's front gate until he came home from a Lockhart · movie theater, then gave him both barrels in the back.[104]

Sometimes the anonymous voices on the telephone made lucrative offers instead of death threats, and the new sheriff soon discovered whether he was as honest as he thought he was. Some "honest men" simply had never been in a position to attract a really good offer, but all sheriffs were in such a position. No sooner had reform candidate Henry Billingsley become Angelina County sheriff in January 1933 than a moonshiner offered him one thousand dollars a year to look for other men's stills instead of his own. The offer was handled discreetly through a third party, and the whiskey outlaw had everything to gain and nothing to lose in making it. Billingsley turned the man down and later caught him at his still, but, with little doubt, other sheriffs came to different conclusions. Illegal whiskey generated big money during Prohibition, sheriffs made low salaries, and such an agreement made small demands on the sheriff. The sheriff only abstained from searching that particular whiskey outlaw's patch of woods. Other whiskey men remained fair game, and the sheriff could still display their ruptured stills on the courthouse lawn. Sheriff Frank Brunt, a ferocious hunter of Cherokee County bootleggers and moonshiners, believed that his predecessor had been "on the take." When federal men planned a raid, this man had called his sponsoring whiskey outlaws to warn them, using an agreed-upon code, "Better bring your clothes off the line, it looks like it gonna rain."[105]

Every sheriff got bribe offers. Retiring at Coke County in 1961 after twenty-eight years as deputy and sheriff, Paul Good jokingly told a reporter that he had been offered many bribes over the years but had never accepted one. Furthermore, "I've got one more week to serve the good folks of Coke County, and I don't think I'll accept a bribe even now."[106] Some outlaws met the sheriff in person and came right to the point. A Dallas lady with diamond rings on all her fingers asked to see Sheriff William Lester Gunn of Bell County on matters unspecified, then, after a few social comments and removing two or three rings and laying them on the table, she came to the point. "Sheriff, I've been inspecting Temple, Belton, Harker Heights, Killeen, and Fort Hood. I want to bring three hundred women down there. Of course, we have to take care of the sheriff, county attorney, and district attorney." Gunn declined the offer and asked the lady if she would be willing to repeat it to the grand jury, but she quickly thanked him, picked up her diamond rings, and departed.[107]

Not all of the new sheriff's tempting offers were monetary. Admitting that "gals have a tendency to take after somebody carrying a darn pistol and wearing a uniform," handsome young Jess Sweeten of Henderson County, known as the "seven foot sheriff," reported that he repulsed many sexual advances during his first term in office. "I was married there when I was young, and I had many chances, but I just never did it," Sweeten said.[108]

As first-term sheriffs such as Marcus Steck of Austin County quickly discovered, some county males had different designs on the new officer—they wanted to beat him up. Nor could the sheriff afford to lose a fight, as Marcus Steck did. Walter Ellison's admonition to his new deputy held equally true for all new sheriffs: "They're gonna try to run over you, if you give one inch you might as well quit."[109] In rural Texas counties about 1950, sheriffs had few deputies and no radios to call them on for help. They worked trouble calls by themselves and faced physical challenges on their own, sink or swim. Rather often, sheriffs personally knew the men who challenged them, and so did everybody else; accounts of the confrontations quickly got around. "The job used to be a lot worse than what it is now," observed Truman Maddox, Steck's successor in Austin County. "You had more privilege to kind of do what you wanted to do and do it like you wanted to, but you had better be able to stand your ground, I promise you that. When you waded in there, it was you or him."[110]

After a while, most dance hall drunks did not hazard to challenge Sheriffs Truman Maddox or H. F. Fenton to hand-to-hand combat, but it took a while for the new men to make their reputations. Fenton recalled: "About the first two years I was in office, I tell you what, I thought it wasn't nothing but fistfighting, cause there was lots of old tough boys here then who would try your boots on. I was just twenty-three or twenty-four years old, and those first two years I had more damn trouble, more fights. Most of the time you'd just start to arrest somebody and they just wasn't gonna be arrested. They'd just start them old fists flying, and you either had to run or stay there."[111]

Even the young sheriffs who enjoyed a good fistfight soon got too much of a good thing and tried to devise ways of handling drunks and rowdies that avoided personal combat. As more than one man discovered, bare-fisted blows, strongly delivered, often broke bones in one's own fingers, hands, and forearms.[112] The trick was to go into a touchy situation, defuse it short of violence, and get everyone involved to do what you wanted them to. A nice mix of intimidation and sympathetic cajolery often did the job, and patience also helped. Midland County sheriff Ed Darnell advised young Dan Saunders never to "'over-do' a situation—he said if you 'under-do' something you can always go back and upgrade it, but if you over-react to start with you can never correct it."[113]

Veteran lawmen advised new sheriffs to use a version of the Golden Rule when dealing with troublemakers—"change boots with him and deal accordingly," one man said—followed only if necessary by swift and effective violence. The old Pampa policeman who told Fenton to "change boots" also knew how to get rough if the Golden Rule failed to work. As Fenton recalled: "He'd always use the palm of his hand, and boy, he could knock one on his bottom quicker than you could turn around."[114] Many officers, including H. F. Fenton, used the shot-filled bag, the "slapper," to quickly subdue fighters, and a smaller number used brass knuckles. Some men relied on striking with the heels of their hands, as did the Pampa policeman, or else used heavy-handed slaps to subdue combatants, as did Frank Hamer and Henry Billingsley. Sheriff Corbett Akins preferred to hit people with his pistol, and he preached another rule, that of "getting in the first lick." "I've had more fights than a jaybird had eggs," Akins told, "but I was always smart enough to get in the first lick, and it's the first lick that counts. First thing he knew, I had him on the ground."[115]

Such things were always the last resort, though often enough resorted to. Montgomery County deputy, later Texas Ranger, Clint Peoples explained that his policy was to

> treat people as I would want to be treated. I always liked to smile at them and treat them as nice as I could possibly could and be kind and help them, even if I was arresting them. I never put myself in a position of trying to embarrass them when I arrested them. But I'll tell you now that when one thought he was going to run over me for one holy second, he had himself a cat on him. When I had to fight, I fought to win. And I fought many a night because you had to fight for your mere survival.[116]

New sheriffs began by strapping guns on their hip, but after a few physical confrontations, some of them took them off. Going into hand-to-hand combat with a holstered pistol potentially provided your opponent with the means of your own destruction, should he gain the upper hand, and multiple opponents and no backup made this even more likely. Over the years, the *Sheriffs' Association of Texas Magazine* reported numerous instances of lawmen's being overpowered and shot with their own weapons. In 1943, for example, Madison County sheriff Rodney Chambless entered a house to arrest a bootlegger, got into a scuffle, had his pistol taken away, and was shot in the groin.[117] Young H. F. Fenton also almost died from his own weapon. Fenton at first carried his pistol in a cross-draw holster, which he soon discovered conveniently placed the gun butt-forward to an opponent facing him. A drunk grabbed Fenton's pistol "and jobbed it in my gut—he was trying to pull the trigger on it, but it happened that I grabbed it and stuck my thumb right there behind the trigger." Fenton fell to the ground with the man, finally wrested the pistol from his hand, and slugged him on the head with it, but a .44 bullet in the stomach had been very, very close for Sheriff Fenton, and he knew it. He changed his way of wearing his pistol, and rather often, at domestic disturbances or roadhouse fights, he left the weapon in his car.[118]

New sheriffs without previous law enforcement experience seldom anticipated what invariably became their most terrifying physical confrontations, the subduing and capture of the insane. Sheriff T. W. Lane reported that twenty-four mentally ill persons had passed through the Wharton County jail during 1950, and that did not include those taken directly from homes or hospitals to the state asylum.[119] Nine days after taking office, Sheriff Paul Ray Jones of Hopkins County went out to pick up a mentally ill man and dodged a bullet. The man told Jones, "I voted for you, and now I'm going to kill you."[120] In 1956, Sheriff Wylie Barnes of Denton asked district Texas Ranger Lewis Rigler for assistance in dealing with "a crazy man holed up in his farm threatening to kill a bunch of people." Ranger Rigler understood Sheriff Barnes's reluctance to face the man by himself, since the sheriff was still recovering from a bullet in the stomach from another insane person, and Barnes's predecessor, W. O. Hodges, had been blinded by a shotgun blast from a deranged young man after only a few days in office.[121]

Sometimes the district Ranger, with responsibilities for several counties, was the only law enforcement assistance the rural sheriff could call upon. When things got rough, city marshals, night watchmen, and local constables often proved reluctant to help the sheriff get the insane man out of the farmhouse. Sheriffs typically had a low opinion of such officers. Sheriff Roy Herrington recalled of the constable at his home community of Neches: "If you were doing something, he'd tell you to go home. If you didn't, he would."[122]

Sheriffs had ambivalent attitudes toward Texas Rangers, and no wonder; beside offering valuable backup and technical assistance to county sheriffs, Rangers monitored sheriffs' official actions for indications of incompetence and corruption and had the right to intervene in their affairs. By 1957, Clint Peoples, onetime Montgomery County deputy sheriff, had risen to command Texas Ranger Company F based at Waco. Company F's territory was subdivided according to population and land area, with a Ranger assigned to each district. For example, from Mason, Ranger Charlie Miller covered nine counties in the northern Texas Hill Country. The duty of each Ranger was to maintain a liaison with the sheriffs, police chiefs, and constables in his assigned territory so he could assist in major cases, offering services not available to those local officers. However, as Peoples noted, "when an officer was not enforcing the law, the Ranger did it for him." Peoples explained: "We operated on the theory that the local law officers were honest. We didn't use it [Ranger power to enforce the law anywhere in Texas] as an ax. But you take some of the places where public officials didn't do their job, they might ought to look back, because there might be a Ranger there."[123]

New sheriffs found that a daunting prospect. Rangers had been part of the Texas Department of Public Safety since 1935, but Clint Peoples and a good many of the old-style officers were still on the job during the 1950s, and that was enough to give any new sheriff pause when considering whether to allow the country club to keep its traditional wet bar and slot machine. Manuel "Lone Wolf" Gonzaullas, with his flashy uniforms and machine-gun–mounted "scout cars," and cold-eyed man-killer Frank Hamer, veteran of fifty-two gun battles, had retired, but other formidable state officers still might show up to inquire into county law enforcement.[124]

No wonder sheriffs were of two minds about Texas Rangers. As Sheriff Ben Murray of Dimmitt County remarked, working cases with the district Ranger could be "like having another badge." Because Rangers had statewide authority, sheriffs could call on them when they needed to cross county lines in a case. Ideally, Ranger-sheriff relations were symbiotic, with each providing what the other lacked to break cases—Rangers the hardware and technical assistance, sheriffs the local knowledge.[125] On the other hand, Rangers might intrude on a sheriff's business and embarrass him. For example, a woman died at Groveton, Trinity County, in 1940 under circumstances so suspicious that doctors present at her deathbed wrote "this may be murder" on the death certificate. Nevertheless, Sheriff Harris Johnson did nothing. A year later, the dead woman's mother complained to the Texas Rangers, and district Ranger R. D. Holliday came down from Livingston and broke the case right under Sheriff Johnson's nose. Disinterred, the body proved to be loaded with strychnine, and the guilty husband had taken out a huge life insurance policy on his spouse.[126]

By 1950 in the more populous rural counties, other officers had joined sheriffs, deputies, Rangers, and constables in local law enforcement, and a new sheriff wisely used his cross-cutting authority to recruit all of them to his side—perhaps almost as extra deputies, but certainly as additional "eyes and ears." At Lufkin in Angelina County, as early as 1941, a reporter noted that Sheriff H. C. Billingsley's office had become a "focal point" for deputies, constables, game warden, Liquor Control Board officer, and Lufkin policemen. Officers sat around the sheriff's office talking about cases, sharing information, and planning how to "function as a unit, with the least red tape." A casual visitor could not even tell who was who, the reporter claimed, so much did the officers look and act alike.[127] Department of Public Safety troopers soon joined this menagerie of local lawmen, and Billingsley and most other sheriffs rejoiced to see them arrive. The carnage on highways after World War II had forced unenthusiastic sheriffs into the traffic control business, but writing traffic tickets did not endear one to the voters.

Municipal police forces were on the rise throughout Texas during the 1950s, and their relations with sheriffs' departments sometimes ran less smoothly than in Sheriff Billingsley's Lufkin. "A good sheriff is a buffer from other law enforcement, they're usually not very popular with the police departments," Sheriff J. R. Sessions observed.[128] After his election in 1961, newcomer sheriff John Lightfoot of Nacogdoches County tried to soothe troubled relations between the sheriff's office and the long-term Nacogdoches chief of police. Lightfoot told the municipal officer, "Now, Chief, I don't care whether you like me or whether you don't like me, your ass is in trouble. I am here until this thing's over."[129]

Close cooperation between police and sheriff's department soon returned to Nacogdoches County, but turf conflicts over authority within the county-seat towns and the natural antagonisms between elected and appointed officers caused trouble elsewhere. At Palestine during Roy Herrington's years as sheriff of Montgomery County, relations between sheriff and chief, deputy and policeman, became troubled, and a gentlemen's agreement to stay out of each other's way was the best that could be arranged. The police responded to calls from Palestine, and the sheriff's department responded to those from the rest of the county, but when the police failed to satisfy a Palestine voter and he or she turned to the high sheriff, the deal was off.[130] Municipal police, game wardens, and DPS troopers enforced the law in a purely mechanical way, but for the elected sheriff, every enforcement episode had political dimensions and consequently was handled a little differently. Sheriffs and their men "interpreted" the law; nonelected officers "went by the book." Like dogs and cats, the two sorts of officers sometimes found it difficult to get along.

New sheriffs everywhere, but especially in East Texas, usually stayed away from enforcement of the unpopular game laws, although most lawmen were willing to come to the wardens' rescue when they got into life-threatening situations. Sheriff Aubrey Cole, who perhaps had run for office on a tacit anti–game law ticket, did this with some reluctance, but for Sheriff Lightfoot the game warden was "just like one of my own deputies, I went to his rescue several times."[131]

Establishing good working relationships with neighboring sheriffs was as important as agreements with in-county municipal police chiefs, and newcomer John Lightfoot took pains to ingratiate himself with veteran San Augustine County sheriff Nathan Tindall and other neighbors. Sheriffs often met with each other, talked on the telephone, and even joined in sheriffs' rodeos, rattlesnake-shooting competitions, and other social and public relations events.[132] Practical considerations strongly encouraged these cooperations, since outlaws tended to cluster along county lines and move back and forth between jurisdictions whenever things heated up. Sheriffs had limited legal rights to pursue wrongdoers into other counties—a major limitation on their power—but informal trespass rights and "hot pursuit" agreements between neighboring sheriffs benefited both officers. Soon after Joe Goodson followed his father into office in Lee County, veteran sheriff Nig Hoskins of Bastrop visited Joe in his Giddings office and told him: "You know, me and your daddy had a thing going. You go in my county any time you want to, and I'll come over here. You don't have to contact me, if you're chasing somebody, you go get him."[133] Other common informal cooperations between neighboring sheriffs involved picking up suspicious locals upon request and holding them for the outsider sheriff to question and answering "hot calls" from foreign communities just across the county line and closer to them than to their official sheriffs.[134]

Neighbor sheriffs sometimes also used each other as undercover officers in sting operations, such as the one conducted at Shelby County in 1954. Rural sheriffs were marked men in their counties, with faces known by most citizens and all native criminals, but not so the neighbor sheriffs. The twenty-six Shelby County bootleggers who had sold whiskey to San Augustine County sheriff Nathan Tindall and Panola County sheriff

Johnny Spradley discovered their mistake after Shelby County sheriff Charlie Christian launched his arrest raid.[135]

Neighboring sheriffs tended to maintain cordial relations even if they personally disliked each other or disapproved of each other's ways of doing things, but not always. Adjacent counties sometimes had different traditions about liquor consumption and other matters, and sheriffs had local political axes to grind; they got no votes from the next county. Consequently, after various citizens' complaints, the Mills County sheriff warned whiskey reformer Gaston Boykin to confine his car chases of bootleggers to his own county.[136] Outlaws who committed crimes in one county, then crossed county lines to their home counties, or to counties with laxer law enforcement, commonly plagued rural sheriffs and often tempted officers into illegal pursuits. Before 1900, Wood County deputy sheriff Bill McDonald "made frequent still-hunts along the Sabine River, the dividing line between Wood and Smith [counties]," waiting for a certain Smith County outlaw to cross into his territory. After a while, however, since "the impulse of the Ranger was already upon him," McDonald crossed the Sabine, hunted down the outlaw, and shot him. Furious at this poaching incursion, some Smith County officials brought the matter to the next grand jury, but District Attorney James S. Hogg told the jury to forget it; if they went ahead and indicted Deputy McDonald for his public service to Smith County, Hogg would refuse to prosecute the case.[137]

Political relations with his own county and district attorneys, and county and district judges, were much on a new sheriff's mind. Ideally, the sheriff worked hand in glove with his fellow elected law enforcement officials, none of whom could effectively do their job without the cooperation of all the rest. The sheriff functioned as executive officer to the courts of the county and district judges, and he worked closely with county and district attorneys to being criminal cases to trial. These latter relationships were particularly crucial for enforcing the law. After a while, new sheriff John Lightfoot's county and district attorneys "were like my own boys," and Ed Darnell's attorneys "would come in at two o'clock in the morning with their britches over their pajamas" to take statements from important outlaws held in the sheriff's jail.[138] The close cooperation worked both ways. Frustrated in his efforts to select local juries who would convict Comanche County's bootleggers, the county attorney soon turned jury selections over to Sheriff Gaston Boykin, who demonstrated an uncanny ability to identify jurors who would vote guilty.[139]

Conversely, if the sheriff "made a case," but if—for whatever reason—the county attorney refused to bring the case to county court, or the district attorney refused to bring the matter before the grand jury for true billing for the district court, the sheriff's case ended there. There could be no prosecution of the crime. County and district attorneys had their own political agendas, which might or might not coincide with that of the sheriff, and their complicated legal cogitations sometimes proved inscrutable to a simple law officer.

New sheriffs offended their public attorneys at great risk, and wars with "courthouse lawyers" accelerated the end of many sheriffs' careers. For Montgomery County deputy Clint Peoples, Hemphill County sheriff Walter Adams, and others, jailing the county attorney for driving while intoxicated proved a politically egregious error.[140]

Sometimes the county attorney joined forces with an incumbent sheriff's enemies at election time, and sometimes he took action before then. Public attorneys had their resources. For whatever reason, at Anderson County veteran constable and first-term sheriff Jack Dismuke found himself bitterly at odds with the county attorney, who swiftly brought the new sheriff to trial on a misdemeanor charge of "stealing meat valued at more than $5 and less than $50."[141] After the first trial ended in a hung jury, the county attorney quickly tried Sheriff Dismuke again. County attorneys' inquiries to the state attorney general sometimes indicated local political agendas directed at sheriffs and would-be sheriffs. In 1946, the Liberty County attorney asked if a candidate for sheriff had to be able to read and write and was informed that he did not.[142] In 1962, the Jasper County attorney inquired if a sheriff could permit a jail prisoner to spend nights at home without supervision, leave the jail to buy cigarettes, and go on jail errands in his private car and was told that such laxities were illegal.[143] Henceforth, the Jasper County sheriff's favorite prisoner would have to remain locked up.

District judges and district courts served judicial districts that included several counties, so a sheriff's most fateful and intimate relationship was with his county judge. Sheriffs brought most of their criminal cases in county court, and the county judge also headed the county commissioners court, which held the sheriff's purse strings in an iron grip. Not surprisingly, new sheriffs went out of their way to offer every courtesy to the county judges and their courts, but some still received rude awakenings when they brought cases to trial. "Judge Butler Rolston was a good judge, but he didn't believe in enforcing the whisky laws," Sheriff Henry Billingsley of Angelina County ruefully recalled. Billingsley had taken office in 1933 on a platform of enforcing Prohibition in a county with numerous desperate and unemployed sawmill men recently turned to moonshining. Sheriff Billingsley caught many such whiskey outlaws, but Judge Rolston dismissed every case without explanation—seventy-six cases at one term of court, thirty-six at the next. After the first court day, moonshiners knew not to plead guilty to anything, only to make bond, and, as Billingsley recalled, "They would even make bond in the morning and before leaving town would go get more barrels to set up another still." After a few such humiliations, Billingsley attempted to get his whiskey outlaws convicted at district court in Tyler.[144]

In some counties, county judges were long-entrenched political figures whom newcomer sheriffs alienated at their peril. Some of these men took advantage of their position on the commissioners court to try to tell the sheriff how to run his department, and some seemed to dislike all sheriffs. Courthouse observers at Cameron County in 1949 believed that County Judge Oscar Dancy was "allergic to sheriffs and their departments." As he had done in the past with earlier sheriffs, Judge Dancy recently had claimed that Sheriff Boyington Fleming's department could be "maintained a thousand dollars a month cheaper than it presently was." Elsewhere in 1949, Lamar County sheriff Willie P. Lane quarreled with County Judge T. E. Springer over mileage allowances for the sheriff's personal automobile. Sheriff Lane told the judge, "You're as wet as a goose," at which insult the judge fined the sheriff twenty-five dollars for contempt of court. The county attorney advised the sheriff that he did not have to pay it.[145]

Sometimes such political conflicts persisted for decades. Sheriff Roy Herrington battled the Anderson County judge from the time Herrington first took office in 1948 until the judge's death. The incumbent sheriff had advised his replacement to "just let him run it," meaning the sheriff's office, but Herrington refused. As a consequence, the judge strongly backed someone against Herrington in every sheriff's race and constantly intrigued behind the scenes to "get something" on the sheriff, who did the same about the judge. From time to time both were successful. On more than one occasion the quarrel came to name calling and direct physical threats. Finally, however, the combative old judge passed away, and someone asked Sheriff Herrington if he was going to the funeral. "I said,

'You bet I'm going to the funeral, cause I want to be damn sure that's him!'"[146]

The new sheriff sometimes found his first meeting with the commissioners as shocking as Sheriff Henry Billingsley's first term of county court. The county commission, comprised of the four precinct commissioners and the county judge, directed all county operational and fiscal affairs and determined the budget of the sheriff's office. If the sheriff wanted an additional deputy or even new tires on his patrol car, he had to ask the commissioners for these things, and rather often the commissioners told him, "Not this year."

In the scuffle for scarce county tax money, each commissioner had his own political and fiscal agenda, always directed—first and foremost—at improving the county roads in the home precinct, and a larger piece of the fiscal pie for someone else meant a smaller piece for him. As every grassroots politician well knew, roads mattered more than anything else to precinct voters—so much so that they often referred to their elected officials as "road commissioners."[147] The family farm still lingered in 1950, and the state of the rural roads determined if a family got cotton to the gin, medicine from the store, or the sick baby to a distant hospital. A commissioner who allowed his precinct's roads to languish while the sheriff bought two-way radios and put a new roof on the jail risked swift political defeat. County tax money was limited, and roofing the jail might mean living with the rickety, dangerous wooden bridge over a precinct creek for yet another year. Consequently, as sheriffs often complained, county commissioners seemed all too willing to agree with the Cameron County judge that their sheriff's office could be "maintained a thousand dollars a month cheaper" than the present and that prisoners in the jail "should be thrown in the Black Hole of Calcutta and fed in a bucket."[148]

Sheriffs had to get along with their commissioners, and they did everything in their power to do so. They turned on the charm, watched what they said, and put on their most humble faces; if the voters did not like to see a proud sheriff with "hairs" on him, as Leon Jones observed, commissioners liked this even less. Furthermore, the high sheriff had no power to compel his commissioners to do anything they did not want to do. Even a long-term sheriff relatively successful at dealing with his commissioners ended up with a bitter taste in his mouth. "There's very few counties where the sheriff and the commissioners court get along," Sheriff Jess Sweeten of Henderson County admitted. "We didn't get along too, too good. I thought of it many, many times, there could be a better way figured out. A sheriff is more or less at the mercy of the commissioners court, and if he's got enemies on that commissioners court, he's in trouble."[149] Commissioners came and went, and even master politician Big Ed Darnell admitted that sometimes he got one that "would kind of lay it on you and hold you down." Since Darnell had no more coercive tactic to use on his troublesome commissioner than the encouragement of guilt, he used that, telling the man: "You're cutting your nose off to spite your face. All we're trying to do is take care of our people, and if you can't help me, that's all right. You just go on. If you can live with it, I can live without it, and we'll do the best we can." Sometimes, Darnell said, "I'd get 'em ashamed of themselves."[150]

During the 1950s and 1960s, after despairing of ever getting such innovations funded, many Texas sheriffs went around their commissioners with direct appeals to the public for voluntary contributions to buy two-way radios and other modern law enforcement equipment. No sheriff did this with the success of T. W. "Buckshot" Lane of Wharton County, who circumvented his county commissioners for a state-of-the-art radio system, fingerprint lab, photography lab, lie detector, and sheriff's department airplane, the latter funded by a public "Buck for Buck" campaign. Lane developed enough political power to overawe his commissioners, at least some of the time, and to deal with them as many other sheriffs doubtless wished they could have. Lane explained: "The county wouldn't pay for much, our cars were as cheap as they could buy. You see, the county fought me, the county commissioners fought me, cause I made 'em count the gravel trucks. Commissioners can rob the county quicker than anybody in the world and get by with it, but I stayed after 'em. They didn't like me. It's hard to get along with your commissioners if you count the gravel trucks."[151]

Desperate sheriffs rather commonly forced public confrontations with their commissioners over the bone of greatest contention—maintenance of the jail. County money spent on the jail did individual commissioners no political good at all, most of them believed. However, sheriffs and their families lived in the jails with assorted vermin, leaking roofs, and prisoners threatening to escape, and the lawmen sometimes tried to publicly embarrass commissioners into jail reform.

After two fourteen-year-old boys broke out of his Trinity County jail by twisting window bars out with a "leg of an old hide-bottom chair" in 1937,

Sheriff Carl Busch told a Houston newspaper that "the only way I could keep anybody in my jail here in Groveton is to feed 'em well and beg 'em to stay." The commissioners became furious, but they reluctantly diverted WPA money for a new jail.[152] In 1946, Sheriff Homer Casey of McLennan County took a reporter on a tour of his jail and demonstrated to the newsman that "a severe shaking would just about open a jail door and the bars on the outside windows were so insecure that a horse or an automobile could pull them out." Furthermore, the first floor was "uninhabitable" as a result of falling plaster and "the continual dripping of water from defective plumbing which pools up on the concrete floor."[153] Sheriff Louis L. Willard of Burleson County went a step further in 1954; he had his jail condemned by the county health officer, then informed reporters that "the law says that if the county will not provide a suitable jail the sheriff can rent a building and hire guards to protect the prisoners at county expense, and if the county does not provide us with a jail soon, that's what I am going to do."[154]

Endless quarreling over jail minutia was the common pattern, however. Legally, commissioners had no say about sheriff department policy, but their control of the department budget tempted them to try to do just that. In Howard County, they forbade the sheriff from feeding deputies at the jail dinner table.[155] In McLennan County they turned down the sheriff's request for repair of a jail heating system and suggested that prisoners "should wrap up Indian style," then they cut the sheriff's subsequent request for blankets from forty-eight to ten.[156] In Jasper County, commissioners shut down the jail kitchen and ordered the sheriff to feed prisoners from a local café at so many cents a meal per prisoner, but they did not stop there. Jasper County commissioners also confiscated Sheriff Thomas Nixon's official car and returned it to the county to be sold, fired his radio officer, and denied car and mileage allowances to his deputies. The county judge would clear all sheriff's office purchases in the future, commissioners announced.[157]

Sheriffs occasionally heard even worse news at their dreaded commissioners court meetings. For example, in 1944, Sheriff W. A. Scholl learned that his official salary had been cut from $2,130 to $1,000 a year by the commissioners, who offered no explanation for their actions.[158] In 1955, the Duval County sheriff discovered that his department's yearly budget had been reduced from $40,900 to $19,950 and that commissioners had raised their own salaries from $5,400 to $6,750.[159]

Grand juries, another ancient Anglo-Saxon institution, lurked like sleeping tigers in the new sheriff's political landscape, and sometimes the beasts awoke. When Dan Saunders first took office as Martin County sheriff in 1953, the county commissioners and the county judge paid the new sheriff little mind. They had their own terrible problems with a secret grand jury investigation into county fiscal affairs. Early in Saunders's first term, the grand jury indicted the county judge and all four commissioners for fiscal mismanagement, and after conviction the judge went to the penitentiary. Martin County was bankrupted, Texas Electric cut off power to the courthouse, and the new sheriff set roadblocks to catch bootleggers for fines with which to operate his department and shot jackrabbits to help feed his jail prisoners.[160]

Normally, grand juries of citizens served the district court for six-month terms, hearing secret evidence presented to them about potential felony cases by sheriffs and district attorneys and deciding to true-bill (indict) or no-bill the persons charged. Indicted individuals faced jury trial in district court and if convicted were sent to the state penitentiary.

Grand juries usually functioned as a docile part of the ordinary machinery of county law enforcement, but grand juries had a right to call witnesses and investigate any part of local government they wished— including the sheriff's office. The grand jury might get out of control: an agent of reform to some, perhaps a corrupt county's last hope, to others it became the dreaded "runaway grand jury," a loose cannon on the frail ship of local government.

Sheriffs paid close attention when they joined the district judge in choosing the five "grand jury commissioners" who then met to come up with the secret names of the "good honest, home-grown, hard-working, God-fearing people" who served on the grand jury. At least Sheriff Joe Goodson hoped such adjectives described the citizens who ended up on his Lee County grand jury. Otherwise, the grand jury might "get off on a tangent, send out subpoenas," and delve into who knows what. "Look how many political people have been ruined by grand jury indictments," Goodson observed.[161]

Somebody often was behind the runaway grand jury, directing it off into its tangent, people commonly believed, but even local political observers were not always certain just who this somebody was. Grand juries might subpoena witnesses to investigate fiscal corruption in county government across the board, as they did in Martin County in 1952, Crosby County in

1959, or Greg County in 1961.[162] They might praise county sheriffs for their good work, recommend that certain deputies be fired or rehired, or suggest detailed modernizations in the sheriff's department—matters that, properly speaking, were none of their business.[163]

Rather often, the sheriff brought touchy matters about his or his deputy's use of violence or deadly force before the grand jury so the actions could be no-billed and tacitly approved, and even ugly rumors might be treated the same way. In Wharton County, for example, persistent rumors that a man named Horelica had been beaten to death by officers at the scene of a traffic accident were laid to rest after Sheriff Lane brought the matter to the grand jury.[164]

Conversely, for whatever reasons, grand juries could turn on the sheriff and try to destroy him. During 1957, without notifying Sheriff Owen W. Kilday of Bexar County (who was sick at home) or Assistant District Attorney J. Lawton Stone, who was supposedly in charge of grand jury activities, a grand jury marched down to Kilday's jail, poked into every nook and cranny of his operations, and took statements from prisoners.[165] During 1951, a Montgomery County grand jury recommended that Sheriff E. T. Anderson "be removed for official misconduct." Beyond that, the grand jury did not elaborate, but the sheriff soon supplied the details. "It's all politics, a frame-up," Anderson told reporters. "I've been accused of throwing wild parties for women prisoners in the county jail, that accusation is baseless." The witnesses who told the grand jury about the wild parties "were after my scalp—I don't want to mention names, I'm too big for that. It's all politics. They said I was drunk and that's a lie. I drink only four ounces of whisky a night, and that is on doctor's orders."[166]

Runaway grand juries might go after almost anybody. After investigating constable-operated speed traps, a Harrison County grand jury noted, "Your grand jury is of the belief that the office of constable is outmoded and should be abolished."[167] A Tarrant County grand jury criticized the sheriff of nearby Parker County, John Young, for laxity in enforcing gambling laws, prompting Young to tell reporters: "You can just tell the grand jury of Tarrant County that I haven't been bought off and that we don't need the grand jury of Tarrant County to act in our county over here. We have a grand jury of our own." Furthermore, Sheriff Young informed the media, he could pinpoint several flagrant gambling dens within blocks of the Tarrant County courthouse.[168]

Considering the heavy demands of the job of sheriff, the long hours, nagging requests, physical challenges, and political minefields the new man had to learn his way around, it was no wonder that many sheriffs served only one term in office and then decided not to run again. As did Marcus Steck of Austin County, they said to their deputies, "I've had all of this I want!"[169] Steck had lost a fight, but other disasters stalked new sheriffs from their first days on the job. At Titus County in 1959, for example, two trustees broke jail and took to their heels during Sheriff Alvis Redfearn's swearing-in ceremony. The sheriff pursued them with department bloodhounds, the bloodhounds would not trail and catch, and the whole affair reached local papers in humiliating detail.[170] New sheriffs were ever on the spot, and one mishandled incident could end a career. After hauling away a young man's truck while the young man's mother held a gun on him threatening to shoot, Sheriff Tom Brown told his companion, "I'd have rather been shot and died right there than to have you come back telling that woman run me off."[171]

Some men did not make it to the end of their first terms. In oil-boom Winkler County during the 1920s and oil-boom Lee County during the 1970s, sheriffs resigned rather than face the new influx of wild oil men and all their hangers-on.[172] In Martin County in 1949, the sheriff served for ten days, then resigned, citing "personal reasons."[173] Coleman Babb of Terrell County also resigned in his first term in 1961, the third consecutive Terrell County sheriff to take this action.[174] New sheriff David C. Hale of Erath County ran two red lights, caused a "negligent collision," and resigned in 1966.[175] The district judge removed newly elected Panola County sheriff J. H. Spradley from office for "alleged repeat intoxication, hampering law enforcement," and the sheriff subsequently resigned.[176] The stresses and strains of the job, unlike anything most men had experienced, also took a swift physical toll on some. More than a few sheriffs suffered heart attacks during their first terms, as did Sheriff Monroe Walbridge of Hudspeth County, who died suddenly in 1960.[177]

However, for some people, playing the role of high sheriff came as a heady draught, and having once experienced it, they strove to remain in office, serving their constituencies, all the remaining days of their lives. Texas sheriffs served two-year terms until 1956, so the successful sheriff never really stopped campaigning. Sheriff Frank Brunt of Cherokee County explained: "People still say I'm campaigning. I was blessed, I guess, with a gift of getting around to people, though I don't stay very long. Every time they had a graveyard cleaning or a memorial service, I'd go out there and visit with those people, and I'd go to Jacksonville and Rusk and get out on the street and shake hands with people. I kind of electioneered the year round. I went day and night."[178] Sheriff Frank Biaggne of Galveston County articulated Brunt's political dictum more succinctly when he told a reporter, "If you go to enough places, meet enough people, and shake their hands, they'll re-elect you."[179]

Abrasive, combative, and hot-tempered sheriffs sometimes amused the voters—at least for a while—but the men who lasted through reelection after reelection usually were not of that sort. Jim Scarborough II of Kleberg County regarded himself as everybody's friend at the courthouse, a "personal sheriff," and Big Ed Darnell recalled that "everybody was my dear friend, that's why I like law enforcement, I love people, I don't think I ever had an enemy, and I catered to the old people and children."[180] As Darnell told his interviewer, some men with underlying motives of greed and power might successfully fake love of their fellow citizens well enough to get themselves elected, but they never lasted; their constituents soon saw through them. Ed Darnell, Jim Scarborough II, Brantley Barker, Wallace Riddell, Dan Saunders, Nathan Tindall, Sonny Sessions, and other long-term sheriffs stated their basic goal while in office in virtually the same words as Darnell's: "taking care of my people."

Successful sheriffs emphasized this public service aspect of their role over that of technical law enforcement, though it was useful to have made a name for oneself by winning a public gunfight, as Truman Maddox or Buckshot Lane did, or turning over a few bootleggers after hot pursuits in your souped up patrol car, as did Frank Brunt. Sheriffs often echoed the political stance of Rufe Jordan, who claimed that "over 95 percent of the people in Gray County don't need a sheriff, my work with the criminal element includes mostly outsiders who drift in."[181]

Resident law breakers did exist, however, and successful long-term sheriffs such as Jordan approached these wayward voters with tact and discretion. Trivial violations of the law often were ignored by the sheriff and his men, who left traffic offenses to the municipal police and highway patrol and game law violations to the game warden. Sheriffs had better things to do, and such matters only lost votes. When rural sheriffs had civil papers or criminal arrest warrants to serve, rather often they called the citizens on the telephone and asked them to come by the office to talk it over. Sheriff John Lightfoot of Nacogdoches County did this as a matter of basic procedure—always being courteous, even to the people with criminal warrants against them, taking time to explain their situations and their options, and politely requesting that they come down to the county jail. Normally, they did exactly that, thus avoiding the embarrassment of a sheriff's department car driving down their road and stopping at their house. Such law enforcement applications of the Golden Rule made political sense for sheriffs such as John Lightfoot. Ideally, your sheriff could arrest you, remain your friend, and retain your vote. Sheriff Truman Maddox explained this basic political reality: "You have a two-fold purpose, you want to enforce the law, yet you want to do it in such a manner that you keep on everyone's good side. If you're a county sheriff, you have to have everybody as your friend, or you'll get voted out."[182]

By about 1950, in Truman Maddox's Austin County, John Lightfoot's Nacogdoches County, Nathan Tindall's San Augustine County, and many other places, the people the successful sheriff needed to have as his friend once again included African Americans, and the long-term sheriffs of midcentury successfully appealed to the new black voters. In Wharton County, Sheriff Buck Lane rode to the peak of his political power with the help of the returning black vote. At San Augustine County during the early 1950s, Sheriff Nathan Tindall publicly greeted blacks on the street and shook their hands. As Tindall noted, recalling these early days in his career, "I was just treating blacks the way they make you treat em now."[183] Tindall's Anglo supporters were of two minds about his familiarity with local African Americans—an ambivalence that persisted throughout the sheriff's forty-year career. "A lot of white people supported Nathan Tindall down the years because they believed he kept the blacks in line," an elderly Anglo woman explained. However, other Anglos thought that "the blacks pretty much had the run of the county when Nathan was in office," and some even called Tindall "the nigger sheriff."[184]

Effective control of the local media also typified the successful careers of long-term rural sheriffs, although in many cases this meant nothing more than remaining on reasonably good terms with the editor of the weekly newspaper. When relations with the editor worsened, as they did for Gaston Boykin during his third term as Comanche County sheriff in 1952, sheriffs found out about the power of the press. Week after week the enemy editor pounded away at Sheriff Boykin with negative stories and critical editorials, even writing speeches for Boykin's opponent. Boykin had no way to answer the newsman, and he lost the election and remained out of office until the mid-1960s.[185]

Successful sheriffs often had a flair for media and public relations, but perhaps no midcentury rural sheriff demonstrated as much native political talent in this field as did the remarkable T. W. "Buckshot" Lane, Wharton County sheriff from 1940 to 1952. Buckshot, usually called "Buck" by his friends, already had a good nickname for a sheriff. An uncle had bestowed it in Lane's childhood to commemorate his nephew's black, beady, close-set eyes. Small of stature, weighing perhaps 130 pounds, usually well dressed in business suit, white starched shirt, felt hat, and wing-tipped shoes, .45 automatic in a hip holster, Lane looked very little like a typical Texas sheriff and a lot like an FBI agent. Nor was this accidental; Lane had attended the FBI academy for local officers and remained on good terms with J. Edgar Hoover. However, none of Hoover's agents would have dared wear Buck Lane's extremely loud ties, which hinted at the Wharton County sheriff's essential nature.

"I was broke, was how I come to get into law enforcement," Lane told a historian, "All I had was a big paper route. I was married and had to make a living." Running for constable, he adopted a confessional, just-one-of-the-boys style, admitting that "during the bootleg days, I had bought a lot of whiskey, drank a lot of whiskey" and that once he had been thrown into the Houston jail. "I know what's it's like to be in jail and out of jail," Lane told the voters, who liked his honesty. Lane became constable of Precinct 1 at the county seat of Wharton, then had a reputation-making highway gunfight with a man who had robbed a bank at Luling, shot a sheriff, shot a liquor control man, and stolen the V-8 Ford of the Beeville chief of police. Blocked at a local bridge, the dangerous outlaw took cover behind the automobile and tried to kill the outgunned Lane with his .30-30 Winchester while Lane desperately hid behind his car's engine block, the only part of the vehicle that would stop a .30-30 bullet. "He put fifty-four bullet holes in my car and shot my hat off," Lane told, but the little constable managed to wound the outlaw in the foot with his pistol and later helped capture him. In 1940, Wharton County voters rewarded Buck Lane by electing him sheriff.[186]

Sheriff Lane wanted to modernize his department but found his commissioners court as hard to deal with as did most sheriffs. By his second two-year term in office, however, Lane had discovered a route around the penny-pinching commissioners. He began a popular sheriff's

Dressed like an FBI agent, Sheriff T. W. "Buckshot" Lane of Wharton County poses for the local media about 1949. (Author's collection)

column in the Wharton and El Campo papers, then a daily radio show, and periodically he asked his Wharton County readers and listeners for direct donations—first, for a two-way radio system; then, for a lie detector machine; and then, in 1949, for an airplane. Some people laughed at the "Buck for Buck" campaign to establish a Wharton County Air Force, with every contributor's name displayed on the side of the first airship, but a few months later the sheriff's plane lifted off the ground.

Lane's column began with an occasional jail report in 1941. By late 1943, longer columns occasionally appeared, and on July 7, 1944, the first column entitled "The Inimitable Style of Sheriff Lane" appeared. It was shorter at first, commonly five hundred to a thousand words, but by 1948 it had swelled to take up most of a page in the Wharton paper and averaged four thousand words. Other papers picked it up, including *The Houston Post*, and reporters from *Life* magazine and the *Saturday Evening Post* came down to do stories on Lane and his column.

An editor aptly remarked that Buck Lane "has no more sense of punctuation than a hog," but Lane's readers did not seem to care. Reporter Wesley Stout noted: "He uses an electric typewriter. When he hits the trigger, the words gush forth like a 4,000-barrel well and as scrambled as the contents of an overturned produce truck." Readers loved Lane's writing style despite "non sequiturs, bleeding syntax, skids, drift, blowouts and other lapses painful to grammarians. Writers at work commonly cloister themselves, snarling at intruders. The sheriff, who hasn't yet heard of the artistic temperament, bats out his columns amidst nagging phones, radio alarms and excursions, visitors official and social, and the jail routine." Certainly the column was good politics, the reporter thought, but it also contributed to law enforcement by converting much of the public into sheriff's snitches. "In Wharton County, half the people, white, brown, and black—and the upper half—are Buck's stool-pigeons, trained to report the unusual instantly. Each report is a secret strictly between Buck and them."[187]

For years, no sooner had Wharton County citizens received their weekly papers than they opened them to the sheriff's column and read Buck Lane first. Almost anything might be there. Lane's column was a fascinating mix of elements, including detailed crime reports (often with an amusing slant put on them, especially if minorities were involved), "news of the weird" items, big-picture political commentary, exhortations to the public encouraging better behavior, warnings about crooks on the make, warnings about dangerous public practices, cease-and-desist warnings to wrongdoers, pedagogic notes about the officer's job, out-and-out lobbying for the officer, pleas for public support of sheriff's department policies, discreet listings of sheriff's department kudos and achievements, occasional confessions of personal failures and embarrassments (especially when already known to the public), and attempts to defuse negative rumors and other political trouble.

If Buck Lane's sons were caught shooting county property with a pellet rifle, or Lane mislaid his .45 auto and launched a panicky search, he put those things in his column. "Sick at heart, my one and only pistol stolen from me," Lane tried to think who might have taken it. "I hated for the news to get out, but it was seeping out and fast." Finally, the jail cook located the pistol where Lane had put it down, and, "Then did I feel cheap? Well, folks, from now on I won't even cuss folks for running in here all out of breath reporting a theft or something wrong."[188]

On December 20, 1946, a friend told Lane that a man had wondered out loud to him "if all that Buck wrote about really happens or happened?" The sheriff wrote, "I can truthfully say, it all happens, and a darn-sight more happens than I do write about." Readers will simply have to take his word about things like the El Campo fat lady who tried to smuggle four pounds of butter from a store by holding it between her upper thighs. Her walk was so peculiar that the store owner investigated and found the butter. She talked the resident deputy into allowing her to pay for the butter and leave, but the next day, in another El Campo store, she tried it again, and "this time she had a dressed, frying sized chicken up in between her legs—this time her pleas of help me, I won't never do it again, did her no good."[189] Then there was the strange demise of Bill Armstrong, an old, retarded, eccentric man from Wharton, who "resembled a long hairy-armed ape rather than a man." Armstrong was harmless, though he had a clothes obsession, often sneaking into people's back yards to steal items of clothing from the lines. When discovered, he ran away, crashing through people's back-yard fences. Armstrong often wore three or four suits of clothes at the same time, as many as he could get on his body. But Armstrong would steal no more. Lane wrote, "Early last Monday morning, I found out what the big rats along the Colorado River can do and will do to a human body." Armstrong was dead, with "half of his face eaten away by rats, not a good sight for any person to see."[190]

By day and night, at Buck Lane's Wharton office and at the offices of over three hundred other Texas sheriffs, the phone rang and citizens walked through the door to talk to the high sheriff, and no one could predict what was on their mind. Sheriffs knew only that they were supposed to "take care of their people." On October 25, 1946, Lane wrote in his column:

> The following is an idea of how things happen, and all nearly at once, first in comes a negro man wanting to make bond for a woman, hardly is this done than in comes a woman wanting to bond out her man, while handling this in comes a fellow hardly able to toddle, he is drunk, he says, "have you got time to go with me? I got trouble," before I can get him latched up good, a call comes in, someone stole a bicycle, and while answering that the other phone rings, it is a report of a negro man whipping a negro woman, hardly hung up before asking that we locate a fellow someplace in town for a death message, and within seconds a fellow calls and reports a dog having bit a child, the child in Houston and then it rings again and it is inquiring as whether the fellow has been located yet, and so on into the night she goes, in other words, there is never too many dull moments, yours very truly, Buck Lane.

CHAPTER TWO

LIFE IN THE JAIL AND TRADE CRAFT

Before 1960, many rural Texas sheriffs and their families lived in special apartments provided for them in the county jails, and officers' wives and children often served as jailers, cooks, office deputies, and drivers for the understaffed sheriffs. Families tended to take these collaborative operations of the jails in stride, since similar sharing of labor had been required back on the family cotton farms or cattle ranches, and everybody was used to customary chores.

Admittedly, the chores had changed. Sheriffs' wives now cooked for thirty or forty instead of four or five, and their daily processings of dried pinto beans reached monumental proportions. Fresh from feeding chickens and slopping hogs, sheriffs' children now rose in the morning to push tin plates of food through jail door slots to inmates. Under the increased pressures of food preparation, some children now moved beyond feeding prisoners and bringing in wood for the cook stoves. For example, in Burnet County about 1950, sheriff's son Pat Riddell "cooked 48 biscuits from scratch every morning" as part of his daily duties.[1]

No one confused life in the jail with life on the farm; by comparison, life in the jail was a sojourn on the wild side of things. When young Leona Bannister carried food upstairs to feed prisoners in the Coleman County jail about 1917, she knew she would once again confront the insane man who refused to wear clothing, squatted continuously on the floor of his cell, and periodically screamed at the top of his lungs. Outside the Bannister family's jail apartment, Leona followed a normal round of school, socializing, and piano lessons, but she found her jail life as helpful sheriff's daughter much more interesting. Leona fed the prisoners, kept the departmental records (including the jail log), and chauffeured her horseman father and his deputies around the countryside in the Model T Ford that most of them could not drive. Around the sheriff's jail apartment it seemed that almost anything might happen. Once, a man killed by a railroad detective lay, arms properly crossed, outside the Bannisters' front door all night. Every Saturday evening, a procession of wayward Coleman County citizens passed through the corridor and booking area outside the sheriff's apartment on their way upstairs to the jail, and Leona Bannister often peeked around the door to watch the action. "Some of them would ask for a lawyer, some would want to make a telephone call. The local gamblers hated the situation, the prostitutes were usually laughing, the drunks steadied themselves as well as they could, the fighters were angry and torn. Papa and the deputies were always courteous and imperturbable."[2]

Chauffeuring her father on law enforcement business also greatly amused young Leona Bannister. She became an expert rough-road driver and fixer of flat tires, familiar with every nook and cranny of rural Coleman County. Leona's mother even devised her daughter a kind of uniform for these excursions—a khaki dress; white blouse; brown, wide-brimmed Stetson; and high-topped, laced-up woman's shoes. Furthermore, Leona carried a weapon. Rather often, she sat alone in the car at night while her father moved out on foot to slip up on gamblers or bootleggers, and Sheriff Bannister had purchased a .38 revolver for Leona's protection in these circumstances, though he instructed her to use it only in dire emergency. On one memorable occasion the Bannisters drove home "loaded down with Negroes from a crap game—two were on the front fenders, two beside me on the front seat, and Papa sat on the right in the back with several others. All the way he kept telling me, 'Now, don't you go to sleep.' We were going from Rockwood to Coleman, probably not faster than twenty miles an hour, and it seemed to take hours."[3]

Occasionally other sheriffs' sons, daughters, and wives accompanied them on calls. Thirty years after Leona Bannister rode with her father, Pat Riddell of Burnet County and Joe Goodson of Lee County accompanied their fathers on calls involving the removal, dead or alive, of dogs, cats, raccoons, possums, and other varmints from attics, crawl spaces, and treetops. Sheriffs Wallace Riddell and J. R. Goodson had separately concluded that half-grown boys were perfect for such duties. At about the same time, during the late 1940s, Loretta Fenton often accompanied her new husband

Sheriff H. F. Fenton of Coleman County and wife, Loretta, about 1950. (H. F. Fenton family, Coleman, Texas)

on sheriff's calls in Coleman County. Loretta waited anxiously in the car while H. F. went inside home or roadhouse, and if he arrested someone, she sat in the back seat and held her shoe or her "do-right stick" over the person's head on the way home to jail. Loretta Fenton also carried a .25 automatic until the night she leaped from the car waving the pistol while H. F. scuffled with two drunks in a dark yard. Immediately, all three combatants stopped fighting and looked fearfully at Loretta. Sobered, the drunks went quietly, but H. F. took Loretta's pistol away. Loretta ceased riding with H. F. after her children were born, but when Loretta's oldest daughter, Ginger, reached the age of six, she began accompanying her sheriff father, at least on some calls.[4]

E. A. "Dogie" Wright was only two years old in 1903 when his father, Will Wright, moved his family into the Wilson County jail at Floresville, converted his jailer into his only full-time deputy, and put his wife and family in charge of jail operations. Dogie lived at the jail until he joined the

Texas Rangers in 1917. The sheriff's apartment at Floresville had four rooms, two up and two down, with no window screens or electric lights. Dogie's older brothers, Charlie and Jack, pitched in immediately to help run the jail, and young Dogie joined them in feeding prisoners at age nine or ten—"just as soon as I could turn the keys in the locks." Later, Dogie Wright's duties expanded beyond the jail. He or his brothers were dispatched on horseback to carry messages to Sheriff Wright or his deputies, to serve subpoenas to grand jury members, and to deliver election boxes to county polling places. The last duty also served as a vacation, as Wright explained: "We'd start out in the western part of the county, be gone four or five days. We'd camp out and stay all night with people some. Particular in that November election, we'd take a shotgun along, kill some bobwhite quail."[5] Still later, Dogie Wright often chauffeured his father and the deputies around from place to place in the department's Model T, which none of the adults could drive.

Dogie Wright's life as sheriff's son was far from mundane, and "for a kid with eyes and ears, it all went in," he said. Once, as Dogie carried an armload of firewood up the back steps of the jail, an escaping prisoner knocked the boy into his mother's flower bed. Dogie shared a bedroom with Chief Deputy Wade Lawrence, who lived with the Wright family. As Dogie told it: "Wade and I slept in the same room, we were real buddies. I went with Wade lot of times when he had to go places, in horseback and into the Model T times." Beyond the occasional companionship of Dogie or one of his brothers, Wilson County officers had little backup, though they often needed it. Floresville was a "wide open" county-seat town about World War I, and two saloons and a pool hall did a booming business directly across the courthouse square from the jail. Especially on weekends, drunks, fights, and shootings abounded, and wounded combatants ended up at the jail. Dogie Wright often helped a local doctor "while he sewed on a fellow laying there on that concrete floor in what we called the runaround." Despite everything the sheriff and his family could do to prevent these, major fights sometimes broke out among prisoners inside the jail, again soon requiring extensive use of the doctor's needle and thread.[6]

A rural sheriff's son like Dogie Wright often found himself almost as much of a marked man as his father; everybody watched what he did and seemed quick to criticize, though his special status as the high sheriff's son also allowed certain privileges. As Jim Scarborough III, Sean Fenton, Joe Goodson, and the sons of Buck Lane discovered, adolescent trangressions

often were severely punished by lawman fathers concerned with setting
a good example to other parents. Jim Scarborough III grew up a little rebellious, but Jim still thought twice before going on watermelon-stealing
expeditions with his friends, and his friends thought twice about inviting
him along.[7] Caught throwing rocks at passing trains, Sean Fenton received
a severe whipping with a belt from Sheriff H. F. Fenton, who remarked,
"I have enough trouble with everybody else's kid in town without my own
son giving me more."[8] However, certain special rights and privileges also
accompanied the status of sheriff's son. Jim Scarborough III discovered
that he had an automatic free pass to every movie, carnival, and circus that
passed through Kleberg County. In Wilson County, Dogie Wright enjoyed
certain special privileges, most of them providing pocket money. Wright
picked up beer bottles after lawyers' gambling parties at court time, shined
shoes in the county courthouse, collected "message fees" after people
received long-distance calls and were summoned to the sheriff's phone,
distributed circus fliers, and guided generous drummers to remote country
stores.[9]

Some prisoners remained in county jails so long that they developed
special relationships to sheriffs' children. Loretta Fenton recalled that her
youngest daughter often summoned a particular long-term prisoner, a
trusty, to swing her on the jail lawn. Still barely able to walk, she would
run her tricycle down the hall at the Coleman jail, smash into the bottom
of the staircase with it, and cry out, "Eeee, Eeee, come out and swing me!"
and trusty Lee Dodds would descend the stairs and do just that. Dodds
also painted the sheriff's daughter's rocking horses and swing set.[10] As her
father told the story, should Dodds finally tire of the prolonged swinging
and seem about to stop, "if he didn't do just what she wanted him to, she'd
call him a name and say, 'I'm gonna have my daddy put you back up them
stairs!'"[11]

Long-term associations led to other relationships between sheriffs' children and jail prisoners. Having gotten in trouble for throwing rocks at
trains, Sean Fenton also soon got in trouble for providing Coleman County
prisoners with girlie magazines.[12] At Buck Lane's jail in Wharton, black
prisoners in the cell immediately over the son's bedroom took pains to go
through proper channels with their request of the sheriff's son. Prisoners
could faintly hear the boy's radio, so they passed a note to the sheriff
asking him to tell his son to turn it up especially high during the next Joe
Louis title fight. Lane instructed his son to do this, and soon afterward a

thank-you note arrived, duly reported in Lane's newspaper column: "Honorable T. W. Lane, esteemed sir: We, the negro men of cell #3 wish to make known our pleasure and gratitude to you and your admirable son for your gracious cooperation and considerate consideration this in making it possible for us to listen to the title fight of last night."[13]

In some rural jails, trusties became so friendly with the sheriff's family or made themselves so helpful that sheriffs sent them out on jail errands— a matter that occasionally drew critical attention from county attorneys, newspaper editors, and other jail watchers. Wallace Riddell once sent a prisoner in a patrol car to pick up items for the jail at a Burnet grocery store. Asked by a newsman what he would do if the prisoner escaped, Riddell said: "Aw, Ned, he ain't going to run off. Even if he did, I know all the places he could go to hide, and I'd just pick him up. And then he couldn't go anyplace anymore and get a little exercise. If I hadn't sent him, somebody would have had to go on county time. It saved the taxpayers a few cents."[14] As Modina Riddell explained, Wallace and Essie Riddell had taught their children "that the prisoners were people in trouble and we were to respect them as human beings—they really all became our friends."[15] Sheriff Riddell made most long-term prisoners his trusties, and they often came into the kitchen to help in food preparation, or they helped paint the jail walls. Trusty labor played a large role in Essie Reddell's low-budget makeover of the run-down old jail apartment, kitchen, and jail cells.[16]

Essie Riddell regarded herself as jail matron as well as jail cook, and she took a special interest in the Burnet County jail's occasional long-term female prisoners. She took books and magazines to male and female prisoners, ran the jail library (which soon became the first Burnet municipal library), and escorted prisoners to church on Sundays. She also landscaped the jail grounds, which included "many rare plants" and the bamboo grove in which Burnet County children traditionally cut their fishing poles. When female prisoners were moved to and from the county by the sheriff, Essie Riddell went along. Once, after two young women finished six-month sentences in the Burnet jail and no one could come to escort them home, Mrs. Riddell and her daughters took their former prisoner friends back to Chicago, Illinois.[17]

Insane prisoners also often remained in county jails for many months, waiting for admission to the state's crowded mental hospitals, but they rarely became close friends of sheriffs' families, and some, the "dirty insane and the noisy insane," became the greatest burdens that sheriffs' families had to bear. At Coleman County, however, one lady committed by her children for a return to the Texas State Lunatic Asylum at Austin immediately set up cheerful quarters with rocking chair and privacy curtains in the jail misdemeanor room and soon ingratiated herself with Sheriff Bannister's family. The lady seemed normal, if a trifle feeble-minded, though she cleaned her jail cell compulsively, over and over. Allowed to remain in her cell with the door open after promising not to escape, the woman confided that she looked forward to her return to the pleasant asylum—and the compulsory provision by the county of her "new traveling case, three dresses, three underslips, three pairs of drawers, six pairs of cotton stockings, six handkerchiefs, and a coat—all new."[18] Finally, after several months of waiting, Sheriff Bannister and his daughter Leona came to escort the lady to Austin, and "no bride going on her honeymoon could have been happier than Mrs. Moss as she packed the traveling case."[19]

While Leona Bannister served as office deputy, chauffeur, and prisoner escort, her mother administered the detailed, day-to-day operations of the jail, including food purchases, cooking, and jail maintenance. Most sheriffs' wives did this, and some, such as Essie Riddell of Burnet County, even made periodic reports to the county commissioners on jail finances. By 1950 some rural sheriffs were on full salaries, but most received a complicated mix of payments for their services, typically adding up to less than four thousand dollars a year. Sheriffs got so many cents for each jail prisoner for each day the prisoner spent in jail, fees for papers served and arrests made, mileage, and salaries.

Fiscal realities were complicated, though sheriffs neglected the details at their political peril. Should one's enemies compel a departmental audit, the least discrepancy—even a matter of a few dollars—could bring a felony charge of "misappropriation of public funds" and removal from office. When Gaston Boykin took office as Comanche County sheriff in 1947, his tangled finances typified those of many rural sheriffs. Boykin lived in the jail apartment with his mother and received a per diem of ninety cents per prisoner (seventy-five cents a day for each prisoner's "upkeep" and fifteen cents for his or her "safekeeping"). Boykin kept any profits he made on running the jail, and he received a monthly salary of $75, ten cents a mile for line-of-duty operation of a county vehicle, and fees for serving civil and criminal papers. Salary, mileage, and fees could add up to, but not exceed, $3,750 a year for the Comanche County sheriff in 1947, but to reach that lofty sum the officer had to take warrants and civil papers in hand and be constantly on the hunt. Most of his income came from fees.[20]

County commissioners liked the fee system, because sheriffs received payments only for services rendered to the county, services that often brought in revenue from fines. In 1948 there were still 167 "fee counties" in Texas.[21] Critics of the fee system, including most sheriffs, claimed that fees brought in inadequate revenues to maintain lawmen's families and also encouraged a "head-hunter mentality" in lawmen desperate to maintain those families.[22] Many sheriffs admitted the partial truth of this latter claim; every fall, for example, outsiders came in to rural counties to pick cotton, make money, and drink and gamble on Saturday nights, and rural officers went on the prowl to catch them for fines for their counties and fees for themselves. From a sheriff's perspective, the gambler-outsider with cotton picking money in his pockets provided the perfect arrest—immediate payment of the fine for the county, a nice "bounty" fee for the sheriff, and no possible loss of a vote.

Complexities abounded, differing from county to county. Sheriff Gaston Boykin explained: "If you got a misdemeanor warrant for a man and arrested him and he paid off, you got four dollars. If you arrested him and he laid it out in jail, you got two dollars." Different fees were paid for serving various civil papers. Boykin received ten cents a mile for travel expenses for going after a misdemeanor offender, but only if the offender subsequently paid his fine, and ten cents a mile for bringing in a man to serve a felony arrest warrant, but only if the man subsequently was tried and convicted. Transport of multiple convicted felons to Huntsville netted the sheriff ten cents per prisoner per mile up to a cap of forty-five cents a mile. Should the sheriff be so foolish as get in his car for a ride to the state penitentiary with five desperate felons, he would received only a partial compensation for the fifth prisoner.[23]

After the county sheriff's combined salary, fees, and mileages added up to a certain sum—in Gaston Boykin's case, $3,750—all department income generated by fines was returned directly to the county, with no fees taken. Most sheriffs struggled to reach their income caps, as did Boykin, but a few managed to take advantage of cotton pickers and passing bootleggers to run their departments at a profit, and they invariably announced this to their county commissioners and the general public. In 1941, for example, Sheriff W. J. Corrigan of Bee County told reporters that during 1940 he had "refunded to Bee County taxpayers" $1,320.19 in excess fees collected over the costs of running his department, and in 1952, Crosby County sheriff Roy Hillin reported net departmental profits for 1951 of $10,735.48.[24]

Capturing outlaws beyond his income cap still put some money in the sheriff's pocket as long as the outlaws spent time in his jail. Income generated by the jail over the county's fixed daily payment per prisoner went directly to the sheriff and his family, so it was in their interest to operate the jail as frugally as possible. Food austerities were common, with meals running heavily to pinto beans, though sheriffs' families consumed (or claimed they consumed) exactly the same fare. Sheriff Gaston Boykin, a practicing Christian, prided himself on treating his prisoners as he would have wished to be treated—so much so that once, when the jail had its roof replaced, all cell doors were unlocked and the prisoners went on the "honor system"—but he still pinched pennies in jail food expenses. Boykin got ninety cents a day for each prisoner, a reasonable amount for the late 1940s, and management of the money was up to him. Boykin recalled: "That went to the sheriff, but he bought the groceries out of his own pocket. If he made a profit or loss on the jail, that was just on his management. I've bought can goods out of the [Rio Grande] Valley by the truck-load—rejects, but good stuff, you know. If you were real careful you could run it to where you could break even or even make a little money."[25]

Sheriffs normally had little time for such things, so the challenge of providing good, cheap food for the jail, the better to make a profit, commonly fell on the shoulders of sheriffs' wives. In Lee County, Sheriff J. R. Goodson's wife and children worked "three big gardens" to provide jail food and "to survive."[26] In Burnet County, Essie Riddell made the most of the "back lot" behind the jail to keep a milk cow, four hogs, and numerous chickens to help feed family and prisoners. The sheriff's chickens had no hen house, so they roosted in trees around the courthouse square. Late fall hog butcheries took place at the Riddells' jail home just off the courthouse square just as they had previously at the family's farm, and the pork went into the smokehouse. Several times a year, Essie and her children visited Sheriff Riddell's parents at the Shovel Mountain community to harvest "Grandfather Riddell's garden," can the produce, and truck their portion back to the jail. Every autumn, Wallace Riddell went out with his father and brothers to kill several whitetail deer to cook and can for the jail.[27]

At Coleman County in 1950, Sheriff H. F. Fenton made a "straight salary" of $240 a month, and Loretta Fenton received fifty cents a day to feed each prisoner. This was not enough, and Loretta purchased "red beans" by the hundred-pound bag and mastered every conceivable way of serving them. Beyond that, the Fentons relied on support from the community. "My family had gardens," Loretta explained, "and everybody in town would have gardens and bring it to our door, give it to Fenton. We'd say, 'If you got any peas y'all don't know what to do with, Fenton will take it.' I picked a lot of gardens, too. People would say, 'I got a turnip patch out here,' and I'd go get turnip greens, and all—everything I could salvage—just a lot of times. Then, the game warden would bring in the deer or wild turkeys that somebody had illegally killed, they all knew we could use em."[28]

Feeding inmates as well as possible promoted prisoner morale and helped prevent trouble, many sheriffs thought, and jail trouble could reach monumental proportions. Jail trouble could so humiliate sheriffs that it could drive them from office. Sheriff G. W. Blanton of Grayson County told a reporter: "It's amazing how far good food goes in keeping down trouble. I don't have to be told when the food starts to get bad. I can detect it in the rebellious attitude the prisoners develop. When things get boring for fifty or more persons confined in jail, they are going to start something on the slightest excuse." At the Grayson County jail, prisoners' "rebellious attitude" was rather easily detected; they tore up blankets, stuffed them into toilets, flooded the jail floors, and began rasping metal cups on the bars of their cells.[29] At the Tarrant County jail in 1952, the appearance of mustard greens on dinner trays caused prisoners to stop up drains, litter the floor with torn-up paper and food scraps, turn on the water faucets in their cells, and use magazines to channel the water into jail corridors. Furious at the indignity to his jail, Sheriff Harlon Wright told reporters that he ate mustard greens himself and that there was nothing wrong with them. Newsmen even obtained Mrs. Wright's jail recipe for preparing mustard greens, "just boil them in water with a little salt."[30]

Life in the jail already was stimulating enough for the sheriff and his family, and they did what they could to keep food riots, fights, suicides, and escape attempts from breaking out above their jail apartments. Jails already echoed to the shouts of fighting drunks being hustled upstairs on Saturday nights, the angry voices of family members trying to argue their relatives out of jail, prisoners' shouts and sing-songs, the relentless cries of the insane, and the ever-ringing telephone. One night in December 1949 in Wharton County, Sheriff Buck Lane and his wife and children awakened

Sheriff Frank Brunt and captured gang of drugstore burglars in the Cherokee County jail, Rusk, Texas. (Author's collection)

to a bedlam of fifty prisoners screaming at the top of their lungs, "just for fun, I think." That same month, Lane concluded his column by noting: "Folks, I started this tale early this Sunday morning and it is now 5:45 P.M., and I have answered 32 phone calls, talked to 7 people, and been listening to that insane woman upstairs hammering for the past three hours, now I am about insane. Yours very truly, Buck Lane."[31]

Lane followed the dictum of other sheriffs and "tried to stay on top" of his jail at all times; for the sheriff at one of the busier rural jails, eternal vigilance was the price of security. Some sheriffs at smaller jails in quieter counties than Wharton, however, passed through long careers with little or no jail trouble. Sometimes sheriffs avoided embarrassing jail events by working the system to incarcerate fewer prisoners; sometimes they operated trouble-free jails "on trust," keeping prisoners always in their debt and on their side.

During the early 1950s, Bastrop County occasionally became so peaceful that Sheriff Nig Hoskins found himself without any prisoners, and at such times he "give the kids here in Bastrop the keys of the jail—many a day they played in the old jail."[32] During his forty-year career, Sheriff Nathan Tindall of San Augustine County disliked the trouble, expense, and potential problems of keeping prisoners in his old, two-story brick jail, and he hustled them in and out of it at great speed. A wealthy sawmill owner as well as sheriff, Tindall had no interest in gleaning pennies from prisoners' per diems. A reporter noted that Tindall "went to great lengths to process prisoners swiftly, so that the county wouldn't have to feed them. Anything to avoid holding them for a week. He'd let them go and tell them to come back Monday [for county court], or else call the judge, get the person's attorney, if they had one, down there, and do it right in the sheriff's office."[33]

In Winkler County in 1967, Sheriff Bill Eddins and his wife retired from their jail apartment after running the Winkler jail like one big happy family for twenty years. No significant bad events, and no escapes, had occurred during their tenure, they told a reporter. Potential trouble proved easy to discern, Sheriff Eddins explained, since "every time anyone's up to anything, the rest of the inmates generally try to cover it up by whistling and singing."[34] In Burnet County, Sheriff Wallace Riddell did things much the same way as Eddins did. Riddell periodically examined the soft steel jail bars of his old jail and had someone weld up the new partial hacksaw cuts, but he ran his jail practically on the honor system. Cell windows opened directly to the outside, and visitors came and went unsearched, but prisoners respected Riddell, appreciated how he treated them, and made few serious attempts to break out or otherwise cause trouble that might embarrass their sheriff friend.[35] Sheriff Dan Saunders of Martin County "ran the jail on trust" from the time he took office in 1953 until his retirement in 1992 and "never, never in all my years had a prisoner betray my trust that I let out of jail by failing to return." Sheriff Saunders emptied his jail during the Christmas seasons, allowing prisoners—even murderers awaiting transfer to the penitentiary—to go home "on furlough" for the holidays. Furthermore, "I have never searched a visitor in my life that went down in the jail to visit or I never examined a sack or box that visitors were taking down to the jail. It may not work for the next Sheriff but it worked for me. I ran the jail on trust."[36] Once, Saunders received a call that his fourteen-year-old son had been thrown from a horse and knocked unconscious, and he rushed to the hospital. About 8:30 that evening, prisoner George Hite, a convicted murderer, called to report an unlocked jail. "I'm up front in your office. You left the jail door unlocked when you left here and we were afraid you would get in trouble." Saunders thanked Hite and told him to ask the other prisoners to return to their cells. He would come by in a while to lock them up.[37] Just before Sheriff Dan Saunders retired from office, former inmate David Boutwell wrote him: "You showed me a care and concern that is rare these days. I realize now that it was God's love manifest through you. I just wanted you to know that you touched my heart and my life. Thanks for being there when no one else cared."[38] Many other sheriffs received similar letters.

Because of his personal concern and careful observation of prisoners, Dan Saunders never had a suicide at his jail in over four decades—an enviable record—but there had been near misses. Many persons were profoundly disturbed by the shock and humiliation of incarceration. "I've had them cry when you locked them up, cry the next morning, too," Sheriff Walter Fellers of Comal County recalled. "It's a shame, most of the time—especially for an old boy who was never in jail before. It kind of hurts his ego."[39] The first few hours were especially dangerous for an inmate, who often entered the jail under the influence of alcohol or other drugs.[40] Once, a new Martin County jail inmate twisted a sheet around his neck, tied it to the bars, and sat down, cutting off blood supply to his brain. After another prisoner gave the alarm, Dan Saunders rushed the man to the hospital, and doctors saved his life. Another time, two drunk brothers took the "lace leather out of their heavy shoes" and hung themselves, only to be cut down just in time. Saunders and his jailer always carried sharp pocket knives just for this emergency.[41]

As Buck Lane of Wharton County discovered in 1948 after his first jail suicide, self-homicides were hard to predict, people were ingenious about devising ways to kill themselves, and the process took little time. A black man well known to Lane and not suspected of being suicidal pulled bedsprings from his cot, made a noose, and successfully hanged himself. Lane, like other sheriffs, found his jail suicide disturbing and humiliating—a person had died on his watch and in his care.[42] Sheriff Dan Saunders wrote in his journal: "The crucial time to watch for a suicide is right after putting someone in jail. Usually they are drunk, mad, and depressed and want attention, but when they hang themselves and it cuts the blood supply off to their brain they are just as dead as they would be if they had been planning it for six months."[43]

Over long years of service and the daily rush of events, rural sheriffs forgot many remarkable things they had done or seen, but they invariable recalled jail suicides, particularly gruesome murders, and insane persons that they repeatedly dealt with and held in their jails. Sometimes all these memorable things came in one package, as in the case of the deranged Fayette County woman who killed her hired hand, burned his body for days in a bonfire, buried the remnants under a new chicken house, then starved herself to death in Sheriff William Loessin's Fayette County jail.[44] Insane people in their jails often plagued sheriffs beyond anything else. Not surprisingly, in 1953 three of the top four items on the seven-point legislative wish list of the Sheriffs' Association of Texas involved the creation of alternative regional holding jails for criminally insane persons, "sex perverts," and the "lunacy patients, who are jamming local jails where proper treatment and care are impossible."[45]

Sheriffs had the legal responsibility to take deranged people into custody and to hold them in their jails until the local courts determined if they should be committed to a state mental hospital. Then it was the sheriffs' duty to jail those adjudged *non compos mentis* until the hospital had a place for them in its overcrowded wards—a waiting period that might last months. Some of these deranged jail inmates proved docile and gave sheriffs and their jailers little trouble, but many were noisy, dirty, dangerous, and hard to handle. Some passed on their way to the state hospital never to return, but many—perhaps most—achieved "institutional cures," returned to their home counties, and—after a time—relapsed to previous insanities. In Wharton County in November 1947, for example, Sheriff Buck Lane winced when he received a call that a certain man from the Louise community once again threatened his family with the customary butcher knife. The man had proven dangerous to subdue and dangerous and noisy in the jail, and it had all happened five times before. Five times the man had been subdued, jailed, and processed into the state hospital, and five times he had been returned to Wharton County as cured. On this occasion, well aware of what his men faced, Lane sent four deputies to capture the crazy man, and they found him armed with an ax as well as his usual butcher knife.[46]

Three years later, Sheriff Lane counted twenty-four insane persons as having passed through his jail during 1950, including—once again—a certain deranged preacher. The man was harmless, but very insane and noisy, preaching incessantly at the top of his lungs from his cell. When deputies approached him to sedate him, he "squealed like a two-hundred-pound hog" and made the deputies back off. To persuade the man to take a sedative, Lane dressed up like a doctor in coat, brown hat, black bow tie, and white shirt and successfully appealed to the retired preacher's courtesy as a fellow professional. The man seemed normal after a long sleep, but a few months later Lane's deputies found him sitting in the middle of a busy highway putting mud balls into a discarded tire. Brought before the judge and grand jury to determine his sanity, the old preacher showed them his feet, sang them a hymn, and asked what they were going to give him. The grand jury members signed over their small jury fees to the insane man and remanded him to the state hospital—after another long sojourn in Buckshot Lane's jail.[47] Lane remarked of this man: "Those insane cases are simply pitiful and a jail house is certainly not a place for an insane person. We move them out as fast as we can, but then there are times the state institutions are full up and can't take them."[48]

Insane inmates were unpleasant and annoying, and jail suicides depressing and unnerving, but nothing so preoccupied the sheriff as the threat of jail rebellions and escapes. Voters and county commissioners cared very little about the sheriff's operation of the jail beyond how much it cost, and the sheriff could make few political points by initiating jail reforms, but jail disasters could humiliate a sheriff and end his political career. Every jail riot and jail escape was certain to make the front page of the local newspaper, and the sheriff and his family resided at the epicenter of such disorders and breakouts.

County jails varied greatly in age, construction, and resistance to escape, and over the years H. F. Fenton's Coleman County jail proved about average for an older jail. Sheriff Fenton had several humiliating escapes to endure at his jail and in the local media. Once, he and Loretta came home to discover "plaster and everything all over the living room floor and a dad-gum hole in the ceiling right over the couch." Two young prisoners in the cell above had dug away their concrete floor until they encountered roofing plaster, then waited until the Fentons left before they broke through the ceiling of the sheriff's jail apartment, dropped down onto the Fentons' couch, and let themselves out the front door. Fenton quickly recaptured the young escapees, which helped lessen the political damage caused by the escape. Later on, he also caught the prisoner who escaped by climbing down from the jail roof on a long rope made of twisted blankets and the man who risked his life by a leap into a big pecan tree. An internal escapee caused Fenton the most political embarrassment. After a pleasant conversation with a female prisoner in a distant cell, this long-term inmate somehow crammed himself through his feeding window, reached the female prisoner, spent the night with her on her bunk, then failed to cram himself back through the feeding window into his own cell. Fenton found him sitting forlornly on the "runaround" floor outside his cell. A few days later, the inmate came down with venereal disease, Fenton had to take him to the doctor for treatment, and "I had to turn in expenses [to the commissioners] on a prisoner with gonorrhea in the jail that had been up there three years."[49]

Sheriff Fenton's first jailbreak attempt in 1947 had perhaps been his most dangerous. One of the sheriff's problems was that he was not always certain just who he had in his jail, especially when the man was a stranger from outside the county. A person arrested on some petty local offense might be a career criminal from somewhere else, with hard time or an electric chair facing him once his true identify emerged. Such outlaws were desperate to escape, and some of them went around with hacksaw blades concealed in their shoe soles, just in case, as Sheriff Fenton discovered. A Pennsylvania man jailed at Coleman County turned out to be a dangerous escapee from the Pennsysylvania state penitentiary. After a day or so in his cell, his true identity still unknown, the man took out his hacksaw blade, sawed from a flattened bean can a key to fit his cell door lock, opened his door, and began sawing the outer jail door to let himself out. Finally awakened by the sound of saw teeth on steel, Fenton armed himself and timed his charge up the dark stairs to coincide with the noisy passage of a nearby freight train, only to meet the Pennsylvania man coming down. The outlaw stopped in his tracks when he saw the sheriff, who admitted: "If he had done one thing I'd have blown him away. You don't forget something like that. I can lay in that room and I won't hear that train, but you can make an abnormal noise up there, jump off of a bunk, and I'll hear. I'm the soundest sleeper you ever saw, but I can hear a noise upstairs that's not normal."[50]

Some jails were much more modern and secure than Coleman County's during the 1950s, but some were much less so. In 1955, Sheriff Leon Jones of Angelina County announced a new, state-of-the-art jail at Lufkin that was "modern, sanitary, and escape proof." All cells had plumbing, cell doors opened and closed by remote control, bars were of tool-proof steel, cell doors had slots for passage of food trays, and a narrow corridor "walkaround" surrounding the cell block offered excellent surveillance. Prisoners could not escape from this jail without a gun, Sheriff Jones believed, and new inmates went through a rigorous strip search before they went in and were not allowed any physical contact with their visitors, who conversed with prisoners through sealed, bulletproof windows. Furthermore, should the worst happen and somebody escape, Leon Jones's prize pack of biting man-hounds, headed by lead dog "Satan," would be on his trail inside of twenty minutes.[51]

At about the same time, however, Lampasas County sheriff Luther B. Person told reporters that his century-old jail was "not really a jail, it is a residence with some bars over the windows."[52] No wonder that prisoners were always escaping, the sheriff said. In Hardeman County, the ramshackle jail was so inadequate that the sheriff often took jail inmates with him when he went on calls, rather than leave them behind to menace his wife, who doubled as jailer. When the Hardeman sheriff left town for a day or so, he placed his prisoners in jails in the surrounding counties for safekeeping.[53] At Leon County in 1958, three years after Angelina County got its new jail, a prisoner escaped and hitchhiked to Houston before his absence was noticed. Municipal officers saw the familiar outlaw walking the streets, recalled that he was supposed to be in jail somewhere, and picked him up. Sure enough, James Erasmus Reed, age thirty-four, admitted that he had escaped from jail at Centerville. After receiving a call from the Houston officers, the Leon County jailer at first insisted that Reed was safely behind bars, then, after checking, admitted that he was not. Reed had battered a hole in the outside wall of his jail cell with a window sash weight. Escape had not proven difficult. "Eight licks and I was out," Reed told the Houston officers.[54]

Leon County commissioners had been loath to repair the Centerville jail, let alone to build a new one, but it was the Leon County sheriff who endured the public humiliation of this "eight-lick" breakout. Ramshackle jails and departmental understaffing caused many jail escapes until the Texas Commission on Jail Standards forced county governments to find money to fix their jails during the 1970s. Most of these escapes and escape attempts were duly reported—briefly, factually, and usually without comment—by the editor of the *Sheriffs' Association of Texas Magazine*.

Inadequate searches and supervision of jail visitors often allowed hacksaws, knives, and guns to be put into prisoners' hands to set up many escape attempts. No trick seemed too old to work. At Menard County in 1961, a prisoner escaped after sawing his way out with two hacksaw blades smuggled into the jail in a loaf of bread,[55] and at Hopkins County in 1962, jail security had become so lax that visitors smuggled in components that allowed prisoners to build a homemade bomb.[56] Unscreened cell windows, sometimes at ground level, often opened directly to the outside, permitting prisoners' accomplices to pass them contraband. At the Anderson County jail in Palestine on Christmas Eve, 1950, a typical escape occurred. After prisoner Otis Fitzgerald's girlfriend handed him a pistol through his outside window, Fitzgerald forced a deputy to unlock his cell and take him to the radio room, where he pulled all the wires on the radio. Then, Fitzgerald and his girlfriend drove away to California. A little later at this same jail, a black prisoner's girlfriend smuggled a hacksaw, coiled inside her bra, into the jail, and several black prisoners sawed their way out. Only at this point did Sheriff Roy Herrington realize that, although the "white side" of his Palestine jail had "hard cast steel bars," the "black side" had soft steel bars—a commissioners' economy measure, justified because "blacks wasn't bad about breaking out back in the thirties."[57]

In small, understaffed jails, opening cell doors to feed prisoners or to move them around or subdue them presented a constant danger to the sheriff or his jailer. One escape tactic in undermanned jails was to stage a jail riot, shouting, tearing up the cells, setting things on fire, and waiting to attack the officer when he came inside to stop the disorder. In 1949, Sheriff F. F. Hackler of Camp County sustained a knife wound in the throat when he fell into this trap, although the district Texas Ranger arrived in time to save his life.[58] At Sheriff Buck Bennett's Lamesa jail, several Chicago natives attacked the facilities in a similar fashion, but Bennett refused to be lured inside, even when one man tossed a stove through the jail window and "sawed himself to freedom."[59] The jailer also refused to unlock cell block doors at Lamar County in 1956 after inmates broke into a loud and

out-of-key rendition of the popular song "Tutti-Frutti" while other prisoners assaulted the jail wall.[60] Because cell doors in older jails often lacked
food slots, doors had be opened at mealtimes, presenting prisoners with
a daily chance to attack the officers. Sometimes, having no other resources,
a sheriff routinely posted an armed family member at the bottom of the jail
stairs when he went upstairs alone to feed prisoners or to move them from
cell to cell. Sheriff Ennis Tittle's son held the stairs at Franklin County in
1936 when prisoners overpowered the jailer and tried to escape, and Sheriff
Fred Yeary's wife did the same at Uvalde County in 1951 after her husband
had been felled with a broom.[61]

True escape artists sometimes passed through sheriffs' jails, setting the
stage for officers' potential public humiliation. At Wharton County in 1949,
Buck Lane reluctantly accepted a federal prisoner who had previously
broken out of five jails and penitentiaries. Sheriff Lane watched the man
carefully, but the inmate still somehow got out of his cell and mingled with
workmen painting the outside of the jail. Lane found him half by accident,
diligently "sand-papering rust off of window frames" while waiting for
the hue-and-cry occasioned by his escape to move far enough away to
allow him to run for it. Workmen next to the man had been completely
fooled.[62] Sometimes the escape artist broke out of jail in such a flamboyant
fashion that the sheriff's political career never recovered; sheriffs could
survive many things, but not being made to look entirely ridiculous. In
1964 a trusty at Sheriff Ray Markowsky's De Witt County jail in Cuero
escaped from his cell, took a .45 Thompson submachine gun from the
sheriff's office, left the jail, and machine-gunned his former wife and her
male companion in their bed.[63] In 1965, well aware of the cat-burglar
proclivities of prisoner Renaldo Treviño, Sheriff W. J. Allie went home one
evening after chaining Treviño by leg irons to an iron bar in the locked jail
kitchen. The resourceful Treviño, however, picked the lock on his leg irons,
picked the lock on the kitchen door, picked the lock on the front door of
the jail, hot-wired Sheriff Allie's personal car (fully equipped with pistol,
rifle, and radio), and drove it to Zavala County, where he disappeared.[64]

With disasters always lurking just around the corner, sheriffs tried to
"stay on top" of their jails and to keep prisoners friendly, if possible, but
certainly cowed and under control.[65] Like many other sheriffs, Buck Lane
took pride in his Wharton County jail and even encouraged local teachers
to bring schoolchildren to tour his facilities. Wharton jail loudspeakers
played carols to the passing public in the week before Christmas, and

inmates looked forward to a festive meal on the holiday. As did Sheriff Dan Saunders of Martin County, Buck Lane also received occasional thank-you letters from former inmates and sometimes printed these in his newspaper columns. Wharton County prisoners, however, also knew that Sheriff Lane had a sterner side and that they crossed him or challenged him at their peril. It was Lane's jail, after all, and what went on inside it remained his business. During torrid Texas summers, the Wharton jail had "cool cells" or "hot cells" that a prisoner might find himself in, and the cook might serve him the usual tasty jail meals or what Lane called "my famous pickle-juice sandwiches." Hot cells and pickle-juice sandwiches ensured an unpleasant stay in jail, and—even in his newspaper columns—Buck Lane admitted that he sometimes went beyond those measures to maintain jail discipline or to encourage criminals to quickly depart Wharton County after their release. During August 1949, for example, three young Hispanic men in custody for public drunkenness continued to "whoop it up" past Saturday midnight. After stern warnings and an order to go to sleep, they stopped, but on Sunday morning after daylight they began shouting at churchgoers from the jail windows. At that point Lane got "rough." Well aware that the word about the shouting incident had gotten around, Lane wrote in his weekly column: "Well, this time they were removed to a different cell and I did a little more than warn and talk. I don't think they will give us more trouble now before they can be taken to see the judge. No doubt they will go out and tell that they were treated rough, well, they were, the only reason they were was because that was the only language they understood."[66]

Other sheriffs also found it necessary to treat people roughly in their jails. In the days before the Miranda warning, the rise of civil rights lawsuits under the Fourteenth Amendment, and the Texas Jail Standards Act, the county jail was still the sheriff's castle, and when he took a man into custody, he really "had him" in a way that is not true today. Perhaps to increase their psychological impact and to deter local crime, many older Texas jails were constructed to look like Gothic fortresses, and behind their walls the quality of the sheriff's power was medieval as well. It was no idle threat when Sheriff Tom Brown of Caldwell County, exasperated at a prisoner's complaints and demands, told him, "The first time you begin wanting to do something like that, I'm coming in there and stomp you through that damn floor!"[67] Local custom tacitly permitted sheriffs to use force in their jails, providing that they acted with discretion and did not use it on the wrong people. Most citizens expected their sheriff to be appropriately rough should the need arise (and it always did) and expected that this necessary roughness would peak behind the walls of the jail. Jails needed to be kept under stern control, most people agreed. "I'll be frank with you," Nig Hoskins said, "Back there then, I'd go out here and just grab one, far as that goes, and just work him over. Everybody expected it, and they respected the sheriff, and that was all."[68]

With little doubt, such public expectancies and the sheriffs' near-absolute control of their jails occasionally led to abuses of power, even as defined in rural Texas before 1950, abuses that might or might not be punished in the local courts. When a prisoner offended Deputy Sheriff E. L. Bracken at Garza, Texas, in 1931, the enraged officer stuck his pistol between the cell bars and shot the man dead.[69] The story of the prisoner killed while in custody because he attacked the officer with a knife, somehow missed in a previous body search, had become a dark joke among lawmen. Knives commonly were "found" in such circumstances. In 1945, a Madison County grand jury refused to indict Sheriff Rodney Chambless for a jail shooting of the bootlegger who had wounded Chambless in the groin two years before, had served time, then had impru-dently returned to Madison County. Choosing his words with unusual care, the sheriffs' association editor tersely reported this legal demise of Bill Adams, twenty-nine, "who allegedly attempted to stab the sheriff while being jailed for the alleged non-payment of a fine."[70]

As perhaps it had for Bill Adams, the sound of a cell door closing seemed heavier and more final during the decades before federal court activism under the Fourteenth Amendment and the Jail Standards Com-mission. Until August 28, 1961, Texas sheriffs were not even required to tell their county and district attorneys who they held in their jails, and indi-viduals, especially if "off the record," could be held almost at the sheriff's whim. At any given time, who the sheriff had in his jail, and how long the inmate had been there, remained virtually the sheriff's secret.[71] On one occasion, recognizing that he was very drunk and unsure how to get home, a friend called Sheriff Tom Brown and asked to be picked up and placed in the Lockhart jail. After four or five days in jail, however, this man told Mrs. Brown, "I never am gonna call Tommy to get me again. He don't know when to turn me out."[72] From time to time, at many other county jails across Texas, other inmates must have felt the same.

To the sheriff, the jail was the cross that he had to bear, a constant headache and a potential "powder keg," as Sheriff Lon Evans termed it, but the lawman felt he could not do his job without the jail.[73] Sheriffs used their jails to "soften suspects up" before interrogation and solved most of their cases by confessions obtained at the jail. Hard treatment in the jail prepared undesirables for informal banishment from the county, a basic tactic of the rural sheriff. Information flow peaked in the jail, the center of a sheriff's power, and good information and a good "snitch network" to obtain it functioned as the undermanned rural sheriff's secret weapon against crime. Sheriff H. F. Fenton explained:

> What you can do there, when you're working on a subject, a suspect, is to put him up there in that jailhouse and just have somebody else feed and water him, not go back up for about three days. Lots of times them old boys get a lot softer after they stay up in that jail awhile. And another thing, you can get lots of information out of that jail if you get somebody up there that you can halfway trust. It may not be information you can go to court with, but it's information you can use to go ahead and solve your crime. That old jail, you can use it in a lot of ways, you can put your [microphone] receivers in it, there's just a lot of ways you can use that jail to get information.

The sheriff recruited informers in the jail, saying, "Without informers you're not gonna get no big lot done, far as that goes. You got to have about every walk of life of informers, an old thug that's been in the penitentiary, he can be your informer. A preacher can't give you much information about what's going on out here in the underworld. An old thug can get around and find out more, if he trusts you, and an officer has got to be trusted by his informer."[74]

After a few days "softening" in the jail, many criminals became motivated to ingratiate themselves with the high sheriff to help themselves out—perhaps not by admitting their own crimes, but by giving valuable information on the crimes of others still on the outside. Later, after release, such persons might remain the sheriff's eyes and ears in the outer darkness, feeding him information and trying to stay in his good graces, expecting that at some point they would fall into his snares once again and the favor would be returned. Rather often a sheriff launched an informant on his career with an immediate favor. "There's a lot of ways to get a snitch going," Truman Maddox said. "Maybe you pick an old boy up, some of 'em are pretty easy to get to, and maybe you don't have a real good case on him and you're gonna have to turn him loose anyhow. You might just get to talking to him and tell him, 'Now, we gonna cut you loose and let you hit the ground, but you need to help us a little bit.' And a lot of time they'll do that—a lot of time you do help people, and then they help you."[75]

Buck Lane admitted, "You had so little, you just had to have the information, had to have 'bird dogs.' I had a bunch of niggers here that would keep me posted on things that went on, and I had people like this Joe Yamada, this Jap. Joe was my friend, and boy, anything happen in Harris County, I'd know it 'fore the sheriff down there would know it." Harris County information was important for Lane, since many of his outside criminals drove in from nearby Houston. Another important "bird dog" of Sheriff Lane was Pete Traxler, a former member of Pretty Boy Floyd's gang who had narrowly escaped the electric chair, done his time, and come to Wharton County to live—now as a honest plumber, or so he claimed. Probably because he thought he had to, no sooner did Traxler relocate to Wharton than he came by to cut a deal with Sheriff Lane. "He said, 'Now, listen, I'm gonna talk to you, but I ain't gonna talk to no other officer. When you see me walk by that jail, you come on down to the river, 'cause I'm gonna tell you all about it. And there ain't gonna be no safe robbers, nothing like that, in this county long as I'm here.' He was on the level. Pete was a bird dog, he kept me in touch."[76]

Inside and outside of his jail, to obtain good and detailed information the sheriff had to associate with outlaws, active and retired, and critics always claimed that those who lie down with dogs wake up with fleas. At San Augustine County, Nathan Tindall developed a first-class snitch network, but his association in the public mind with a motley crowd of jailhouse hangers-on, many of them former inmates and some of them blacks, hurt him politically. Tindall shrugged it off; forming and maintaining such relationships were essential to his role as high sheriff and master of county turf. "I never had no preacher come to me with no information," Tindall told a reporter. "It's the thieves that come to you with something, after they done got themselves into something. That's the ones that tell you what you need to know."[77] Many local observers thought that Sheriff Tindall's informant network verged on the uncanny. Officer Charles Mitchell, who often worked with Tindall in the early 1960s, recalled: "You couldn't do a thing here without the sheriff knowing about it. He just pretty well *handled* it. One thing you have to say for Nathan: he is good at solving crimes."[78] A decade later, a state narcotics officer discovered that he could not even drive across San Augustine County without the sheriff's learning about it. "When I got back to my office the phone would ring and it would be Tindall wanting to know what I was doing. The man had *resources*."[79]

Some policies that voters might not understand derived from the sheriff's need to maintain his informational resources. After saving Freestone County from its plague of moonshiners and bootleggers, reform sheriff J. R. Sessions nonetheless allowed the continued operation of a few discrete black "beer joints" in his dry county. The owners of these joints commonly picked up information from the county's black community and passed it on to the sheriff.[80] Sheriff Leon Jones of Lufkin also worked with several "undesirable people," minor bootleggers and gamblers, in Angelina County's black community. Jones perhaps disliked the necessity of doing this, but he did it, keeping his promises and his secrets. "People knew they could tell me anything," he said, "and they knew I'd die before I'd tell anybody who told me. That's worth a lot to a sheriff."[81] Local business people with the highest volume of shady customers often collected the most information and made the best informants. An experienced sheriff once told Texas Ranger Lawrence Rigler, "Give me a whore or a bootlegger, a cab driver or a pawn broker, and a guy could solve any case."[82]

Pat Riddell said of his father, Sheriff Wallace Riddell, that he had no informants, only friends who supplied him with all his information, and perhaps that was true. Over time, snitches and friends became the same people, at least for some sheriffs. Sheriffs often set out to befriend their jail prisoners, both genuinely to warn them about the error of their ways and to solicit their help, now and in the future, and over the years the process created a cadre of loyal informants. Aubrey Cole of Jasper County often did this, and

> when I left the sheriff's office, I expect I had fifty snitches over the county. These people you have to cut some slack, these people you have to help out of some binds themselves. You have to befriend a person to be his friend and maintain his friendship. I had to keep an eye on [them] real strong—they would steal, they would do things they shouldn't do, and I had to watch [them]. But, by the same token, I maintained a good enough relationship with these people that if I had an old crime anywhere in their community I'd go sit down on their porch and ask their help.[83]

One sheriff's valued informants, however, often were the bothersome criminals of the sheriff across the county line. Outlaws often "housed" in one county, paying that sheriff off with information, and did their criminal business somewhere else, setting up curious interactions between neighboring sheriffs. In Henderson County, Jess Sweeten had "built up a good informant structure, a system set up that was second to none. The criminals respected me and they trusted me and they would talk to me. There's one man that can help you, and that's an old criminal, cause he thinks like a criminal, and you better listen to him when he's talking to you." Informed by one of these snitches that the man responsible for a ten-thousand-dollar drugstore robbery resided in Tyler, Smith County, Sweeten called Sheriff Bill Baker on the phone and asked about the man's whereabouts, and "I could tell the way Bill was talking that Bill was using that son-of-a-gun for an informant. I couldn't help it. Bill was disappointed, but he said, 'You come up here, I'll have him in jail when you get here.'"[84] Although Dallas County sheriff Bill Decker played the same game they did, Sweeten, Frank Brunt, and other East Texas sheriffs occasionally complained about Decker's hundreds of resident snitch outlaws who moved out into rural counties to ply their trades, but the same deal obtained: If the outside sheriff identified the home outlaw, Decker would call him in. "Anytime I had a safe knocked in Cherokee County north of Rusk, you could bet they were out of Dallas," Frank Brunt said. "There was a gang of 'em, and Dallas was full of 'em—they wouldn't bother Bill Decker, he had an understanding, they housed up there. He told 'em, 'You can live here, but don't you bother anything here.' I'd go up there and I'd want somebody and he'd send after 'em. He'd pick up a telephone and call 'em, just say, 'Come in.'"[85]

Whether or not he was deemed good snitch material, every time a new person passed through a rural sheriff's jail, the sheriff usually took time to look at him, talk to him, get to know him, and mentally file him away in his rogues' gallery of local outlaws and wayward voters. Many sheriffs prided themselves on their memory for names, faces, and even telephone and license plate numbers, and a how-to-do-it book about improving one's memory often stood on the sheriff's bookshelf. In populous Wharton County, Buck Lane personally got to know his prisoners in the usual way, but he also fingerprinted and photographed every person who passed through his jail using the most up-to-date FBI trade craft.

All of this had a serious purpose. More than by any other means, rural sheriffs broke cases and solved crimes by local knowledge, and they prided themselves on this. Jess Sweeten once informed visiting FBI agents: "Gentlemen, maybe I'm over-rating myself, but I feel like that if I can't break a case in this county that other people can't break, I'm a damn poor sheriff. Cause, I'm supposed to know my people here, and I'm supposed to know my thugs." Sweeten told a historian: "I broke 21 murder cases, and I went out without an unsolved highjacking, and I didn't have an unsolved rape case or an unsolved murder case. I was proud of my record, it did represent some hard work. In your homeplace, you catch a man many, many times by knowing the manner he operates. Some burglars will drill holes in the ceiling even if every window and drawer is open, and there's other burglars that'll break in that window if it didn't have no roof over it—they're crazy, there's just one way they see it."[86]

Working "their thugs" and well-known county landscapes, rural sheriffs such as Sweeten often compiled impressive arrest records, which they sometimes shared with appreciative professionals at the *Sheriffs' Association of Texas Magazine*. In November 1947, for example, Sheriff Boyington Fleming of Cameron County reported that he had cleared 96 of 108 cases handled during the previous month, including thirteen burglaries, two aggravated assaults, six thefts, four auto thefts, two swindles, two uses of narcotics, four missing persons, thirty-six traffic violations, eight stock law violations, and thirty-nine miscellaneous violations.[87]

Rather often, a long-term sheriff such as Jess Sweeten knew his county, people, outlaws, and rural communities so well that he consulted with informants and gathered evidence only to confirm what he already suspected. After learning that his druggist friend had just been murdered, Sheriff Gaston Boykin of Comanche County sat for a while in his car in his driveway thinking who might have done the deed. Before Boykin turned the key in his ignition, he had a suspect, and before very long, he had a confession. "I thought I had a natural ability," Boykin said, trying to explain this. "I've always studied people, and people interest me. I put myself into the sheriff's office to the extent that, if something happened, I could usually pretty well guess who did it, if it was local."[88]

Conversely, the sheriff might know immediately that some local person had *not* committed a crime. After hearing over his car radio that a certain elderly lady had been brutally murdered and his deputy and the Texas Ranger had a man in custody for the murder, Sheriff Dan Saunders immediately concluded they had the wrong man. "I *knew* Travis didn't commit the murder. By 7:30 P.M. I had a statement from Mrs. McDonald's

19-year-old grandson, admitting to the crime. It pays to know people and know their background."[89]

Often, as Jess Sweeten noted, the local outlaw's characteristic *modus operandi* identified him to the investigating officer, studying the crime scene, as surely as if the crook had signed his name. About World War I, Kleberg County sheriff Jim Scarborough I could examine the butchering site of a rustled cow and determine from the details of the butchering who had done the deed, and thirty years later Jim Scarborough II often solved Kleberg County house burglaries and car thefts in much the same way.[90] Crooks, especially true professionals, often went about their business in precise and rigid ways. Only a few minutes into examination of a Gray County safe-cracking job, Sheriff Rufe Jordan knew the culprit had to be "Knob" Ash, working, as usual, with one of his brothers. Ash "knocked" safes in exactly the same way every time, always observing the same fixed precaution; if he had not penetrated his target safe in twenty-six minutes, Ash walked out.[91] Crooks behaved obsessively, and strange repetitions of events often jogged sheriffs' memories and put them on someone's trail. After a citizen reported his horse stolen to the Lamar County sheriff, the officer recalled that a certain man, recently returned from the penitentiary after serving time for a horse theft, had taken the same animal two years before. Sure enough, a quick check confirmed a repeat offender, though this time the thief had received five dollars less for the horse.[92]

Outlaws, crimes, and trouble were not distributed evenly across the county's landscape; as the sheriff was well aware, they clustered at certain places and times. After a few years on the job, a sheriff knew every highway, county road, dirt track, stream course, county line boundary, and back-country settlement in his domain, and in most cases he could call off, one by one, the family names of people who lived down any particular rural lane. If the county allowed alcohol, the sheriff knew its regular bars and roadhouses and the "fighting joints" where people looking for trouble (or wanting to look at trouble) went on Friday and Saturday nights. If the county was dry, the sheriff knew its ordinary roads and the roads that ran towards the Devil's siren song at the nearest wet county—thoroughfares of disorder and outlawry that caused officers endless trouble. The 10-mile stretch of Highway 94 from Lufkin in Angelina County to the river-bottom joints of Trinity County typified many such eventful liquor runs. In 1952, state road crews picked up more bottles and cans from this 10 miles than from the other 185 miles of state roads in the Lufkin district combined.

Along with the twenty dump-truck loads of liquor containers collected monthly, road crews found false teeth, eyeglasses, articles of outer clothing, underwear, purses, and even stranger debris tossed out by drunks and folks on a spree.[93]

The county-seat town and other larger towns also had their trouble spots, but by the mid-1950s such places usually had municipal police forces to help the sheriff watch over them. Beyond the city limits signs, the countryside belonged to the sheriff, and the sheriff knew that the cross-roads communities and dispersed rural settlements of his domain were not all alike. Deep in the countryside, at the end of dirt roads, many small Texas communities still maintained their nineteenth-century distinctive-ness for a decade or so after World War II. Some were Godly communi-ties centered around a rural church and school, but there were other sorts of places that drew most of the sheriff's attention. Every sheriff had his disorderly outlaw settlements, more often than not poised, as if to escape, along county lines. Frank Brunt's "Dogtown" in Cherokee County was one such, and when Brunt roared down the county road towards Dogtown on a whiskey raid, carefully loosened boards at every creek-bottom bridge rattled like thunder, and residents fired off shotguns as he passed to further give the alarm.[94] At San Augustine County, Sheriff Nathan Tindall occa-sionally ventured into "Greertown," a strange, close-knit black commu-nity founded by freed slaves deep in the pineywood sand hills of a part of the county known as "the Pre-Emption." As at Dogtown, locals often engaged in moonshining but were hard to catch, even for Tindall. Later, they branched out into marijuana farming, and, still later, they became regional distributors of crack cocaine. Some rural communities were not outlaw zones but traditional forbidden areas for the county sheriff. In Bastrop County, for example, sheriffs and their deputies customarily did not go into Red Rock, a small cotton community on the railroad near the south county line. Until Red Rock's first native-son sheriff, Nig Hoskins, discreetly ended this tradition, if the distant Bastrop sheriff wanted some-body from Red Rock, he sent him a message or called him on the tele-phone. Red Rock citizens believed they could keep order in their own community without outside help or interference, and they refused to vote for a sheriff who overly intruded in their affairs.[95] As in the case of Hoskins's own family, past conflicts at Red Rock had sometimes ended in killings, regretted but unpunishable acts of violence between consenting adults, usually white males. Some rural communities had so much of this sort of thing that people called them "killing communities"; one such was Possum Walk in Trinity County, of which people said, "They kill a man there every Saturday night."[96]

Besides the trouble places, there were trouble times, and the experienced sheriff recognized these and distributed his scarce resources accordingly. A weekly cycle of trouble peaked on Saturday nights at dance halls and beer joints, and a yearly cycle peaked during fall—the harvest season of cash-in-hand cotton-picker camps, county fairs, country dances, and football games. A sheriff with reserve deputies often stationed them at likely trouble spots during harvest season, with dances and football games usually heading his list, while the sheriff and his regular deputies waited by the phone. At Lee County, Sheriff Goodson at first had no deputy, and on Saturdays he usually left the county seat of Giddings to its municipal police and drove south to the rival community of Lexington, where he prominently displayed himself downtown—sitting on the hood of his car, talking with passers-by, and waiting for dark and trouble.[97]

As sheriffs well knew, fierce athletic contests on the field or court often spilled over into scuffles among rival fans, and sometimes even the presence of the sheriff and his men failed to prevent violence. Martin County sheriff Dan Saunders wrote in his journal on February 17, 1969: "A terrible fight broke out last night at a basketball game in the high school gym between the Stanton team and the McCamey team. I was the only officer there. Fans were fighting all over the court. I pulled the master switch and it was pitch dark. I caught some heat over that but I had to 'take the bull by the horns.'"[98] Again, on November 11, 1979, the Martin County sheriff tersely noted, "Had hell on top of hell at the ballgame at Grady tonight."[99]

Before the mid-1960s, cotton was still king in many rural counties, and crime and trouble followed the cotton cycle. Autumn was the season of picking, ginning, and cash in hand for rural families and town merchants, and it was also the time that rural outlaws, home-grown or imported, went on the prowl. Bootleggers and gamblers came into the county to work the cotton-picker camps, and legitimate peddlers and a wide array of scam artists went door-to-door across the countryside, selling fake watches, dyed rabbit fur coats, and a wide variety of other dubious goods and services. As Buck Lane noted, thieves now broke into people's smokehouses to get their hard-won hog meat, stole their fall turkeys from pens or woods, and even drove away in their automobiles. At Lee County during the 1950s, Sheriff Goodson's jail logs filled with listings of turkey thieves and bootleggers.

Crimes by local people perpetrated upon local people were the rural sheriff's specialty, and he often solved them by a mix of acute local knowledge, clever information gathering, and vigorous interrogation. More often than not, sheriffs collected physical evidence to buttress their cases only after the process had worked its way to the end and confessed culprits were in his custody.

After the murder of a woman in San Augustine County, Sheriff Nathan Tindall considered who might have done it, consulted his informant network, then set out personally to confirm his suspicions before picking up the dead woman's son-in-law. "I'll do about anything to catch a thug," he told an interviewer. "This old boy had murdered his mother-in-law, and I knew how these boys always liked to talk about what they done, so I saw them all in there one night, and I crawled up under the house where I could hear them clear as could be. And here was that old boy telling them others, 'Don't tell the sheriff that.' After a few minutes, I heard pretty much everything I needed to know."[100] Tindall "hauled him in" and began the process of eliciting a confession.

As in this case, sheriffs' detailed personal knowledge of the suspects and their families, friends, and rural communities often helped elicit swift confessions. This was especially true of repeat offenders, whom sheriffs had in custody a number of times. Sheriff Truman Maddox observed: "There used to be a saying that if you want to check a man's history, go into the county where he was raised and ask the sheriff about him. If he doesn't know him, you know damn well he's all right, because he would know him if he wasn't."[101]

A sheriff rarely took a suspect into custody until he believed the person was guilty, then he often took advantage of the legalities and customs of an earlier day to get a quick admission of guilt. Usually this did not involve the laying of one finger upon the suspect, but there was no "reading him his rights," and some sheriffs planned their arrests to have maximum psychological impact. For example, Frank Brunt of Cherokee County liked to take a man in at about two or three o'clock in the morning so that this experience might disorient and bewilder him and serve to loosen his tongue.[102] The sheriff might also conduct prolonged off-the-record interrogations of the suspect before ever taking him to jail, sometimes driving the person around the county for hours. Truman Maddox explained:

Terrell County sheriff Lee A. Cook and a woman accused of poisoning her husband, 1931. (Institute of Texan Cultures, San Antonio)

I liked it a lot better in the old days, because my motto is, "To free a man if he's innocent, prosecute him if he's guilty." I'd pick a man up and tell him, "I'f you've got a reason to show me that you're not guilty, you've got a chance to do it right now. I'll do this, I'll go with you anywhere and we'll check your story out. We'll check it out one end to the other, and I'll not be prejudiced in any way. If you can prove to me that you're not guilty, that's what I want to do. Let's get in my car and take out and we'll do this and do that and I'll find out you're not guilty." I've cut a many a man loose thataway. The record does not show that he's been in jail or anything.[103]

With the rougher sheriffs in the older days, as the officer's degree of certainty about the subject's guilt went up, so did his impatience for a quick confession. Having identified to his satisfaction the butcher of someone else's Kleberg County cow by the technical details of the butchery, Jim Scarborough I might just go and get the man, take him somewhere in his car, and then have a rough conversation with him under a mesquite tree, emerging with a full confession.[104] Likewise, Frank Brunt sometimes improved his information about county bootleggers by judicious application of a persimmon limb to one of their fellows before he took the bootlegger in to jail—"putting a little pressure on him," Brunt and other officers termed this illegal process.[105]

Once at the jail, a sheriff might immediately follow the shock of arrest with the shock of interrogation, or he might put the man in a cell and leave him for several days to "soften him up" before talking to him. After a few days in jail, boredom, long hours to reflect and to worry, an absence of accustomed drugs, and the experience of imprisonment sometimes shook a suspect's confidence to the extent of encouraging a confession.

Then the sheriff brought the man down from his cell to talk to him, and more often than not the officer was low-key, friendly, and seemingly sympathetic. Many sheriffs spent a good bit of time conversing with their prisoners, playing the fatherly listener, getting them to repeat their stories over once again (if they still maintained their innocence), listening carefully for some tiny part of the oft-told tale to slip and change and turn vulnerable, waiting for any signs of weakening. Truman Maddox explained:

If you could keep an old guilty guy there very long, he's gonna begin to trip himself up, and the more you can talk to him, and the more

you can remember, the better off you are. And the minute he makes
a slip, you better be able to jump right in on him. Then you get him
excited, and then he says, well, I meant this or I meant that, and he'll
get to stuttering. Then the first thing you know he'll throw up his
hands and say, "Hell, I'm guilty, lemme go!" That happens time and
time again. There's an old saying—tell the truth and you won't have
to remember what you said.[106]

Every sheriff had his special tricks of interrogation. Walter Fellers of
Comal County placed himself very close to the prisoner, looked him
directly in the eyes, and made sure that the suspect blinked first.[107] Sheriff
Gaston Boykin positioned the man in a lower chair than his own, or stood
while the man sat, and fixed him with a piercing gaze. After years of experience as a horse and mule trader, the Comanche County sheriff believed
that no man could successfully lie to him. Boykin also sometimes used the
"good cop, bad cop" routine; he interviewed the suspect in a fatherly way,
a deputy took over and talked roughly and abusively for a while, then
Boykin came back in. At that point, one young suspect told Boykin,
"Sheriff, what that fellow did didn't help one bit—nothing, nothing he
did—but you been so nice to me I'm gonna tell you the truth."[108] When
Brantley Barker arrested two prisoners suspected of involvement in the
same crime, and he believed they had not had sufficient time to rig up a
story, he immediately separated them, made one explain in detail exactly
why they could not have committed the crime, then went to the other and
followed a careful formula of words: "Now, I hate a liar. Tell me just like
your partner did how come you two didn't do it."[109]

Sometimes in serious felony cases the multiple interrogations went on
around the clock and day after day. H. F. Fenton admitted: "Some of those
old hard things, I've had five or six officers lined up and we'd interrogate
them for a good many hours, swapping out. If I knew in my mind that a
man was guilty, I've done that. I never did like to do that if I wasn't certain
a man was guilty."[110] Jess Sweeten once interviewed a kidnapping suspect
"for sixteen days and nights without letup,"[111] and on another occasion
Sweeten carried murder suspect George Patton from sheriff to sheriff and
jail to jail to avoid Patton's lawyers while continuing to interrogate him.
Texas Rangers often aided in this tactic, sometimes known as the "East
Texas merry-go-round." Repeatedly brought in for questioning, Patton
held out against the relentless sheriff for three and a half years until he

Confessed ax murderer Ernest Herwig poses beside Blanco County sheriff J. S. Carpis, who displays the murder weapon. (Institute of Texan Cultures, San Antonio)

finally gave in and told Sweeten where he had buried a murdered family.[112] By that time Patton may have preferred his visit to the electric chair to yet another conversation with Sheriff Jess Sweeten.

As interrogations wore on and sheriffs' patience wore thin, a few of them turned to third-degree methods, placing a premium on techniques

A Bexar County deputy questions a witness to a tavern homicide, 1938. (Institute of Texan Cultures, San Antonio)

that left no marks on the body. Gaston Boykin knew a sheriff who made suspects stand with their feet in a little wooden box while he interrogated them; after a while, maintaining their balance became very difficult. One sheriff (who wished to remain anonymous) told of a technique he claimed he had learned at the Texas Department of Public Safety's school for new officers in Austin. The officer handcuffed a man, then he stood on the handcuff chain, pinning the man's hands to the floor and cutting off blood flow to his hands until they began to turn blue. Then the officer reached down and straightened the man's fingers. This was intensely painful, and any marks on the prisoner's wrists could be dismissed as having been caused by his struggles to escape the handcuffs. During his interviews, Buck Lane proved even more forthcoming about law enforcement realities than in his newspaper column. Officers sometimes "took one good lick" at a stubborn suspect to shake him up and start him talking. Once, Lane caught a cattle thief from the Hallettsville area and soon lost patience with his continuing professions of innocence. "It used to be that you could really enforce the law," Lane said. "I got him and knocked him in the head one time, and he started spilling his guts."[113] The man served time in the pen, then Lane helped get him a job with the county. As Lane well recognized, by the early 1950s knocking people in the head during interrogations had become somewhat dangerous for sheriffs. In 1952, for example, a federal grand jury at Houston indicted the incumbent Walker County sheriff and the retired Grimes County sheriff for roughing up a black prisoner suspected of theft of cotton seed.[114]

Besides the lengthy interrogations and the occasional use of physical force, a good many sheriffs admitted to using tricks to elicit confessions—the sorts of things possible in the unfettered days before Miranda warnings and civil rights litigation under the Fourteenth Amendment. Corbett Akins of Panola County found that prisoners captured with his pack of man hounds normally confessed very easily; they believed that the dogs had physically linked them to the crime scene in an incontestable way, allowing no possible denial of the crime.[115] Likewise, suspects faced with Buck Lane's or Roy Herrington's lie detectors often assumed the machines' infallibility and confessed before even being hooked up to them.[116] Sheriff George Humphreys of King County used a bogus doctor in a "frock-tailed coat" and a specious "truth serum" to get a killer to admit his crime during the 1930s,[117] and forty years later Sheriff J. C. Parker of San Jacinto County used an ordinary Xerox machine as a phony lie detector to accomplish the same thing.[118]

Tricks and irregular methods seemed most common when the suspects were African Americans. Frustrated by two black youths in his custody, each accusing the other of a theft, Sheriff J. E. Holbrook gave up further interrogation and forced the youths to settle the matter with their fists. Presumably, the loser became the liar.[119] After locking up a black man suspected of killing his wife, Lockhart sheriff Tom Brown crept down to the jail hall after midnight to "squall and groan" in a woman's voice outside the man's cell, crying, "Ennis, how come you kill me? My goodness, Ennis, you ain't ever gonna sleep or have no rest unless you tell Sheriff Brown that you knocked me in the head with the ax."[120] At Angelina County, to frighten a murder suspect's cousin into revealing the suspect's hiding place, Sheriff Henry Billingsley put on a chilling little jail charade with lynch mob and rope, and Sheriff A. J. Spradley of neighboring Nacogdoches County once feigned a mass execution of blacks to make a man reveal a killer.[121] In February 1933, a note from the *Sheriffs' Association of Texas Magazine* discussed the use of a skeleton and scare tactics to force admission of guilt from a black burglar. The unnamed sheriff wrote, "In one minute the negro gave us his life history, so my motto is, do not use brutal third degree methods, USE A SKELETON."[122]

By the 1950s, R. C. Pace of Jasper County had gained the reputation of being a "rough sheriff," which benefited him in several ways. "Mr. Pace had a pineywoods polygraph machine," Sheriff Aubrey Cole explained, tongue-in-cheek. "It was a big nail keg, and he'd put that defendant on that nail keg, and he'd run him on polygraph. And if he lied to him, he'd fall off that nail keg, and when he fell off of that nail keg about the third time, he'd failed his polygraph examination, and he got his business straight."[123] With Pace's rough interrogations in mind, outside outlaws tended to "go around" Jasper County to ply their respective trades, and local criminals minded Mr. Pace when, as Cole told it, "he put the sun on them," banishing them to somewhere else before the solar orb rose once again above the Jasper County pines.

Establishing a reputation for meanness, diligent law enforcement, dogged pursuit beyond the home county, an excellent informant network, the ability to break cases, and an unpleasant jail helped deter many criminals from doing business in a sheriff's county, or so most sheriffs believed, and they actively worked at creating these impressions in the criminal mind. Rural sheriffs had good reason for this deterrence strategy. In truth, such sheriffs had inadequate resources and manpower to effectively combat professional criminals who moved into the county, struck quickly, then swiftly moved beyond the county lines. Sheriffs solved a high percentage of crimes committed locally by locals but a low percentage of crimes perpetrated by these professional, highly mobile outlaws from outside—safecrackers, hot check writers, scam artists, and all the rest. The best thing a rural sheriff could do was to try to establish a formidable reputation that served as deterrent to professional criminals and made them avoid his county, just as barking dogs and security signs convince house burglars to move a few homes farther down the block.

Since each sheriff had only a deputy or two to help him, the criminal knew he probably would not get caught in R. C. Pace's Jasper County, Leon Jones's Angelina County, Frank Brunt's Cherokee County, or Jess Sweeten's Henderson County, but what if his luck ran out and the worst happened? Didn't it make more sense to do one's business in some other sheriff's county?

Consequences of capture could be severe and to some degree extralegal. Frank Brunt combated the professional safecrackers from Dallas County by harsh treatment of the few he did catch. Brunt noted, "Them old safe burglars, they're real hard to catch, but I'll be honest with you, I treated 'em pretty rough. Treat a couple like that and they'd go around you."[124] While Jess Sweeten went out of his way to rehabilitate wayward Henderson County youths, "born criminals" were another matter. Sweeten noted, "I don't think anyone could've been harder on real criminals than I was, or more gentle with those who deserved it. But if a cold-blooded criminal decided he was gonna take things into his own hands, well, he ran into a saw. I've always had the opinion that a cold-blooded criminal was born— he's born, there is no doubt in my mind about that. The day he was born, he became a criminal."[125] At Wharton County, Buck Lane similarly distinguished between "accidentals" and "habituals," with the latter receiving the harsh treatment.

"Civil rights" remained an unfamiliar phrase in Sheriff Sweeten's Henderson County about 1950, and in Sweeten's view born criminals could not be rehabilitated and did not deserve to have their rights respected. At another East Texas county at about this time, the sheriff did things much as did Sweeten. He explained: "We had a reputation for catching you one way or another. I think if you do the job, well, you got to get that kind of reputation. We used whatever method was available to get it straightened out. They don't even start to do it like we did it back in those days, it was a different game altogether. They had the FBI down pretty regularly to check on you, but you didn't leave any tracks for them."[126]

Corbett Akins of Panola County remained equally unrepentant of his harsh treatment of outside outlaws. "The sheriff had to be mean," Akins explained. "Do you realize that the world started with 50 percent crime? Adam and Eve had two boys and one killed the other, and that was

Sheriff Andrew Jackson Spradley of Nacogdoches County posed with his favorite trailing hound. (Texas Ranger Hall of Fame and Museum, Waco)

50 percent crime. It may be nothing to brag about, but I been tough all my life. I enjoyed fighting and enjoyed doing things I guess what you call mean. A preacher can't be a sheriff, cause he's going to hell if he don't watch out. Else, some guy will kill him. I'm not boasting or bragging, but I was mean as hell."[127] Perhaps Akins exaggerated, but students from the Gary High School magazine, *Loblolly,* for years tape-recorded his hair-raising accounts of dragging reluctant arrestees behind his patrol car, beating up and banishing undesirables, making hip-pocket bootleggers chugalug their products at gunpoint, torching the feet of sleeping oil-field transients, and carrying out even more drastic extralegal acts. Most of Corbett Akins's recounted incidents of illegal meanness involved outside criminals or local nonvoters, especially African Americans, a fact that tends to support their authenticity. It was politically expedient to build up one's reputation at the expense of such people rather than at the expense of misbehaving local citizens with numerous family members and friends.

Akins, Leon Jones, Buck Lane of Wharton County, and others did not rely on roughness alone, however, but also tried to "make them go around" by establishing regional reputations for diligent law enforcement. Akins and Leon Jones of Angelina County used well-trained packs of man hounds to deter local crime and to make outlaws go around. Both men broke many local cases with their fast packs of mixed-blood fox and coon hounds and often traveled to other sheriffs' counties to pursue their runaway felons, but Akins and Jones believed their dogs did even more good as a deterrent. Any outlaw with imagination did not relish the thought of running through the East Texas pineywoods with such a pack after him. In fact, no sooner did many criminals hear the dogs on their trail than they climbed a tree or walked in to a nearby farmhouse to give themselves up.

Jess Sweeten rarely used dogs, but he tried to establish a reputation for scientific crime detection and diligent police work, as well as one of roughness, and in Wharton County, Buck Lane did the same. After a few years, criminals contemplating excursions into Wharton County had a lot to worry about. "All them thieves, they dodged this county for a while," Lane said, "We had 'em dodging this county. They called me the 'White Sheriff,' and they'd dodge around me, too! I kept a file on all of 'em, I kept one fingerprint on file for all of 'em, and I took pictures, I kept pictures, of any man. They knew I could clear a case down here."[128] Sheriff Lane had a state-of-the-art radio system linked to several area departments and to DPS headquarters in Austin, three-way radios in all patrol cars, mug shot and fingerprint files for every person who had ever passed through his jail, a lie detector, several machine guns, and a departmental observation plane. Furthermore, Lane seemed indefatigable, rising every morning at 4:00 to drive randomly about the Wharton County back roads on the constant lookout for early morning outlaws. Crooks knew Lane suddenly might show up anywhere, traveled alone, and also had an intimidating reputation for roughness. According to Lane, "Lone Wolf" Gonzaullas once advised him: "When you travel, travel by yourself. Ain't nobody to tell the tale but you. It's a hell of a lot better to be tried for killing some sorry son-of-a-bitch than to have some sorry son-of-a-bitch tried for killing you." Lane took the advice, and in 1986 he bluntly admitted to a historian: "In those days, if a criminal got in a bad way with us, he got killed, and they knew it. Or, he got whipped and they knew it. We were not tried."[129]

Just as Lane's fierce reputation helped to deter outside crooks from moving in, so did it help him enforce banishments. Outside criminals and persons especially repugnant to Lane often got the hot cells and the pickle-juice sandwiches (and probably worse) in Buck Lane's jail, then Lane expelled them from Wharton County, instructing them never to return. Lane especially disliked sex offenders, panhandlers, and scam artists of all kinds. No sheriffs had the legal right to throw people out of their counties, but most sheriffs did exactly that; "putting the sun" on undesirables was one of their most basic strategies of law enforcement. Conversely, however, every sheriff constantly endured the entry into his territory from other sheriffs' domains of banished outlaws, ready to ply their illegal trades. Impelled by sheriffs, outlaws sometimes moved back and forth like human Ping-Pong balls, or they moved of their own volition from areas of greater law enforcement pressure to areas of lesser pressure. Lane recalled: "We'd go over there and get those nigger whores, white whores too, and we'd take 'em out on the road and put a strap to 'em and run 'em off," but then the chastised prostitutes only entered some other sheriff's county.[130]

Wharton County voters clearly perceived Buck Lane as an active, effective, and efficient sheriff—an opinion shared by Lane—but, as the Wharton sheriff's weekly newspaper columns also made abundantly clear, the little officer's intimidating reputation and modern law enforcement paraphernalia failed to deter many outside criminals from preying upon Wharton County. During November 1949, for example, two Gypsies "driving a big shiny red automobile with an Indiana license plate" entered Buck Lane's territory and somehow got word of an elderly Czech farmer who had just withdrawn $1,250 from the bank to purchase a new home. The Gypsies visited the farmer and offered to "bless his money for him," a process supposed to multiply its amount. As Lane described the incident: "They wrapped it up in some sort of a rag with him watching, then they gave it a blessing and turned him around one time, then handed him the rag and told him not to look at it for three days. In two days he looked, and sure enough he had been blessed with a back issue of a newspaper and the $1,250 was flat gone, so were the Gypsies. My idea is that sort of hoodwinkers and robbers of the old, ignorant, blind, sick, and dead should be shot."[131]

Rural sheriffs rarely got the chance to shoot such professionals. Week after week, Lane warned readers of the latest outside outlaws on the make, but his weekly warnings almost always came after the outlaws had come and gone. Perhaps because of its prosperous economy and proximity to Houston, where many outlaws resided, Wharton County suffered the depredations of a wide range of criminals who specialized in driving in, doing their things for a few hours or a few days, and then driving out again, and if local lawmen caught them, they caught them more or less by accident. Lane filled his columns with reports of the outlaws' exploits, rarely followed by any reports of capture. During June 1947, for example, safecrackers of the "knock and punch" school of safe burglary struck three El Campo businesses, including the mayor's, and left a "Kilroy has been here" note on the mayor's typewriter.[132] During February 1951, safe-crackers hit the Danevang Hardware Store, following a characteristic *modus operandi* that involved breaking into hardware stores or machine shops and then using welding equipment and cutting torches from the premises to open the safes. Another group of professionals soon struck elsewhere in the county, Lane reported; this time they were "nitro men" and also with a characteristic method of operation. These robbers broke into a business adjacent to the mainline railroad tracks, waited for the next train to come by, then blew the safe under cover of the train's rumbling passage.[133]

Safecrackers were not the only outlaws passing through Wharton County. On March 19, 1948, Lane warned citizens to watch out for roving junk men from Houston who specialized in cutting farmers' tractors or other equipment into pieces and hauling them away for junk. As so many times before, Lane sounded the alarm. "It don't take a junk peddler long

A Bexar County deputy surveys the work of safecrackers, 1935. (Institute of Texan Cultures, San Antonio)

to cut one to pieces with a torch, load it on the truck, and peddle it for junk iron, watch your tractors, these junk boys are scouring the countryside."[134] In May 1947 the sheriff warned of a specialized gang of milk cow thieves working the whole state of Texas, and in February 1951, of clever liquor store thieves who rode into town on the bus, stole a car, removed its back seat, broke into a liquor store, completely loaded the car, then quickly drove out of the county.[135] In May 1949, "deaf mutes selling sticking plaster" worked door-to-door in the Wharton business district. The sticking plaster cost twenty-five cents, and when the clerk opened his cash drawer to get a quarter, one deaf-mute threw dried peas at the wall behind the clerk, and the other grabbed a handful of quarters when he turned to look. Deputies caught one man with one pocket entirely full of peas and the other entirely full of quarters. Several teams of these deaf-mutes had been working Wharton County, directed by someone in an expensive new automobile with Idaho license places. Although one door-to-door team went to jail, everybody else escaped, as usual.[136]

During the 1950s and early 1960s, before effective networks for the exchange of law enforcement information and good radio systems had become widespread, fast-moving bandits had the upper hand, and even formidable and efficient rural sheriffs such as Buck Lane vainly swung their law-enforcement brooms at them like Loretta Fenton swinging at bats in her jail kitchen. A rogues' gallery of outside outlaws filled Buck Lane's columns, but not usually his jail cells, during the late 1940s and early 1950s. Crooks peddled fake fur coats, diamond rings, lightning rods, "Bulov" watches, and pedigreed baby chicks door to door. Bogus roofers, plumbers, insurance salesmen, magazine salesmen, photo salesmen, and gas-stove repairmen hoodwinked rural housewifes. Short-change artists, "bill splitters," professional shoplifters, and a wide array of hot check passers plagued local merchants. Motorized rustlers stole cattle, horses, milk cows, and tractors from the fields. Specialized bandits robbed liquor stores, businessmen's safes, and even banks. And Gypsy healers, faith healers, and "electric" curers cruelly cheated the old, sick, and dying.

Buck Lane admitted to his reading public that the bats were hard to hit with the broom, but he made dire threats against the outlaws and still claimed to be optimistic. On May 14, 1948, he wrote in his column: "Fact is, at this time, we got rice thieves, saddle thieves, chicken thieves, junk thieves, and gasoline thieves still running on us. Oh yes, cattle thieves too. But here is how it goes, they get all the breaks for a while, and then we get a few. We are a whole lots like a fast cotton-tail rabbit and an ol' long-eared bloodhound. The thieves hop around and skip around and dodge around, and finally the old bloodhound gets a smell, and here he comes, when he gets there it's too late for the rabbit."[137]

Some of the rabbits had teeth, however. Even in 1950 rural sheriffs still policed an armed society, where petty criminals and law-abiding citizens alike carried pistols under their car seats, shotguns on their pickup gun racks, and knives and straight razors in their pockets. In the undermanned rural sheriffs' departments, officers usually went out on calls alone, and if many of them had primitive two-way radios in their patrol cars by the mid-1950s, this made little difference. After the officer left his car and approached a house to serve a legal paper, arrest a petty criminal, take a drunk into custody, quell a domestic disturbance, or perform any of the common duties of his daily round, he acted on his own, with no immediate backup. Eternal caution and vigilance were required, though sometimes hard to maintain in the daily grind of twelve-hour days on the job. Marion County sheriff George Whatley's policy was that "Everybody is guilty, as far as I'm concerned, when I go to arrest him," and Leon Jones said, "I never did get relaxed, I watched everything."[138]

The so-called common drunk caused officers endless problems, and some rural people became just as berserk on the traditional drug of alcohol as modern Texans do on angel dust, speed, or other exotic substances. Most sheriffs believed that public drunkenness and other alcohol-related offenses caused more problems in dry counties than in wet ones, where alcohol consumption was regulated, out in the open, and under better control. For example, at Lufkin, the county seat of Angelina County, a dry town in a dry county, 673 of 1,045 misdemeanor arrests in 1951 were for public drunkenness. "Affray" followed in second place, with 190 arrests, and "disturbance of the peace" followed in third with 173, and most of these 363 fighters and peace disturbers had been intoxicated as well.[139]

Local drunks got that way over and over, and sheriffs came to know them well, especially the ones that underwent Dr. Jekyll–to–Mr. Hyde transformations under the influence of alcohol. A friend of Sheriff Will Wright, "a fine fellow," came into Floresville every Saturday in 1910, got drunk, began to rope people from his horse, and got thrown in jail by Sheriff Wright. This man varied who he chose to rope, but he always roped someone; one week he roped a woman giving music lessons, the next, a railroad engineer on a train.[140] Forty years later, a Coleman County man with a deformed hand drove to Coleman every Saturday, drank heavily, started a disturbance, then confronted Sheriff Fenton for his customary weekend fistfight. The man always lost, but the next week he would say once again, "Well, I guess I'll go into town and give old Fenton a try."[141]

Other habitual binge drinkers threatened an officer's life every time he subdued and arrested them. Sheriff Tom Brown of Caldwell County often got calls on a certain Lockhart man. Sober, the man was one of Brown's better friends in town; drunk, he turned homicidal and suicidal. As Brown approached the man's house after a disturbance call, the man said, "'Brownie, don't you come in here.' I said, 'I'm coming in.' He said, 'If you are, I'm gonna kill you.' I said, 'Naw, you ain't gonna kill me.' He cocked that old .45, says, 'If you get any closer I'm gonna kill you.' I knew if I made a move for my gun he'd shoot. I grabbed him and we wrestled—I was a pretty good-sized batch of man then. I finally got the gun turned round and stuck in his belly, and the old devil says, 'Pull the trigger! Pull the trigger! Pull the trigger!'"[142]

Sheriff Brown chose not to fire the pistol, though he admitted that the thought crossed his mind as a way of solving a recurrent life-threatening problem. The next day he told the man in jail: "Now, you're sober. I'll never take that chance again, I'm gonna kill you. If I ever have to come get you again, I'm gonna say, 'Come on,' and if you don't follow me, I'm gonna shoot.'" Brown arrested the man many times after that warning, "but he always followed me, and I never had a better friend."[143]

Drunks and friends often were the same people. Sheriff Dan Saunders wrote in his journal: "Got a call out north of town tonight on ———. When I got there he was drunk and stuck a .22 rifle right between my eyes and cocked it. He kept it on me for several minutes. Finally he let it down and started laughing. Asked me if he scared me. I told him no you didn't scare me. I just didn't think it was funny."[144]

Over long years of experience and many such confrontations, which came with the job, a sheriff like Saunders developed a command presence that cut through people's fogs of alcohol and emotion and caused them to consider what they were doing. Saunders, Jim Scarborough II, Wallace Riddell, and many other sheriffs regarded themselves as peacemakers— moving into potentially violent situations, defusing them, and protecting drunken, overemotional, or temporarily deranged people from the conse- quences of their actions while at the same time protecting themselves. The experienced officer talked things over with drunks and fighters and did not prematurely force the issue. As Truman Maddox noted, you had to be willing to finish what you started, so you tried not to start it. "It's a whole lot easier to spend fifteen or twenty minutes talking a man into something than it is to spend five minutes forcing him into it," Maddox said.[145]

A willingness and an ability to be effectively violent lurked just behind the veteran officer's conciliatory demeanor, however—perhaps close enough to the surface for the wayward citizen to sense its presence. Tall, unblocked cowboy hats, high-heeled boots, badges, and prominent pistols made intimidating nonverbal statements for some, such as Jess Sweeten, "the seven-foot sheriff." Jim Scarborough II acted as a peacemaker and never carried a gun, but barely visible in his back pocket was a pair of "knucks"—as his son said, "just in case he got hold of some big guy he couldn't handle."[146] Like any sheriff, Scarborough could not afford to lose a fight, and some people always forced one. At Burnet County, kindly old Sheriff Wallace Riddell specialized in shaming fighting drunks and quarreling family members into sobriety and submission. "He would make you feel so badly that you had done something bad enough for him to be there that you would go willingly just to please him," Riddell's son Pat explained. However, with one group of local brothers, persistent troublemakers, this approach just did not work. They refused to go quietly and started fights with Sheriff Riddell over and over again, and "then he'd whip hell out of 'em, I mean, just literally whip the hell out of 'em!"[147]

The use of deadly force was another matter. Some sheriffs found frequent occasions to use firearms, as part of law enforcement, during the dangerous confrontations with drunks, insane people, and criminals. Others passed through forty-year careers without firing a gun at anyone. County-to-county differences in local traditions of violence doubtless explain some of this variation in law enforcement practice, but to a considerable degree the decision to shoot or not to shoot seems to have been a matter of personal taste.

Although they might carry backup weapons in their cars, a good many sheriffs chose to go about their daily business unarmed. Some nineteenth-century Texas sheriffs had done the same, and this at a time when many men still went openly armed. Sheriff A. J. Spradley of Nacogdoches (himself a lawman of the "shootist" school, with several notches on his gun) told his biographer about several Texas sheriffs who went unarmed during long and successful careers. One of them, Rufe Perry of Harrison County, arrested many bad men unarmed, including famous killer John

Wesley Hardin, who offered no resistance, paid his fine for disturbing the peace, and left Harrison County. According to Spradley, Sheriff Delmas E. Teague of Washington County once stood off a mob threatening to take his prisoner away by "baring his breast and telling the men who composed the mob that they would have to kill him first, and no man wanted to take that responsibility."[148] Perhaps, in an armed society, going unarmed both demonstrated impressive courage and allowed lawbreakers to surrender without damage to their personal reputation or sense of honor. Michael B. Wright served seven terms as Nueces County sheriff, beginning in 1902, and he arrested many dangerous men without carrying a gun. On one occasion a rancher got into a quarrel and killed someone outside a saloon, then left the message, "Tell Mike I'll kill anybody who comes after me." But Mike Wright rode out unarmed to meet the rifle-holding rancher at his door, talked to him for a time, then put the man up behind him on his horse and carried him to jail.[149]

Jim Scarborough II served as a rifleman during World War I, and while still in France, as his son said, "He made a little pledge to himself that if he ever got out of there alive, he'd never raise a gun against a man as long as he lived. He never did." Scarborough once told a reporter, "If I ever had a gun, I probably would have killed somebody, a six-shooter never solved a problem." Once, a murderer had returned to visit his parents and became trapped in their house, exchanging shots with lawmen outside. Sheriff Scarborough slowly walked to the front door while the outlaw shouted verbal warnings then fired warning shots; he then surrendered to Scarborough. During 1942, this happened again, and Scarborough brought a black man out of a house "with the man's pistol in one hand and his arm around him."[150] Sheriffs Nathan Tindall and John Lightfoot also successfully pulled off some unarmed "walk-ups," aided by the fact that local people knew they never carried guns. On at least one occasion Lightfoot raised a sobering point as he approached, saying to the man barricaded in the house, "Why would you want to shoot me? And besides, it'll just get you into the electric chair."[151]

Even sheriffs who carried guns often seemed reluctant to use them, especially when drunken or deranged people were involved. Sheriff Houston Brantley of Delta County absorbed a terrible beating for twenty minutes from a huge, drunken, former serviceman outside a Cooper bus stop before the sheriff reluctantly shot the man in the leg. Both men went to the hospital, with the sheriff in by far the more serious condition.[152]

Hardeman County sheriff Malon Owen came under fire from a service station operator on the streets of Quanah but refused to shoot him. Owen took bullets in the hand and chest as he approached the man, then felled him with an axe handle.[153] In Limestone County, a deranged black man assaulted another man, then stood off officers with an ax. Sheriff Harry Dunlap talked to the insane man for more than half an hour, trying to get him to put down the ax, then Dunlap approached him holding a sawed-off shotgun on the ready. The man swung the ax, striking the sheriff in the right arm and shoulder, but Dunlap subdued him without firing the shotgun.[154] Heroic attempts to save insane people did not always end successfully, however. A year later, Sheriff Dunlap stepped from behind the shelter of two oil drums to reason with berserk farmer N. J. Tynes, who had barricaded himself in a house, and Dunlap took a fatal .22 bullet through the head. Soon thereafter, Ranger Clint Peoples and other officers killed Tynes.[155]

During long years of service, most sheriffs found themselves in one or more situations in which they had to shoot, and some regretted these occasions all the rest of their life. In six terms in office, Buck Lane had to kill one man, a drunken Hispanic who had terrorized a roadhouse with a gun. After Lane shot him, he told a reporter that he and his wife "had a good cry—that's right, nothing womanish about a man crying. I'm not in the fighting business. I'm trying to stop fighting. If I have to fight, I fight to win, and quick."[156] Retiring in 1941 after eighteen years in office, Sheriff Frank Hunt of San Patricio County told a reporter about the only man he had killed in line of duty—a story almost too painful for him to repeat. Hunt had taken an admitted murderer to a brushy area, where the man said he could find the murder weapon, when the man suddenly sprinted into the woods. Hunt ran in pursuit, yelling for the murderer to stop and thinking that he could not let the man get away. Hunt shot over the running man's head, he shot under his feet, and finally he shot to wound the man in his shoulder, but the man ran on. Finally, with his last bullet, Hunt shot to kill.[157]

Even for pacifist sheriffs, in time one's luck tended to run out. Sheriff Dan Saunders tried to "initiate an image of law enforcement that would extend to the kids. I never wore a pistol. I would have felt silly standing at the counter registering a car with the pistol on. I wanted the kids to know that you didn't have to have a pair of mirrored sunglasses on and a pistol and a billy club hanging on your belt with two sets of handcuffs to be a peace officer."[158] However, at 3:00 A.M. on Saunders's birthday in 1965, an eight-year-old boy knocked on his door and woke him up and told him the boy's father was drunk and about to kill his mother. Domestic violence calls were part of Saunders's daily round, but this time he felt a strange foreboding.

> I hurriedly dressed and took the little boy with me to his house. I felt an intuition that only a person in danger of his life can feel. I was by myself and of course had no radio contact with anyone. I stuck a pistol in my belt. When I entered the house and saw the drunken father sitting at the kitchen table with his wife and six more children terrorized I knew that one of us was going to die. I could tell by the look in his eyes. He was drunk and had a knife. A drunken friend was with him. He attacked me and tried to get my pistol. I knew if he got the weapon he not only would kill me but would also kill his wife and even perhaps some of the kids. My first shot took his finger off but he kept coming. My second shot killed him. This is one of those things that an officer faces every family squabble he makes.[159]

Often, the moment of deadly violence came in a split second, out of nowhere, with no time for foreboding. Asked by a hunting club to check on the increasingly eccentric behavior of the club's watchman, Sheriff Frank Brunt and a constable drove out to talk to the man. They saw him walking down a dirt road carrying a .30-30 carbine, stopped the car next to him, and Brunt said, "We're officers, want to talk to you." Then

> he just stepped back one step, it was so close, and, "BALOOM!" The bullet hit that little ventilating window, little steel rim around that glass, that .30-30 bullet grazed that and come over and hit Pete right across his chest, just ripped him. I had bent over to talk to the man, and the bullet caught me right there in the chest and stopped right up close to my backbone. And we started shooting. I shot through the glass a couple of times, shattered glass and cut us all over. A little of it is still in me. Anyhow, I looked at Pete and I saw the blood shooting everywhere. I looked to see if this guy was down, and he was. He was still trying to pull that trigger, but he didn't have no life in him. I looked in the rear view mirror at my face, and there was just a perfect size of a .30-30 bullet right there over my eyebrow. I felt back

there at the back of my head to see where it come out, but I couldn't feel it.[160]

The brass rim fragment of the shattered .30-30 bullet finally emerged from the festering wound in Frank Brunt's forehead, but other sheriffs carried buckshot pellets, pistol slugs, and other inoperable combat shrapnel with them to their graves.

Shootist sheriffs always were far more common than the stalwart souls who went unarmed, and with good reason. During the late nineteenth and early twentieth century, Texans often flashed with anger and proceeded to shoot, cut, and stab their neighbors or to engage in hand-to-hand combats that proved nearly as deadly. Rural Texans still conducted fistfights under the awesome rules of "stomp and gouge," which lumberman John Henry Kirby well described: "A contestant could not use anything but the members of his own body. He could kick, gouge, choke, strangle, pull hair, or resort to anything else with his hands, feet, head, legs, arms, or mouth. He could not use a weapon of any kind, nor a stick, nor a stone, pocketknife, piece of metal, brass knucks, or anything other than his bare body."[161]

People often went armed, however. During 1949, Sheriff Owen Kilday of Bexar County told reporters that by state law his department could file concealed weapons charges only for pistols, slingshots, brass knuckles, and Bowie knives, and that straight razors and pocket knives of any length were entirely legal.[162] Many Texans continued to carry illegal weapons, especially on Saturday night excursions; for example, a man was arrested at Longview in 1940 with seven revolvers "of varying calibers" and a pair of brass knuckles.[163]

A good many sheriffs did not bother trying to talk deranged men into putting down their axes or barricaded outlaws into giving up; they turned their guns on them, as did Sheriff Roy Hillin of Crosbyton on the "rampaging negro" who attacked him with a knife in 1946.[164] Many similar news items dotted the pages of the *Sheriffs' Association of Texas Magazine* over the years. When a Henderson County man, perhaps insane, barricaded himself in a house and shot at passers-by with his rifle, marksman Sheriff Jess Sweeten dispensed with long conversations. He slipped up to the back porch, located the man in the house by the sound of creaking floor boards, kicked in the door, and, as Sweeten described, "'Bam, Bam, Bam,' three hit him right in the belly."[165]

Jess Sweeten shot nine men in twenty-two years as Henderson County sheriff and killed three of them, including Gerald Johnson, the "Dallas Kid," after a high-speed car chase through the county seat of Athens.[166] Without doubt, oil-boom East Texas was a wild and violent place, but sheriffs such as Sweeten who specialized in firearms often found good occasions to use them. Sheriff John S. Spradley of Nacogdoches County killed several men in the line of duty (not including the two brothers Spradley killed before immigrating to Texas), and in time he learned to watch his back. Spradley "owned a bullet-proof vest and wore a gun which fastened to a gunbelt with a swivel so that it could be shot from the hip without having to be drawn from a holster." In his later years, Spradley became well known for always closing the blinds when he came into a room, and other veteran sheriffs did the same.[167] After killing several men in outlaw-plagued Lee County at the close of the nineteenth century, Sheriff Jim Scarborough I spent the rest of his life sitting with his back to walls facing doors, even while attending church. Perhaps a certain family's long-standing offer of several thousand dollars for Scarborough's head in a tow sack had something to do with this practice. Sheriff Jim Flournoy refused to tell a reporter how many men he had killed in line of duty, and other sheriffs proved reticent about such matters. "I wouldn't want to tell you about how many men I killed," Corbett Akins said, "cause, I might have to count 'em before I went to hell."[168] Buck Lane officially killed only one man, but during 1986, at age eighty-three, while allowing an unfamiliar historian (the author) to interview him about his career, a cocked .45 automatic lay next to Lane's gun hand on his rolltop desk.

Possibly Lane feared an attack of blood revenge from a son or grandson of someone he had harmed. In the face-to-face communities of rural Texas, confrontations between sheriffs and local outlaws tended to become personal, and sometimes they turned into dangerous feuds. Well aware of their vulnerability to assassination, sheriffs sometimes considered preemptive strikes on such individuals.

In Comanche County, Gaston Boykin had personal confrontations with a certain bootlegger and with a wild garage owner who enjoyed taunting the sheriff by blasting through Comanche's only traffic light at speeds in excess of one hundred miles per hour. The crime was only a misdemeanor, and officers did not have cars that could catch the man, but the challenge rankled. Finally, Boykin consulted with the county attorney (who promised not to indict him, should the worst happen), then told the man, "I'll dare you to come through one more time!" This time, Boykin said, officers would shoot to kill. The man ceased his hundred-mile-per-hour drive-throughs, although one Saturday (as he told Boykin years later) he sat in his car on one side of the courthouse square contemplating a rifle assault on Sheriff Boykin, who was sitting in his patrol car (and watching the garage owner) from across the square. On this Saturday, nothing happened, but the garage man's hand had been on his .22 centerfire rifle and the sheriff's on his .30-06 Springfield.[169]

After this shootout that did not happen, the garage owner left Comanche County. Sheriffs sometimes tried to solve such problems by banishments, as Henry Billingsley did with a black man whom he had wounded and who had then returned to Angelina County.[170] Sheriff Frank Brunt became locked in a serious feud with a Wells man who ran a car theft ring out of several auto repair businesses. After Brunt learned from informants that the outlaw businessman had sent four assassins to waylay Brunt on one of his midnight patrols, narrowly missing the sheriff when he chose to take another turn on the back road, Brunt took action. "I went down there to Wells one day with my shotgun and called him outside. I says, 'John Mason, you're gonna kill me or I'm gonna kill you, or you're gonna get out of this county in two weeks and don't ever come back.' Thank God, he gave me back a week of that, he moved to Lufkin."[171] Once, Jess Sweeten testified about the bad character of a man named Hood who was on trial for maiming a Henderson County youth with a knife. Furious, Hood started "gunning" for Sheriff Sweeten, carrying a double-barreled shotgun with him wherever he went. Sweeten well recognized his danger and considered his alternatives. "I was watching him. I knew he was gunning for me, he was doing a little talking. But I couldn't get him right where I wanted him. You know, I wanted to kill him, but just can't go out there and just shoot him. So, I kept watching him. He was trying to get me in the right place, too." Fortunately for Sweeten, the formidable Hood also threatened other people, one of whom shot Hood to death in his car and then was no-billed by the grand jury.[172]

At Trinity County during 1937 and 1938, a personal conflict between young Sheriff Carl Busch and elderly bar owner and former convict Ed Chandler ran its full and deadly course. A local man with important family connections and a reputation as a killer, Chandler returned to Trinity County soon after the county voted itself wet and opened a legal road-house and illegal gambling den just inside the county line. Chandler had a partner and numerous friends and henchmen, but Busch did not even have a deputy. One evening, with the dubious backup of a young constable, the sheriff went out to try to make his writ run on Chandler, who got the drop on Busch with a rifle and humiliated him in front of a crowd gathered outside Chandler's roadhouse. Faced with almost certain death, Busch backed down, walked off, and drove away while spectators laughed. Afterward, Busch got a warrant for Chandler, who remarked in public, "Let the son of a bitch try to serve it, he hasn't got the guts." The gauntlet having been thrown, and Busch's only other option being to "paint my back yellow and run off," the sheriff made up his mind to "serve that warrant or die in my tracks." He accosted Chandler on the Groveton courthouse square, and when Chandler reached in his pocket, Busch shot him through the body, felling him, then "gave him one right through the head between the eyes, cause I didn't want no wounded tiger like him on my hands." Despite this rather deliberate coup de grâce, a local grand jury soon readied itself to no-bill Sheriff Busch (keeping faith with a long-standing county tradition of no-billing such affairs), but the sheriff insisted on an indictment, a trial by jury, and an acquittal to put him in the clear once and for all.[173]

Perhaps no Texas sheriff of midcentury killed so many men as did the controversial Vail Ennis of Bee County. Sheriff Jim Scarborough II of Kleberg County and his son of the same name knew Ennis well. According to Jim Scarborough III, shootist sheriff Ennis "was better than an expert, he just loved to shoot, and he'd do trick shooting. You could flip a quarter up and he'd pull his pistol out and shoot a hole in it. And Vail Ennis could put up a sheet of copper and punch the outline of an Indian, shooting from the hip. He was a sniper in World War I, a very successful one. He believed in the gun, and that's the way he ran Bee County." Ennis once went so far as mounting a Citizen's Model Thompson .45 submachine gun on the hood of his car—a fixed-mount weapon aimed by pointing the whole car like a fighter plane and fired by pulling a chain from dash to trigger.[174]

An immigrant from Nacogdoches County (where he doubtless knew gunman sheriff A. J. Spradley), Vail Ennis came to Bee County as an oil-field worker in 1941, became a deputy, and served as Bee County sheriff from January 1945 to the end of 1952, during which time he killed eight men. Ennis seems to have wounded no one, since people in gun battles with this sheriff invariably died.

Bee County seems not have been an especially violent place, so Sheriff Ennis's four-term career demonstrated just how far grand juries, trial juries, and voters were willing to go in giving a shootist sheriff the benefit of the doubt, even at midcentury, provided that he shot the right people. Sheriff Ennis shot mostly Hispanics and blacks. He killed one man while still a deputy, and he shot a black prisoner fifteen days after taking office as sheriff. Ennis said the latter man grabbed for his gun, but there were no witnesses. Then, in July of Ennis's first year in office, the sheriff machine-gunned a Hispanic father and his two brothers to death after they failed to obey a court order to turn over two young children to their mother. Ennis, the two officers accompanying him, and a survivor in the house told different stories about this incident. Ennis was true-billed by the grand jury, tried, and acquitted. Then, on August 1, 1946, Bee County voters swept Sheriff Vail Ennis to overwhelming victory in the Democratic primary.

Ennis's gun battles continued, however, and eventually Bee County citizens began to have second thoughts. Ennis entered a phone booth with two handcuffed hot check artists, one pulled a hidden pistol foolishly missed by Ennis in a body search, and prisoner and sheriff exchanged pistol fire at very close range. Both prisoners died, Ennis spent hours on the operating table and barely survived, and a nearby filling station operator took a stray bullet. A couple of shootings later, Ennis killed his last man, a Hispanic prisoner who recovered from being slugged with a chain to jump Ennis from the back seat of his patrol car on the way into Beeville. The man grabbed Ennis from behind, the sheriff struggled to keep his car on the road, then Ennis got a pistol free to fire back over his shoulder into the man's face. Soon thereafter, as Ennis readied himself for his fifth election campaign, he told reporters that he had in truth killed eight men. "I don't have any more room for notches [on my pistol]," Sheriff Ennis said. "I certainly do not relish the idea of having to kill anyone. In every instance where I have had to act, it was either him or me, and I don't propose to let anyone consign me to a casket if I can prevent it. It just so happened that the men I have had to kill or get killed were that desperate type of individual. Perhaps they have been accustomed to getting away with a lot of rough stuff. They can't do that in Bee County so long as I am sheriff."[175]

By the Democratic primary of 1952, however, although Sheriff Ennis still had his strong supporters, the body count had climbed too high for the majority of Bee County voters. Two candidates faced Ennis, one of them the sheriff who had first hired him as deputy. In May 1952, this man withdrew from the race in favor of the other candidate, commenting: "Better than many people I recognize the need for a change. In a sense I feel responsible for the condition that has existed. I brought Ennis into the sheriff's office when I hired him in 1941. I want to make up for that mistake now."[176]

Vail Ennis lost the election, but he remained unrepentant about having run Bee County "by the gun." Two decades after his electoral defeat, Ennis lay dying of lung cancer, and in his last days he summoned new Kleberg County sheriff Jim Scarborough III to his side to offer him some advice. Scarborough recalled:

> I went around to his room—he couldn't talk, he had to force a whisper. He pulled me right down into his face, had me lean over, and said, "Jim, I'm gonna give you the best advice that you ever had in your whole life. I want you to remember it." His voice was raspy and everything else. It took him forever to say it. All this time he had a death grip on my hand. He said, "Now, your dad won't agree with this at all, but I'm telling you, don't never get caught without your gun. When you go after a man, you get him and you kill him. Don't bring him back to the hospital. When you bring him in, bring him in dead. Take him to the morgue. Now, that's the best advice I can give you." I said, "Mr. Vail, coming from you, I appreciate it from the bottom of my heart, thank you very much," and I shook his hand. That's the last time I spoke to him. He was dead a few days later.[177]

Sheriff Ennis's hood-mounted machine gun and his troubles with back-seat prisoners suggest two recurring dangers faced by rural sheriffs at midcentury: perilous one-on-one car chases of the preradio era, and life-threatening lone-officer prisoner transports. From the 1930s into the 1960s, officers injured on the highway in collisions or turnovers and officers over-powered and injured by prisoners received constant mention in the *Sheriffs' Association of Texas Magazine*. At one point, listings of the deceased reached such proportions that the editor quoted fatalistic lines from "The Revel," a poem by early-nineteenth-century poet Bartholomew Dowling:

> We meet 'neath the sounding rafter, and the walls around are bare;
> As they shout back our peals of laughter, it seems that the dead are
>   there.
> Then stand to your glasses steady! We drink in our comrades' eyes:
> One cup to the dead already—hurrah for the next that dies![178]

During the 1920s and 1930s, and afterwards, automobile bandits like Clyde Barrow lived and died in their motor cars. If a lawman wanted to catch Clyde Barrow and others like him, he had to outrun them and outgun them, and that was not easy to accomplish. At a time when most rural officers went around armed with handguns and .30-30 carbines, the Barrow gang drove the highways with Browning automatic rifles (BARs) stolen from National Guard armories. Furthermore, the outlaws had faster cars and better drivers. Beginning about 1933, Dallas County deputy Ted Hinton chased Clyde Barrow on various occasions in a Ford V-8, a Cord V-8, and a Cadillac V-8, and Clyde ran off and left Hinton every time. By constant practice, Barrow had made himself a masterful dirt-road driver and race-car tuneup man, and his favorite car to steal and to drive was the popular Ford V-8. He knew just how to tune it for performance driving, and its heavy steel sides and doors stopped pistol bullets (but not BAR rounds). Barrow drove very fast all the time, not just when pursued, so he became very good at it. The Barrow gang and others like it typically hit a bank or some other target, drove day and night to get hundreds of miles away from the crime scene, then hid out. From time to time they went to ground for more extended periods in certain safe areas, such as Panola County, Texas, where Barrow or other gang members had family, friends, and protectors, and Barrow knew every back road in the countryside. As Ted Hinton noted, Clyde Barrow was a professional, a daring and inspired driver who demonstrated an uncanny ability to second-guess officers in automobile cat-and-mouse games across the countryside. Clyde Barrow, Bonnie Parker, and other gang members lived in their cars and slept in their cars and more or less constantly moved about over several states. Jess Sweeten and other sheriffs recounted the common tale of just missing Bonnie and Clyde—of learning of a suspicious car parked under a back-road bridge somewhere in their county, of massing officers and weapons for an assault, and of going out to find the birds had flown. Like many professional outlaws from outside a sheriff's county, Clyde Barrow had an excellent sense of timing for how long to stay and when to drive swiftly on.[179]

On numerous occasions, until Ranger Frank Hamer, Deputy Ted Hinton, and others caught up with them in 1934, the Barrow gang and others like them outran and outshot rural lawmen, leading to sponsorship by the Sheriffs' Association of Texas in 1935 of special legislation "providing for the authority of the County Commissioners Court in each county in the state of Texas to purchase one or more machine guns, or sub-machine guns, to safe guard sheriffs in the discharge of their duties." Rural lawmen felt inadequate, the association said, because "the ordinary equipment of the sheriff is usually far inferior to the equipment of the big shot gangster. The gangster is provided with high powered automobiles, machine guns, and sufficient funds to make a quick get away."[180] In 1939 the *Sheriffs' Association of Texas Magazine* announced a technological breakthrough to help sheriffs equalize firepower in their car chases of "big shot gangsters": the electrically operated "Stockholm machine gun," designed to replace the hood ornament on a sheriff's car and fire fully automatic rounds at a rate of eight per second. A pursuing officer simply aimed his car at the quarry vehicle and touched off a deadly burst of fire.[181]

The machine-gun bill did not pass, and the Stockholm gun fantasy did not materialize for most rural sheriffs, though the weapon itself continued to be promoted in the sheriffs' association magazine until 1960, at which time it had evolved into a .357 magnum, semiautomatic "Electric Pursuit Gun," fired by push button, capable of penetrating a vehicle from back to front and cracking the engine block.[182] Car chases remained a problem. When crooks fled in a car, the sheriff raced after them, siren screaming, and the only way he could stop them was by shooting into their car, forcing them off the road, or pursuing them until they crashed. Over and over again, if the outlaw's car was faster, or the outlaw a better or a more daring driver, he got cleanly away, leaving the sheriff, quite literally, in his dust.

Every sheriff who held office during the 1950s experienced harrowing car chases, most of them unsuccessful; county commissioners rarely provided sheriff's departments with really competitive automobiles. During the 1930s, Sheriff J. R. Sessions of Freestone County often chased moonshine-laden trucks leaving the county on Highway 75. Truck drivers straddled the center of the narrow road, blocking officers from getting around them, so officers' only option was to shoot. The sheriff's son recalled, "I've seen 'em bringing in cars that was literally shot all to pieces."[183] Lengthy hot pursuits still went on twenty years later, well into the two-way radio era, since early radios often proved inadequate. Sheriff Paul Bone of Somervell County chased two bootleggers across three counties in 1959 while the outlaws threw bottles of whiskey at the pursuing patrol car and the sheriff fired his revolver. Eventually, radio contact worked well enough to set up a roadblock.[184] Frustrated sheriffs often fired at the tires of fleeing vehicles, leading to regrettable tragedies when bumpy

roads made shots strike high. Sheriff Ben Waldrip severely wounded a
Texas A&M College student after a long road chase in 1949, and Sheriff
Wallace Riddell accidentally killed a young man from the Oatmeal com-
munity in a similar automobile pursuit that same year.[185]

Some sheriffs liked the excitement of road chases and helped make their
reputations with them. Jess Sweeten, Truman Maddox, Gaston Boykin,
and Buck Lane all had epic car pursuits, usually ending in gunfights beside
the highway. In Cherokee County, Sheriff Frank Brunt often gave his
professional whiskey outlaws a run down dirt roads on the way into
Nacogdoches County. Forty years later, Brunt managed to communicate
some of the thrill of these hot pursuits:

> Most times we'd catch 'em before they got out of there to the high-
> way. Some of 'em had their cars tuned up professional, but I had
> mine that way, too. We'd block those roads, I like to get killed chasing
> em, get on those dirty roads in summertime and that dust fogging
> up, you couldn't see where you was going. It was worse than driving
> in the dark. Had a bridge over there just as you cross to go over into
> Nacogdoches County, on that slough bridge there's a curve where
> we wrecked two or three. That was a good place to catch 'em, crowd
> 'em on that curve and wreck 'em. I was young and I'd give 'em a
> pretty good race, wonder I didn't get killed.[186]

Successful high-speed car chases sometimes ended in prisoner transport situations more dangerous than driving dirt roads at eighty miles per
hour. Well into the 1960s, sheriffs and deputies worked alone, patrol cars
had no barriers between back and front seats, and an officer placed a handcuffed prisoner beside him or in the back seat. In these tempting circumstances, even common drunks, fighters, and petty criminals often made a
break for freedom or grabbed for the officer's pistol. In 1963, for example,
experienced Panola County deputy A. C. Henigan arrested two short-
change artists after a high-speed chase and put one in the back seat and
one beside him in the front. On the way to Carthage, the front-seat prisoner went for Henigan's gun, holstered in plain sight on the officer's right
side. They struggled, the car weaved down the highway, and the gun went
off twice, wounding the deputy and killing the prisoner. As Henigan
stopped the car, the back seat prisoner jumped out and ran, and the
wounded deputy shot him dead.[187]

In the course of long careers, such incidents happened to most sheriffs. In 1962 a back-seat prisoner slashed Sheriff H. R. "Mike" Flournoy with a knife, and Flournoy stopped the car and killed the knife wielder.[188] In rural Montgomery County, Deputy Clint Peoples was securing a prisoner beside him in the front seat when the man seized People's tie, jerked him off balance, and began beating him with his fist. Peoples had almost lost consciousness from the combined beating and choking before he unholstered his pistol and cracked the prisoner's skull with a deadly blow.[189] Sometimes it was the officer who paid the ultimate price for this precarious situation. For two decades after the first ad for a steel barrier between front and back seats appeared in the *Sheriffs' Association of Texas Magazine* in 1954, most patrol cars still had none. At Lavaca County in 1969, Sheriff Ronnie Dodds and his chief deputy both died after picking up two men for disturbing the peace and refusing to pay a bar bill of $37.50. The prisoners jumped the sheriff from the back seat of the car, got his gun, shot both officers and pushed them out of the car, then took the time to shoot them again. Sheriff Dodds died on the scene, and his deputy died two weeks later without regaining consciousness.[190]

Transporting prisoners to the state penitentiary at Huntsville also proved dangerous, though this situation differed from impromptu transports from roadhouses to jails. Prisoners had sober jail time to plan desperate escapes before the "Walls" prison at Huntsville closed around them, and officers expected trouble. Only luck and an armed prisoner's reluctance to kill saved Gaston Boykin from a carefully planned carbreak during a prisoner transport in the early 1950s, and in 1957, Sheriff C. F. Stubblefield of Mills County had his gun jerked and his tongue nearly shot off in a similar situation.[191]

From 1905 to 1944, "Uncle Bud" Russell, "transfer agent" for the Texas Department of Corrections, often performed this dangerous duty for sheriffs. Nobody escaped or even tried to escape when Bud Russell transported them. Russell rolled into town in "Black Betty," his special armored transport truck, steel-meshed cage on the back, Thompson submachine guns in the front cab. Bud Russell said hello to the sheriff, the sheriff brought the prisoners down from his jail, and Russell and an assistant strip-searched them very, very carefully—shoes, socks, clothes, ties, hair, and body orifices. Then Russell marched the prisoners outside, put them in Black Betty, and triple-chained them. At one time or another, Russell transported Clyde Barrow, Buck Barrow, Joe Palmer, Raymond Hamilton, Clyde

Thompson, and other notable outlaws, none of whom tried to escape. If Russell deemed a warning necessary, he kept it short: "Don't get any wrong ideas in your heads. You're forty years too late if you think you're tougher than I am." Unfortunately for Sheriffs Boykin, Stubblefield, and others, Bud Russell retired in 1944 and died in 1955, immortalized only by prisoner Huddie Ledbetter's second verse of "Midnight Special":

> Here come Bud Russell. How in the world do you know?
> Well, he know him by his wagon and the chains he wo'.
> Big pistol on his shoulder, big knife in his hand:
> He's coming to carry you back to Sugarland.[192]

From the late 1940s into the early 1960s, for use during prisoner transports, car chases, and the more mundane affairs of rural law enforcement, two-way radios gradually arrived to link patrolling officers to departmental transmitters, and, should the need arise, to call for help. Ultimately, radios changed everything, but for a decade or more they proved only of limited usefulness. Sheriff Wallace Riddell acquired his first two-way car radio about 1950, but its antenna was a bamboo pole wrapped with copper wire that had to be removed and hidden from mischievous boys every night, and ten miles from the transmitter, the radio went silent. As Riddell traveled around most of Burnet County, he still stopped periodically to check with his operator-dispatcher on private telephones to see what calls had come in.[193] In Bell County in 1951, Deputy Lester Gunn and the other two deputies also had radios, but "you couldn't hardly read 'em in Killeen from Benton."[194]

Radio assistance began with coded calls put out to officers over ordinary public radio stations during the 1930s. Then, Harris County, Dallas County, Bexar County, and a few other places began to use one-way transmitters to communicate with patrolling officers, who could not communicate back. Primitive, unreliable, underpowered, two-way radio systems like Burnet County's gradually arrived during the 1950s, often paid for not by county commissioners but by fish frys, dances, auctions, and sheriffs' begging pleas in weekly newspapers. True three-way systems, allowing officers to communicate car-to-car in the field without passing messages through central transmitters, did not reach most of rural Texas until about 1970, and only then did rural officers' isolation truly end.

But even the poor systems of the dawn of law enforcement radio had soothed the nerves of anxious sheriffs' wives, listening to "traffic" back in jail apartments. No longer able to accompany Sheriff H. F. Fenton when he went on calls, Loretta Fenton manned the radio and listened for coded messages from her husband, far out in the lonely Coleman County dark. Loretta recalled: "After we started having our babies, I had to stay here. When I'd hear him go out on a call, he did have his radio then, I'd hear him get out of his car, and I'd come in here and listen. I'd wait and wait and wait, it would seem like a hundred years until I heard him say, "Ten-eight." That would be his voice and that code meant he was back in the car. I sat in there and waited because I could get somebody to go out there and help him, if I had to."[195]

CHAPTER THREE

WHISKEY AND BLOOD

No sooner did a new sheriff like H. F. Fenton take office than he found himself in an ambiguous relationship with certain county traditions, extralegal and illegal—matters which, more than anything else, forced the sheriff to "interpret" the law or even ignore its violation. Many voters expected their sheriffs to respect these local traditions and became angry at them if they did not. Rather often, the underlying political dynamics of sheriffs' elections turned on such matters, with candidates friendly to extralegal or illegal local traditions opposed by candidates favoring their reform.

Most dry counties nonetheless had their customary wet spots at country clubs, Veterans of Foreign Wars (VFW) halls, and black "barrel houses." Public drunkenness was illegal but also traditional. Every Saturday night the sheriff had to pick and choose among his many candidates for arrest, and a strict interpretationist could jam his jail with angry intoxicated voters by 11 P.M. Drinkers often also were the fighters, participating in what H. F. Fenton called "just good old fistfights"—another outlaw tradition, fair combats between consenting males. Prostitution and gambling also were illegal, but discreet "red light districts" condoned by important citizens operated in many communities, and zealous gamblers from all echelons of county society wielded cards and dice. Should the sheriff so desire, he could ignore the Saturday night drunks and instead fill his jail with bank presidents, lawyers, sharecroppers, cowboys, pulpwood haulers, and other adherents of the sporting life.

If sheriffs strategically looked the other way at the violation of some state laws, they also enforced certain customary local rules not on the books. About 1950, "Jim Crow" laws still supported segregation, but in every multiracial community many extralegal customs elaborated on the formalities of apartheid to further separate the races, and people expected sheriffs to patrol the invisible lines and enforce the unwritten rules of local race relations. If a black man entered the wrong doorway to a place of business or sat on the wrong bench at the courthouse square, or if white youths prowled the black quarter after midnight, it was the sheriff's job to deal with these matters. Fearing racial troubles perhaps more than anything else, rural sheriffs of the 1950s and 1960s invariably sought to preserve racial harmony by more and better segregation.

Whether the traditional transgressors were drunks, gamblers, fighters, whoremongers, or whatever, a sheriff prided himself on enforcing the formal laws with discretion, common sense, and a degree of leeway, the better to "protect his people from abuse." "I don't think every man that messes up a little bit needs to go to jail," Truman Maddox explained:

> All rules are made to be distributed to the people as the person sees fit. Start with speeding. The law out here says fifty-five miles an hour. There's no one that would agree to give a man a ticket for fifty-six, but that is more than the law says he is allowed to do. There's a law against a man using abusive language, but a man can do that up to a certain point. He might raise a little cain and cuss and cut up a little bit, but go give that man a chance to go on home. If he's got too much to drink, give him a chance, let him go on home.[1]

As Maddox implied, sheriffs often did not operate in the same way as such mechanical enforcers of the law as municipal policemen, state troopers, or Texas Rangers. Sheriff Sonny Sessions affirmed: "A good sheriff is a buffer from other law enforcement. They're usually not very popular with the police departments. A good sheriff's gonna protect his people from abuse."[2] In his study of the Texas sheriff, political scientist James Dickson noted how sheriffs often operated to buffer county citizens and county traditions from the full and immediate effects of enforced legal changes coming down from the state or federal levels of government. "His dual role, both as an agent of local government and state government, enables him to use his unusual brand of discretion in law enforcement to modify and adapt changes intruding from the upper reaches of the system. The sheriff provides the citizens of his county a cushion of time to decide how much of their old ways can be preserved within a facade of compliance with inevitable and unavoidable adjustments."[3]

In truth, within this "facade of compliance" some sheriffs defended their counties' "old ways" with special vigor, and a few developed economic incentives for doing so. A sheriff was supposed "to defend his county against any of its enemies, when they come into the land," legal scholar Walter Anderson noted.[4] Sometimes these enemies of the county were outside criminals, and sometimes, a sheriff might conclude, they were Liquor Control Board (LCB) men, Texas Rangers, or FBI agents.

Sheriffs occasionally might set out to destroy local gambling and prostitution root and branch, but this was not the norm. Most accepted such petty criminal activity as unavoidable, made a show of catching and fining all the gamblers and whores they easily could, and went about their other business. Gambling traditions ran deep in Coleman County, as at other places. Just before World War I, "Coleman was a gambling town, the men of all ages gathering at one vacant house or another, the windows covered with blankets and the games going on by lantern or kerosene light." Sheriff Bannister had good informants to tell him where the gambling party of the night would take place, and on one occasion he caught twenty-four young Anglo males, representatives of most of Coleman's prominent families, shooting craps. All that long night, lights burned at the courthouse as families' lawyers met with the county attorney, attempting to keep the gambling arrests from besmirching their clients' permanent records.[5] Sheriff Bannister also often pursued black crap shooters in the Coleman countryside, and by Sheriff H. F. Fenton's time after World War II, little had changed. About 1947, Fenton kicked in a door at a private residence on the "Hill," Coleman's black quarter, and caught twenty-one African American gamblers in the act. With far too many perpetrators to transport in his car, Fenton "just put 'em in a column of twos and marched 'em all the way from the Hill to the courthouse with a flashlight."[6]

The zeal to gamble ran deep at the Texas grass roots and knew no racial boundaries. In 1947, Chief Deputy Jeff Guthrie heard "an ominous clicking sound emanating from a seldom used room" in the Gray County courthouse at Pampa and broke in to find several men shooting dice on the floor.[7] In Wharton County, Sheriff Buck Lane kept a nickel slot machine as an office souvenir until the night he caught his two oldest sons, ages fourteen and twelve, playing the machine. At that point Lane recalled all the occasions that deputies had come into his office on one pretext or another and put coins into the gambling device.[8] Reminiscing about the Peach Tree community in Tyler County, where he had grown up, lumberman John Henry Kirby noted that card playing and crap shooting were common male diversions, often practiced away from the house and the womenfolks, sometimes "down in a secluded thicket by firelight, rich pine knot constituting the fuel."[9] In the Brazos River bottoms of Washington County, black men had gathered for the same outdoor diversions, as Ed Lathan described. "They would get out there by the wood pile in a great big ring, they'd have a big piece of quilting or cotton-sack duck, and that what they be dealing and shooting crap on. And guys used to take these soda bottles and fill em with kerosene, and get a rag and twist it plumb down in there, and light em, and that would give light to see while they gamble."[10]

Some sheriffs felt the gambling urge as strongly as did the Washington County sharecroppers, and all sheriffs had decisions to make about their policies with regards to local gambling. No sooner was Henry Billingsley elected Angelina County sheriff in 1932 than a local businessmen offered to pay Billingsley two hundred dollars a month for the right to run a few slot machines.[11] Billingsley declined the offer, as did Sheriff Buck Lane of Wharton County after a Corpus Christi man told him, "Just let me put in a few slot machines over here on the county line, and I'll give you a car and so much money."[12] Noting that "you can't be on the take and be a good sheriff," Lane said that he kept his county "clean" of serious gambling and prostitution during his terms in office. As he explained to the public in a newspaper column, his position was "no public gambling allowed, that is to say, no slot machines, punch boards, numbers rackets, however, we are not bad about hunting up these little sporadic games that are had here and there by folks, for they are not what I would class as gambling, more or less a pastime for people at their barbecues and get togethers, and no one loses much or wins much."[13]

Most sheriffs treated local gambling traditions much as did Buck Lane, although less tolerant citizens often lobbied for more stringent enforcement of the gambling laws. "Little sporadic games that are had here and there" were anathema to some—as were the traditional black gambling houses that came under grand jury attack during 1947. "From time immemorial in Wharton County," Lane wrote, "the negro has been allowed to openly run his gambling houses, that is, certain sections of the county, it was generally said, gambling or crap shooting was a religion with the negro."

No more, however; Lane promised to follow the grand jury's request to shut these places down—or at least so he said. Week after week, year after year, Sheriff Lane's jail lists remain devoid of gamblers, black or white, amateur or professional.[14]

Rather often, grand jury probes impelled sheriffs to take action against traditional gambling spots and red light zones the sheriffs previously had ignored. During 1949, for example, the Gregg County grand jury forced Sheriff Noble Crawford to raid Gladewater for marble tables, punchboards, and other penny-ante gambling devices.[15] Minor gambling had flourished in the Conroe area until Sheriff Hershel Surratt died in office and the county commissioners appointed his wife to serve out his term. Working closely with other community churchwomen, Sheriff Fannie Pearl Surratt now launched her department on a vigorous antigambling purge of marble tables, pinball machines, and everything else.[16] In Eastland County in 1951, with grand jury encouragement, Sheriff Frank Tucker shut down "cutthroat gambling gyps" at county fair booths run by the Eastland American Legion, and the veterans' group took out full-page newspaper ads in self-defense.[17]

Grassroots gambling passions remained strong, however, and as soon as active suppression ceased, gambling devices and games of chance popped up like mushrooms in the sheriff's domain. A year after blocking the local businessman's slot machines, Sheriff Billingsley discovered that the man had introduced "racehorse machines" instead and had "paid the district judge at Fairfield $1,500 to enjoin me from bothering the machines."[18] Perhaps serving as front man for local cotton growers (who always needed more pickers), a "colored citizen" approached Buck Lane during 1949 with the idea of "open gambling places" to draw additional workers to Wharton County during picking season.[19] Gamblers were always knocking at the sheriff's front door with offers or sneaking around behind his back. A month before, a slot machine had shown up in a "black beer joint" in the Wharton County hinterland, peddled to the owner by a white salesman with the assurance that "he had it fixed with the law."[20]

Prostitution and professional gambling often went on in closely related circumstances at red light districts as small as Coleman's "Rat Row" and Richmond's "Mud Alley" and as large as Galveston County. At the dawn of the twentieth century, most Texas courthouse towns and all larger cities had such districts, and some persisted into midcentury. At Brenham, seat of Washington County, the red light section was called "Tiperary," and at

the state capital of Austin, "Guy Town." Prohibitionist sentiments closed
Tiperary about World War I, and at the beginning of World War II, army
commanders at Fort Crockett and Camp Wallace forced a temporary shut-
down of Galveston's extensive red light district. Editors at the *Sheriffs'
Association of Texas Magazine* accurately predicted that the banished
Galveston prostitutes, now outside of regulation and medical supervision,
soon would reestablish operations at nearby Houston, Beaumont, Port
Arthur, and other war-industry boomtowns. An editorial of May 1942
argued that experienced law officers knew that "a well restricted and regulated district appears to be the only remedy. The red light district evil is
as old as time, never having been successfully expunged from a community." Running the whores out of town accomplished little, the editors
believed. "Long-nosed, gloom-spreading reformers have sought solution
of the red light district since the days of Nero, but only to realize they were
bucking nature, which has never been done successfully."[21]

Sheriff Buck Lane told a historian that he had joined forces with other
officers to drive the whores from Wharton County, and perhaps that was
true, but the expulsion proved suspiciously effective. Like gamblers, prostitutes never showed up on the little sheriff's lists of jail prisoners, a fact
suggesting that Lane believed he had better things to do. Even into the
1970s many sheriffs had the attitude towards red light districts and
"victimless crimes" that "boys will be boys," a belief that sometimes put
them at cross purposes with local reformers. During 1957, for example, a
political war broke out in Fort Bend County between Sheriff R. Z. Cowart
and Glymer Wright, editor of the *Fort Bend Reporter*. Wright claimed Sheriff
Cowart had allowed vice to exist at Mud Alley, a gambling and prostitution area in the county seat of Richmond, and the sheriff replied that "the
Alley is shut tight," a claim soon disputed by the editor.[22] Over a decade
later, Sheriff Aubrey Cole of Jasper County took public criticism for
allowing black "barrel houses," mini–red light zones, to operate in rural
precincts. Cole explained: "These rough, tough blacks, that Saturday night,
done their thing, they kept it out there and didn't bring it down on the
streets in town." Prominent people came to Sheriff Cole and encouraged
him to leave the barrel houses alone "because they serve a purpose." Cole
did so, and "after a while it got to where we didn't know what was going
on and didn't want to know what was going on—let them have it [out]
among themselves, and most of them licked their wounds and didn't
report it."[23]

In Bowie County, Fayette County, and a few other places, as late as 1970, certain traditional red light zones and houses of prostitution had attained the status of protected local institutions. For good political reasons, a succession of Bowie County sheriffs had allowed Texarkana's five historic whorehouses to go about their business. During the 1960s, politicians from outside Bowie County brought pressure to clean things up—pressure resisted by Homer Garrison, Jr., head of the Department of Public Safety until his death in 1967. After Garrison's death and the retirement of the district Texas Ranger, politicians forced Rangers and other state lawmen (but not the sheriff's department) into a sting operation at the Texarkana whorehouses, but local juries refused to convict prostitutes or madams.[24] In Fayette County in 1972, bowing to outside political pressures, reluctant Texas Rangers forced Sheriff Jim Flournoy to close Edna's Fashionable Ranch Boarding House, a local institution fondly known as the "Chicken Ranch."[25] Sheriff Flournoy glumly told a reporter: "It's been there all my life and all my daddy's life and never caused anybody any trouble. Every large city in Texas has things a thousand times worse. The girls started packing their things Tuesday night, I don't think anyone is out there." The petition to keep the Chicken Ranch open had "as many as several thousands of names. I don't think it will do any good, but I plan to go with several people to see Governor Briscoe."[26] Newsman Lester Zapalac, publisher of the *La Grange Journal*, bitterly protested the demise of the Chicken Ranch. The institution was "beneficial to the community" and had contributed thousands of dollars to the new community hospital. "I've never seen anything bad come from it," the newsman told a reporter, "and I've lived here all my life. The girls buy all of their clothes here, their eats, it brings in business for the community. They pay taxes same as everyone else—city, county, federal income taxes. It's listed on the records as a rooming house. It keeps down rape, venereal disease. I think most of the people here are in favor of it. Sometimes, when there is a barbecue in town, the leftovers are sent out to the girls, and they always send back fifty or a hundred dollars to town."[27]

Sometimes the local red light district took in virtually the whole county, as at the "Free State of Galveston" until 1957. Gambling, prostitution, and illegal alcohol rose to dominate the Galveston economy from the 1920s to the 1950s, a red-light heyday largely coincident with the political career of Galveston County's most famous sheriff, Frank L. Biaggne, who held office from 1933 to 1957. Sam and Rose Maceo, former barbers of Sicilian descent, controlled Galveston gambling, prostitution, and whiskey running from the 1920s, and by 1942 their empire centered on the Balinese Room pier, a two-hundred-yard, T-headed pier built into the breaking surf at the end of 21st Street. An elite restaurant with two bands occupied the land end of the pier, while a fully equipped gambling casino operated farther out in the Gulf. Texas Rangers and other state lawmen sometimes staged raids on the Balinese Club, but the staff often seemed to have been warned about their comings, and the long pier, with its guard stations and heavy glass doors, slowed the Rangers' assaults. No sooner did officers pass the front door than a guard pushed a button, warning casino staff to whisk cards and poker chips out of sight, fold slot machines into the walls like Murphy beds, and convert green-felted craps tables into backgammon and bridge tables.[28] The Balinese pier was lengthy and the Texas Rangers not very fleet of foot, so time after time they found nothing illegal going on when they reached the pier's T-head. Sometimes casino staff added insult to injury along the way, as on the occasion when a band leader announced to restaurant customers, "And now the Balinese Room takes great pride in presenting, in person, the Texas Rangers!" then signaled his band to strike up "The Eyes of Texas" while a squad of Rangers thundered by in cowboy boots.[29]

Sheriff Frank Biaggne once told a state investigative committee in Austin that he had never raided the Balinese Club because it was a private club and he was not a member. Furthermore, although Biaggne often might be seen knocking down free drinks and shooting dice at the Turf Club, another Galveston casino, the sheriff told the chairman of the state committee: "I don't gamble, your honor. I'm not a drinking man, and I don't know the taste of tobacco. Maybe I'm too good to be a peace officer."[30]

For decades, Sheriff Biaggne's confidence was not misplaced. The Maceo brothers remained enormously powerful and friends to several governors, and the county attorney joined the sheriff in keeping Galveston running wide open. In 1951 the attorney noted that the last felony indictment for gambling in Galveston County had come twenty years back. Open gambling and prostitution had become a fact of life, and as long as there was no violence, officials did not bother with enforcement of the vice laws.[31] Furthermore, this profitable "Little Havana" version of Galveston had friends in high places. Candidates for governor courted the Maceos. Texas politicians often ate at the Balinese Room restaurant. When affable

Sam Maceo staged a benefit for survivors of the Texas City explosion of 1947 and asked some of his friends from the entertainment world to come down, Frank Sinatra, Jack Benny, Gene Autry, Phil Silvers, Jane Russell, George Burns, and Gracie Allen showed up.[32]

All good things had to come to an end, however, and by the mid-1950s the people that the Sheriffs' Association of Texas editor termed "long-nosed, gloom-spreading reformers" began to get the upper hand. Texas Ranger Clint Peoples assumed the identity of a Blanco County rancher, reached the Balinese Room casino, and held a dice table, twelve house men, and forty-eight gamblers at gunpoint while Rangers raced up the pier and Maceo employees hid all the other gambling equipment. Other successful "busts" followed this one, in 1954 fire destroyed the Maceo brothers' pleasure pier, and in 1957, State Attorney General Will Wilson and DPS head Homer Garrison launched an elite squad of Texas Rangers and LCB undercover men on wicked Galveston, closing bookie parlors, whorehouses, and gambling casinos. Rangers demolished thousands of gambling devices with sledgehammers and dumped them in the bay—so many that Galveston officials accused the state of creating a shipping hazard.

This outsider attack closely followed the one event most essential for its success, the defeat of Sheriff Frank Biaggne in the 1956 election. Sheriff-elect Paul Hopkins, a former DPS trooper, denied to reporters that he was a "reformer," but he planned "to enforce all the laws of the state of Texas as they are written on the statute book," and this included "waging an all out war on prostitution and its deadly partner, narcotics." Gamblers had come to Hopkins after the first primary and "offered me their help," but "I turned them down cold—I promised to uphold my oath of office if elected, and I intend to do just that." As Hopkins prepared to assume office (and Will Wilson and Homer Garrison at distant Austin readied their shock troops to attack Galveston vice), former sheriffs' association president Frank Biaggne planned his return to private life after twenty-four years in office.[33]

Although every county might have its customary one-street or one-motel version of "Little Havana," policing problems caused by the traditional drug of alcohol took up far more of a sheriff's time. Moonshiners, bootleggers, and—above all—public drunks filled the sheriff's jail, and the sheriff's informal policies on enforcement of the liquor laws remained a hot political issue. By 1950 the Texas law enforcement map showed a

checkerboard of wet and dry counties, each with its own peculiar problems. "Local option" on alcohol matters had ruled the day before the asser-
tion of national prohibition from 1919 to 1933, and a more complicated
form of local option returned after 1933. The Texas Liquor Control Act of
1937, and its subsequent elaborations and amendments, set the rules of the
game. Counties could vote to prohibit alcohol totally; to allow alcohol, but
only beer and wine; or to allow any and all alcohol. Political subdivisions
(municipalities, commissioners' precincts) within wet counties could vote
themselves dry, but subdivisions within dry counties could not vote themselves wet.[34] Of Texas's 254 counties, 123 were entirely dry in 1941 and 142
entirely dry in 1951, and the political scuffle continued. No less than thirty-
two local option elections were held in 1950.[35]

Sheriff Leon Jones took office at Angelina County in 1951, and Jones
found himself confronted with the typical problems of a dry county. "Dry"
did not, of course, mean an absence of alcohol. Drinkers could have up to
one-fifth gallon of hard liquor or a case of beer for personal use at any
time—quantities quite sufficient to induce intoxication and bad behavior.
Local people who despised "drug fiends" from the cities nonetheless
drank themselves into fiendish states every weekend with traditional beer
and whiskey, and after they crashed their cars on the highways or
assaulted their families or neighbors, they became the sheriff's problem.
Other people supplemented their incomes by saving such consumers the
twelve-mile trip to the county-line bars of nearby Trinity County. A white-
clad African American tamale vendor named Eddie pushed his cart
around Lufkin's downtown. Sometimes Eddie cried "Hot!" to announce
his product, and sometimes, when Eddie had more than tamales and
circumstances seemed right, "Hot, and that ain't all!" Local bootleggers
such as Eddie commonly waited wait until 10 P.M., when the Trinity
County liquor stores closed, to begin to peddle their wares at the usual 100
percent markup over liquor store prices. "Hip-pocket" bootleggers walked
the streets with a pint of whiskey in each hip pocket, constituting their
legal fifth. After they sold one pocket "dry" to a customer, they slipped
around to their stash, put another pint in their pocket, and went back to
the street. Sheriff Jones could arrest a hip-pocket bootlegger only if he
caught the person illegally selling liquor to someone or taking additional
bottles from his illegal stash. One Lufkin taxi stand owner sold whiskey all
the time, though the man was careful to keep only two pints in his desk.
Sheriff Jones filed on him many times, but the owner always waited until

he had five or so documents accumulated, then went to the county judge and offered to pay one fine if the judge dropped the other four. This happened over and over again, and the taxi man once informed the sheriff that he could do business like that at a greater profit margin than he could operate a legal liquor store in Trinity County.[36]

Most dry-county sheriffs allowed a few discrete wet spots to operate as part of their compromise with local alcohol traditions, just as they often ignored well-behaved public drunks and prominent citizens with several cases of beer in their car trunk. Pat Riddell noted of his father, Sheriff Wallace Riddell, "He had a certain amount of tolerance, because if he didn't, a sheriff would drive himself crazy trying to look behind every car door and every trunk and under every hood."[37] In truth, a sheriff could spend all of his time and his deputies' time on such minor enforcements of the liquor law, and to his ultimate political disadvantage. Sheriff Leon Jones, however, had been a Liquor Control Board officer, so he cracked down on informal black "joints," the Lufkin Country Club, the Elks, and the VFW, and he paid the political price. A lawyer at the country club asked him, "Do you think you can be Angelina County sheriff and do this?" Jones answered in the affirmative at the time, but he later admitted, "That may be why I'm not sheriff now."[38]

Alcohol was rural Texans' recreational drug of choice during the 1950s, as it had been for many decades before, but problems associated with its traditional use shrank to irreducible, minimal levels during Sheriff Jones's tenure of office in Angelina County. With bonded whiskey available only twelve miles away, few moonshiners chose to operate, and bootleggers remained small-scale. Twenty years before, however, when Henry Billingsley first took office as Angelina County sheriff, things had been entirely different. By 1931, in the depths of the Great Depression, shut-down sawmills and five-cents-a-pound cotton had forced many desperate residents into the risky craft of whiskey making. Sober family men assumed the role of moonshiner and hid out along wooded creek and river bottoms, plying their outlaw trade. The sheriff before Billingsley had allowed his friends and neighbors considerable operating room, but not so Billingsley, elected by the dry majority on a reform platform promising more rigorous enforcement of national prohibition. As a result, Sheriff Billingsley soon found himself in an all-out war with the whiskey men and their customers and supporters, which, as the new sheriff soon discovered, included County Judge Butler Rolston.[39]

The whiskey war in the dry county was an old story in rural Texas, and counties often passed through several cycles of outlawry and reform during the twentieth century. No sooner had the wave of prohibition sentiments caused many counties to reject legal alcohol during the years between 1900 and 1918 than moonshiners and bootleggers stepped in to service thirsty consumers. Every dry county created a market for local whiskey producers and for long-range bootleggers, who hauled in their product from the nearest legal purchase point. Beginning in 1919, national prohibition dried up all Texas counties at once, encouraging major cross-country bootlegging from the Republic of Mexico (at levels anticipating the 1990s drug trade) and stimulating whiskey production in any Texas county with readily available water, good places to hide stills, and less than zealous law enforcement. If a rural county had all these advantages and was close to a major market in an urban area or oil field, it became even more likely to experience a moonshine boom, and counties such as Harrison, Somervell, Falls, Trinity, and a few others became major regional whiskey producers during Prohibition years. As in the case of Angelina County, where several major sawmills suffered quick shutdowns after 1929, the Great Depression overlapped Prohibition and impelled into the trade a new wave of moonshiners, most of whom continued to operate after liquor became legal during 1933. Many counties swiftly voted themselves dry after that year, thus perpetuating both local prohibition and the outlaws who serviced citizens who did not agree with it. Local industries and cotton prices did not revive until World War II, and thousands of Texas whiskey makers began operations during the late 1930s, even though moonshine prices fell drastically after 1933.

Illegal whiskey making did not disappear following the repeal of national prohibition or the return of prosperity after 1941, but it waxed and waned during the 1930s, 1940s, and 1950s with the rise and fall of federal taxes on legal liquor. World War II saw a resurgence in the illegal whiskey trade, especially in counties near major new military bases such as Fort Hood. Sold for as low as two to three dollars a gallon, moonshine was still the "poor man's drunk," and many people had developed a liking for its raw, fiery taste. In Jasper County during World War II, as elsewhere, moonshiners and moonshine seemed to be everywhere. C. W. Gandy recalled: "You used to go to dances around here, and when you'd drive up it'd look like headlights. Every tree top around that place had a gallon of whiskey under it. Well, if you didn't drink with everybody it'd make 'em mad and you'd have to fight with 'em. And we'd generally get so drunk to keep from fighting 'em we'd end up sleeping on the porch at night all night long."[40]

Gandy described local consumption, but a lot of Jasper County moonshine was destined for nearby Beaumont. In every county there were small operators, large operators, and sometimes a relationship between the two. Former sheriff Aubrey Cole explained the situation in Jasper County:

> There were three people in Jasper County that was the big whiskey men. They had the big rigs. They set up more or less like a small sawmill operation, worked a lot of people, ordered their grain, rye, and corn and sugar shipped in on the train. They went in wagons and unloaded it at the depot and hauled it out in the woods to their rig. Now, there were lots of people, topwater whiskey makers, that had a little old rig, little old thirty-gallon rig, ten-gallon thumping kegs, and they just might make a run or two of whiskey after the crop was laid by, mostly to get the baby a new pair of shoes with and to drink themselves. Most of them would sell their whiskey to these three big whiskey men, and they'd carry this raw-made whiskey to Beaumont.[41]

Sheriff Henry Billingsley's predecessor at Angelina County had ignored the "Strain Farm," a moonshining enterprise near the county line that was also "more or less like a small sawmill operation," as Aubrey Cole described Jasper County's three "big rigs." Without doubt the Jasper County sheriff did the same, since truckloads of corn chops and sugar rolling from the railroad into the county backwoods could hardly have been missed. Sheriffs varied greatly in attitudes and policies regarding their traditional whiskey outlaws. Some, such as Henry Billingsley, Frank Brunt, J. R. Sessions, and others, fought them tooth and nail. Many sheriffs went into action only after formal complaints had been filed, captured some moonshiners and bootleggers to seem diligent, and made a show of ruptured stills on the courthouse lawn, but otherwise they looked the other way. Sheriffs often personally disagreed with prohibition, as did, in various formal editorials, the Sheriffs' Association of Texas—the same association that elected Frank Biaggne as president.[42] Especially during the 1930s a sheriff well knew that many locals made whiskey out of acute financial need and that some of them had voted for him in the last election. In fact,

Jasper County officers display captured whiskey-making equipment, 1920s. (Author's collection)

some of them were probably his own friends and family.[43] Beyond this, some degree of collusion and "going on the take" probably was not that uncommon, especially during the impoverished Depression years. As an extreme case, in Jasper County, Beaver Bishop operated as a major moonshiner at the same time that, as the county sheriff, he suppressed his outlaw competitors. Convicted in federal district court in 1940 on a charge of "conspiracy to traffic in untaxed liquor," Bishop resigned as Jasper County sheriff and escaped with a suspended sentence and sixty days' confinement at New Orleans. However, in 1941 officers once again caught Bishop making whiskey.[44]

The story of the reform sheriff, elected to clean up his county and going to war with entrenched moonshiners and bootleggers, repeated itself many times over. More often than not, lawman and local outlaws knew each other. The sheriff commonly viewed native whiskey men as wayward voters just trying to support their families, and many perpetrators recognized that the sheriff was just doing his job. These attitudes often resulted in a strange kind of friendly rivalry. The moonshiner did everything to avoid capture, but if caught, he usually interacted in a friendly way with the sheriff and gave him no trouble. For his part, the sheriff usually treated the whiskey maker with respect and courtesy, often taking his word that he would come into the courthouse to post bond the next day. In Angelina County, moonshiner George Carpenter said of his long-term adversary Sheriff Henry Billingsley, "He was a good sheriff, he never did mistreat nobody that he caught running whiskey."[45] Honest sheriffs who played the game this way were even admired. The operator of the Strain Farm distillery told another man: "Henry Billingsley would not sell out. We ain't got enough money to buy him. He won't sell."[46]

While quail hunting one day, Sheriff Roy Herrington of Anderson County noticed an old house in an open field with smoke coming through its rotted roof. Curious, he walked over, looked inside, and found a local man named Howard Barrett tending a whiskey still and fourteen barrels of mash. "I said, 'Howard, you doing any good?' He looked around and saw me. He said, 'Mr. Roy, I didn't know you was anywhere around this world.' I said, 'I'll tell you what, Howard, you take my car and go on in to town and tell this filling station man to bring his truck out here to get the still.'"[47]

Reform sheriffs sometimes enjoyed the cat-and-mouse games they played with local moonshiners. Local outlaws often had detailed knowledge of many square miles of landscape and made full use of this knowledge to hide their stills. Sheriffs, on the other hand, prided themselves on how well they knew their counties and hired deputies from the same woods-wise communities the whiskey makers came from. The moonshiners' determination to hide was matched by the sheriff's determination to catch them making whiskey "on their still."

Whiskey makers used various strategies to escape detection. Often they set up operations in the most inaccessible place they could get into. They might crawl into the densest thicket or briar patch they could find and cut out a place in the middle to set up their still, or they might wait until the river rose in the fall and then wade or paddle out to one of islands in the maze of backwaters to set up there. Others dug their operations into cut banks on the bends of creeks, placed them under brush heaps, located them in the shattered forests just behind logging "fronts," or buried them completely in the ground.

Some major stills operated in remote locations behind large buffers of private property, and if the whiskey makers kept their mouths shut and sold only outside the county, they might escape detection for a long time. In Montgomery County in 1929, someone finally informed on a major distillery that had been running without the sheriff's knowledge for over three years. The vats, coils, and storage containers for this operation covered an acre. Gasoline pumps brought up water from the creek to fill mash tanks, and finished product rolled out by the truckload after dark to Houston and San Antonio. The still site was in a river bottom one mile from Deputy Clint Peoples's father's filling station and café, but no one had detected a hint of its presence until the informer turned it in.[48]

Moonshiners operating in the deep woods guarded against the signs that might give them away—wood smoke, the sound of metal on metal, or the traces of corn chops left along a trail. Meanwhile, the sheriff and his deputies watched for just these things. They staked out remote roads, sniffed the wind, listened for careless sounds, walked the banks of remote creeks, and checked rural stores for excessive sugar purchases. Outlaws and lawmen played a game of strategy and counterstrategy. Whiskey makers had to have a good source of water, preferably from a spring or clear-water creek, and the sheriff and his men often searched these places for stills. Knowing that they did, the moonshiners sometimes piped in water from some distance away or drilled shallow wells so they could locate somewhere else. Moonshiners commonly walked to their stills down one trail, then walked out by another, as a precaution, so officers checked trails for one-way tracks—the telltale sign of outlaw foot traffic. When a moonshiner walked into the woods to his still from a county road, he usually took care to leave the road from a different point every time, only after some distance joining his main trail. Knowing this, sheriffs and deputies often walked parallel courses to a county road about a hundred yards out, trying to pick up the whiskey maker's primary trail after all his little subtrails had come together. Finding a still without the moonshiner present did the officer little good, especially since many whiskey men took care to operate on other people's property. Officers often found the still, looked it over, then put it under surveillance. Knowing this, moonshiners sometimes strung black threads around the underbrush at knee level so they could tell from the broken threads if their still had been located. After finding broken threads, the whiskey man might move his still. A few old hands operated at several locations scattered through the woods. If they got the idea that the law watched one location, they moved a few miles away to another.[49]

Back-of-beyond still sites had their disadvantages, however. Such locations forced whiskey makers to haul heavy loads of corn chops, sugar, and finished product for long distances, painful foot travel that left many revealing traces, and in time many moonshiners chose a different strategy to avoid capture. As one veteran explained: "How in the hell you gonna hide from the people when you're selling whiskey? If you went in the woods twenty miles you just had the pleasure of toting your damn liquor and all your damn supplies in the woods and toting it out. So, you might as well go in the damn smokehouse."[50] Some men set up near their own homes and vented still smoke from house chimneys and smokehouses. Increasingly, however, moonshiners who operated around their homes in smokehouses, barns, crawl spaces, and house lofts used smokeless home-made gasoline stoves to fire their stills. As one moonshiner described it, a man could rig up an excellent gasoline stove from a twenty-gallon drum with a valve welded on it, a bicycle pump, and the burner from a water heater. With such a rig a whiskey maker could, indeed, "go in the smokehouse."[51]

Whiskey men showed remarkable ingenuity in attempts to hide stills under officers' noses. In Limestone County, one distillery operated in a large room hidden under a smokehouse and vented from beneath a nearby black yard pot, where someone kept a wood fire constantly burning. In

Wichita County, officers discovered a still hidden under counters at the back of a popular café in the community of Bradley's Corner, and near Ranger, a massive, coal-fired steam tractor had been turned into a mobile whiskey operation. The tractor pulled a large trailer, which concealed a huge mash tank and accompanying still. Steam to heat the still and "cook off" the mash was piped in from the tractor's boiler. Operators moved the tractor moonshine rig around from time to time, but after a while an officer noticed that nobody ever plowed with it.[52]

Moonshiners' ingenuity at hiding their stills almost was equaled by bootleggers' cleverness at concealing their stashes. In Leon County, officers caught one man hiding bottled product in a grave in a country churchyard.[53] All one evening in Parker County, Dallas reporters hid behind tombstones in a cemetery to watch a lady bootlegger give curb service to driver after driver from a station beside her deceased husband's grave vault. After a while, according to the reporters, the sheriff drove into the cemetery, met briefly with the lady, then walked over to the newsmen and said, "I want you bastards out of my county by sunup."[54] In Coleman County, Sheriff H. F. Fenton never found where some of his bootleggers hid their stashes, but he discovered that one man usually buried his in soft dirt at various places beside the road. After this pocket bootlegger had sold his two pints, he would drive up beside the buried liquor, crack his door, and reach down to get it, never leaving his car. Another Coleman County outlaw stashed his pints, fifty or so at a time, under the blankets of his baby's crib, and another man hid his beneath the board-sided sandbox by his back door, a play area for his children.[55]

Moonshiners often sold to bootleggers, thus insulating themselves from direct sales of their product to strangers, who might turn out to be LCB agents or undercover men in the pay of sheriffs. Such strangers rather commonly got the goods on bootleggers. Sheriff Frank Brunt found his moonshiners hard to catch, but not so the hip-pocket bootleggers operating around Jacksonville. Brunt got LCB undercover men to buy from many of these, then he picked them up. "We started around there one Saturday," the sheriff said, "and we liked to fill the jail up with bootleggers. And with a few licks like that, well, I had 'em on the run."[56]

H. F. Fenton's sandbox bootlegger had been turned in by the same snitch who revealed his other stash, a fifty-gallon barrel cleverly buried between the tire tracks of his dirt driveway. Informants, many of them whiskey outlaws themselves, told sheriffs where to find most stills and stashes. Henry Billingsley often encouraged whiskey makers to snitch on each other for personal revenge, small sums of money, or the satisfaction of putting a rival out of business. As Billingsley recognized, this often put the snitch out of the whiskey business as well, since he feared retaliation. In Henderson County, Jess Sweeten paid twenty-five dollars for every still revealed, and in Cherokee County, Frank Brunt paid fifteen dollars. Brunt also "put pressure" on captured moonshiners, before taking them in to jail, to encourage them to reveal other men's still sites, and some of them accommodated him.[57] Corbett Akins and Henry Billingsley were woods-men sheriffs, and they often found stills by sniffing for smoke, reading trail sign, and watching for bits of landscape that looked suspiciously rearranged. Billingsley, in particular, proved an uncanny stalker of men. Once, he crept up to one end of a river island to watch a whiskey man on his still. Suddenly suspicious, the moonshiner walked the length of the island, looking and listening, finally stopping close to the concealed sheriff. Then he shrugged his shoulders and walked back to his still, now, however, with Billingsley walking in step just behind him, the sound of his feet in the leaves covered by the sound of the moonshiner's. At the still, Billingsley said, "Hello, Barney!" and the man nearly fainted.[58] On several occasions, Corbett Akins used bloodhounds to trail whiskey makers from their stills to their homes or from their homes to their stills. Once, Nathan Tindall released a whiskey man's mule and followed it on its familiar path to a creek-bottom still, where the sheriff found the mule's owner busily running product.[59]

Not all the outlaws caught operating stills in the woods or freighting bootleg whiskey down county highways were childhood acquaintances of the sheriff and out-of-work family men. Some were outside professionals or hardened local thugs and the sort that Jess Sweeten called "born crim-inals." If Howard Billingsley found a moonshiner carrying a weapon, his cordial manner disappeared, and the man went immediately to jail in handcuffs. Once, Billingsley and a constable approached a still near Broadus, each from a different direction, and the sheriff narrowly averted two young moonshiners' shotgun ambush of the constable. The boys asked to say goodbye to their mother, but Billingsley wrote in his memoir: "No. They had come down there to kill an officer for destroying their still, and they wasn't entitled to any courtesy. We carried them to jail." Later, the boy's father showed up at the jail, started a fight with a deputy, and had his knife taken away.[60] In Cherokee County, Frank Brunt's whiskey men tried to kill him more than once, and they had killed his sheriff brother. In 1923, Dallas County deputy John Wesley Massey surprised a group of moonshiners working their still on a river island, and the outlaws went for their guns. "I never pulled on another man who didn't have his gun out of his scabbard first," Massey told a reporter, but on this occasion two moonshiners died.[61]

Long-range bootleggers, outside professionals running big loads to major markets, were the most dangerous whiskey outlaws, many sheriffs believed. Such men were a far cry from their local hip-pocket brethren working football crowds on Friday nights. Long-range bootleggers helped to explain why sheriffs showed so much interest in the hood-mounted Stockholm machine gun. Sheriffs went after long-range bootleggers by setting up highway traffic stops at places where firefights would not injure noncombatants. In Collin County in 1943, for example, Sheriff W. E. Button tired of bootleggers' running booze across his dry county to military bases and seized $15,656 worth of liquor and twenty-seven automobiles, some of them very expensive.[62] In 1951, major bootlegging routes ran from wet Louisiana to what sheriffs' association magazine editors called "prohibition-ridden Oklahoma," and Panola County sheriff Corbett Akins waylaid one such Louisiana-to-Oklahoma truck carrying $9,000 worth of liquor.[63] By spring of 1952, Cass County sheriff John W. Thompson announced the capture of thirty-one long-range "bootleggers and whiskey smugglers" and that liquor had been found "in every conceivable contraption—coffee trucks, undertakers' wagons, loads of hay, etc."[64]

Sheriff-bootlegger confrontations of the 1940s and 1950s were nothing like the bloody days of liquor smuggling across the Rio Grande during national prohibition. In truth, border sheriffs seemed to have played only a limited role in the whiskey wars of the 1920s, a period when many federal men believed that some of the sheriffs were on the take. Before 1924, only a few Immigration River Guards impeded the flow of illegal alcohol across the 1,932-mile border between the Republic of Mexico and a thirsty United States. Trampled paths through canebrakes on both sides of traditional river crossings indicated the huge volume of the trade. Liquor smuggling went on at every level. Poor farmers made a little mescal and waded across the Rio Grande with tow sacks of their product to peddle in Texas border towns, and major pack trains guarded by groups of armed men carried large quantities of bonded liquor north. Top-level Chicago hoodlums bankrolled some of the latter operations.[65] Sporadic battles broke out between the pack train smugglers and the agents of the U.S. Border Patrol, a branch of the U.S. Immigration and Naturalization Service created in 1924. Young E. A. "Dogie" Wright joined the Border Patrol at the height of the combat during 1927, and Wright believed that period to be "one of the most vicious times in the history of the Border. Those smugglers had been in a revolution since 1910. They were gunmen, they knew how to handle a gun. They were good horsemen, and they knew their brush country just like the palms of their hands. You weren't dealing with a greenhorn, you were dealing with a man equivalent to you. We lay on that river at night, and we were fighting all the time."[66]

Nor did Wright exaggerate; the so-called "Volstead Wild West Show" peaked along the Texas border. During February 1927, according to official logs of the El Paso District, no single twenty-four-hour period passed without an armed skirmish between Border Patrolmen and smugglers. During 1927, thirty-two pitched battles took place, and 3,287 persons were arrested. As Dogie Wright tersely summed things up: "They fought over that liquor. When something's worth money, they'll fight over it, and a $1.50 bottle of whiskey was worth $25 in Kansas City. We lost a lot of men, but we killed a lot of smugglers."[67] Not all border sheriffs hung back from these confrontations, and Sheriff Ron Hall of Dimmit County recalled many dark nights staking out river crossings, including one or two nights that he could not remember without a chill coming over him. In later years Hall told his wife that these experiences had left him deeply afraid of two things: "sitting before a lightened window with the shades up and a knife, I'm deadly afraid of a knife."[68]

Sheriffs such as Ron Hall worked out many delicate adjustments between their enforcement of state laws and their defense of local traditions, some of them illegal or extralegal, but when drillers struck oil, "boomtown" traditions usually overwhelmed local sheriffs, setting the stage for intervention by Texas Rangers. For decades, oil-field workers and parasitic outlaws moved from strike to strike, reestablishing boomtown conditions wherever they went. Some of the outlaw "boomers" passed themselves off as experienced oil-field deputies to the beleaguered sheriffs on the scene, who were eager for help in dealing with the onslaught of humanity. Once hired, enforcing the law proved the least of the deputies' concerns.[69] Trying to explain what had happened to him in Freestone County, adjacent to the Mexia oil boom, where martial law had been declared in 1922, Sheriff Jim Wasson told a committee of the

Texas legislature: "Well, we just woke up one morning and found the crowd here; that is to say, the oil boom came all at once. We were officers without any experience and hardly knew what to do. The crooks were smart and experienced and saw the situation and took advantage of it."[70] Winkler County's oil boom came in 1926, and the underworked sheriff, just elected by the county's "thirteen voting citizens," found himself swamped with twenty thousand wild strangers who arrived almost overnight. Boom culture swiftly seized Winkler County, as Texas Ranger Carl Busch recalled:

> There were twenty thousand people there, all in tents and shacks. They had muddy streets and board sidewalks. I was in the Ranger company then that was headed by Captain Bill Wright, an old-time Ranger that had a big old kind of a handle-bar mustache, and he had boots that went way up to his knees. He was a tough old codger! We would make raids on Saturdays and sometimes arrest 150 [people] and lay 'em on a mattress under a shed. Looked like a trotline, had 'em strapped to the ankles. They paid their fines to the justice of peace, and then the next week it'd be just the same story. The sheriff left in six months. He was a local man.[71]

Early and late in the history of Texas oil, the story of the sheriff who "left in six months" repeated itself at other booms. In Lee County in 1976, Joe Goodson ran to succeed his father but lost to his father's chief deputy. However, as Goodson said, "We had the oil boom in the Austin Chalk and things went crazy." The former deputy endured this for a while, but daily combats with tool pushers in beer joints was not what he had bargained for. He resigned at the end of 1978, and the county commissioners appointed Joe Goodson as sheriff. An oil-field man himself, Goodson noted, "I was tough, I'd been handling heavy steel all my life." Sheriff Goodson usually just walked up to fighters, crooked his finger for them to follow him outside, then stated his policy: "You know, I don't care how much you fight, but it's gonna cost you."[72]

Lee County's 1970s boom was a pale shadow of what happened in earlier times at Mexia, Ranger, Borger, and other places, however, and these instant boomtowns soon generated their own corrupt version of local officials, including sheriffs. Young William Sterling moved to the boomtown of Breckenridge, Stephens County, after World War I and soon found himself appointed chairman of a grand jury investigating local corruption.

"The news of easy money had filled the town with a milling throng, and crime was rampant," Sterling recalled, in words that well described any boomtown. He quickly determined that the sheriff and deputies "were taking bribes by the wholesale. They had placed their graft on a business basis. In exchange for official protection, the local 'laws' maintained a fixed scale of prices. The degree and form of each underworld activity governed the amount demanded." Rather quickly, the "best citizens" asked Sterling to run for sheriff, and he reluctantly agreed. Campaigning on platform promises of a "clean oil field" and that "the first man who offers me a bribe will land in the hospital," Sterling nonetheless lost the election in a runoff against the incumbent. Many flourishing businessmen and the most popular minister—their bread well buttered by the status quo—feared reform and supported the corrupt sheriff, Sterling claimed. However, William Sterling got some satisfaction later on, since "my opponent was sent to jail for bootlegging about the time as I was sworn in as adjutant general of Texas.[73]

Sheriffs did not play prominent roles in the cleanups of Mexia, Limestone County, in 1922, or of Borger, Hutchinson County, in 1928. In fact, lawmen often ended up chained to the Texas Rangers' "trotlines" or thrown into their own jails. Senior Captain Frank Hamer of the Rangers presided over the reformation of Mexia, with some help from Governor Pat Neff's declaration of martial law on February 2, 1922, and the Texas National Guard. After martial law, Rangers freely rounded up gamblers, dope peddlers, moonshiners, and other outlaws. One of their rough-shod techniques was to examine suspects' hands; calloused hands indicated an honest oil-field worker, but smooth, well-kept hands marked an outlaw. Rangers ran over 3,000 individuals out of town, arrested 602 persons, captured twenty-seven stills, recovered fifty-three stolen automobiles, and destroyed 9,085 quarts of bootleg whisky. According to Hamer, Rangers learned that local officials were taking payoffs of up to $250 a day and that out-of-state crime syndicates were behind most of the illegal activities.[74]

After the Borger boom began in 1926, local officials also quickly became overwhelmed and coopted. Forty-five thousand "oilmen, prospectors, roughnecks, panhandlers, fortune seekers, card sharks, bootleggers, whores and dope peddlers descended on Borger," and "in a few months the town was firmly in the hands of an organized crime syndicate."[75] Citizens asked Governor Dan Moody to declare martial law, and he dispatched Ranger Frank Hamer to investigate. After a few days at Borger, Hamer reported that this boomtown had "the worst crime ring I have seen in my twenty-three years as an officer." Hamer found that city and county officials were not just on the take and looking the other way, but also were actively directing the Borger crime scene.[76] Borger ran wide open, eighteen hours a day. Deep mud underfoot and black smoke drifting across from oil-field fires failed to deter pleasure seekers, who jammed the streets until midnight. At wide-open Borger, thugs stalked drunks after dark; gamblers, whores, and drug dealers hung out in the red-light district of Dixon Creek; and legal and illegal businesses alike paid protection to "The Line," Borger's criminal syndicate.

Governor Moody sent in the Texas Rangers in 1926, and officers soon found they had all they could handle with outlaw Borger. Governor Moody ordered Borger's mayor to place all city police officials directly under Frank Hamer, and the Rangers began to make some progress, but soon the honest county attorney was assassinated. In September 1926, Governor Moody finally declared martial law, because "there exists an organized and entrenched criminal ring in the city of Borger and in Hutchison county."[77]

Now, the 56th Cavalry of the Texas National Guard joined the Rangers, and Borger began its second, and more stringent, reform. Nearly all city and county officials were suspended from office, and most were jailed. Rangers disarmed Sheriff Joe Ownbey and his deputy. Captain Lone Wolf Gonzaullas recalled: "Some of them tried to get smart with us, but we just smacked em around and hitched a few to the snorting pole at the jail. That took the wind out of em. You just can't imagine the pile of guns that stacked up as we took them off the Borger officers. And you should have seen how those fellows squirmed when the good people of the town came down to the jail to see em with the rings on em and chained to the snorting pole."[78]

First, Rangers jammed Borger's jail full to overflowing, then they secured hundreds of additional outlaws to a heavy chain running down Borger's main street. Outside lawmen now began to visit Borger to "shop" for their wanted outlaws. Meanwhile, thousands of boomtown residents fled Borger by any means possible, even riding truckloads of drill pipe and the roofs of jam-packed passenger trains. Rufe Jordan of Pampa, age fourteen, came over to view the chastisement of Borger, though his deputy father had explicitly forbidden him to do so. Borger presented a cautionary example for the future sheriff of Gray County. "The soldiers and few

Rangers had a huge pile of slot machines that were being bursted with sledge hammers. The Salvation Army was standing back out here, it was my understanding that the coins from the machines were to go to the Salvation Army, and they were beating the drums and singing rather loud, 'Blessed Be the Tie That Binds.'"[79]

The East Texas boom began with Dan Joiner's well, near Henderson, which struck oil on September 5, 1930, and the field turned out to be huge, extending over twenty miles further north, but by that time the Texas government had learned its lesson. Rangers moved into Kilgore in force early in 1931 and worked closely with the Gregg County Sheriff's Department and the municipal police.[80] Lone Wolf Gonzaullas immediately set up his "trotline" chain in plain sight in the Kilgore street, this by way of intimidation, and Rangers went about banishing known outlaws. Around the edges of the giant East Texas oil field, honest sheriffs held their ground against temptation and vice, though they took some casualties. On March 10, 1937, as the *Sheriffs' Association of Texas Magazine* noted, "shortly after midnight a cowardly and slimy assassin fired a charge of buckshot from the outside into his bedroom, immediately killing [Marion County] Sheriff Brown, who was ready to retire for the night. He was a vigorous enemy of all gambling, vice, and bootlegging, and it is known that the underworld had sworn bloody vengeance on their relentless foe."[81]

Racial boundaries remained somewhat indeterminate during the social chaos of the first weeks and months of the existence of oil boomtowns such as Kilgore, Borger, and Ranger, but things soon sorted themselves out. Drillers customarily hired African Americans as mule skinners and for a few other jobs in the fields, but not for all, and the disorderly tent cities soon segregated themselves along racial lines. Likewise, the characteristic boomtown institutions of "cot houses," "hobo towns," and "taxi dance-halls" developed their Anglo and minority versions.[82]

During a century of existence, however, established towns in Texas counties with large minority populations had evolved far more elaborate systems of racial apartheid, and citizens expected sheriffs to enforce the customary boundaries between the races, maintain the status quo, and keep the peace. Incumbent sheriffs running for reelection might not stand up at political gatherings to brag about how well they had kept local minorities "down" and under control, but—without a doubt—this issue dominated many elections. No sheriff wanted racial trouble, and to virtually all officers racial harmony was best maintained by more and better segregation. At Stanton, county seat of Martin County, Sheriff Dan Saunders told a reporter: "We have not had any racial troubles and don't contemplate any. Neither race fools around in the other's section of town."[83] Most sheriffs and most Anglo voters believed that an officer needed to intimidate minority citizens as his most important contribution to preserving racial order. Sheriffs sometimes chose big hats, big guns, man-hound packs, and selective rough treatment of perpetrators to help overawe the underclasses and prevent trouble. To illustrate the social functioning of this old-time intimidation, Sheriff Tom Brown of Caldwell County recounted an incident described to him by an elderly black man who had became nervous at the attitude of younger men listening to a successful Joe Lewis fight on the radio. "There ain't nobody in the world can whip that Joe Lewis!" one man cried, after Lewis knocked his opponent out, but the old man cautioned, "Sheriff Brown can get him down on Plum Creek."[84]

By 1950 some of this system of racial apartheid had embodied itself in formal Jim Crow laws, but that portion was only the tip of the iceberg. Established towns had many unstated rules and invisible lines of racial segregation that minorities—and sheriffs—needed to know about. Tradition strongly enforced minority neighborhoods and labeled them with informal names often supplied by the dominant race—"Cocklebur" at Lockhart in Caldwell County, "Oxblood" at Wharton in Wharton County, "Fly Blow" at Kountze in Hardin County, and at many places just "the quarter." Minorities lived in their neighborhood, or neighborhoods, often set apart from the rest of town by a physical boundary of railroad, creek, or highway, and a good many places had informal curfews restricting minorities to their part of town after a certain hour of the night.

Certain customs were universal—for example, that of a minority person's giving way to an Anglo on a sidewalk—but local traditions of segregation were complicated, the rules unstated, and the boundaries often unmarked; minority persons unfamiliar with the customs of a town needed to be very careful. Tradition might invisibly mark certain benches around the courthouse square as "whites only" benches, and it would not do for a black stranger to sit on one of them. Stores had doors for whites and doors for minorities, and, once inside, custom dictated that minority customers wait politely until all Anglo customers had been served. It would not do to pass through the wrong door or to insist on "first come, first served." Nor could the minority customer dare to try on his or her article of clothing before purchase; this was commonly forbidden, according to customs of racial pollution, which worked only one way. Whites could not use houses, books, utensils, or clothing after blacks had used them, although the opposite was perfectly permissible. A black purchaser had better know his hat size.[85]

Usually, the transgressor against these informal customs of apartheid escaped with an explicit correction and a rude word, but not always, and in these cases the sheriff often came to cast oil on the troubled waters (though perhaps not to arrest the Anglo perpetrators). Very occasionally, the built-in social trap went off with a vicious thud. Willie Massey recalled riding into Apple Springs, Trinity County, and being told by his father at some point, "Boys, pull off your hats, we're getting into town now." African Americans could not wear their hats in Apple Springs; a black man had been shot dead a few years before for entering an Apple Springs store with his hat on.[86] During the 1970s, African Americans at Lockhart told historians of a deranged or suicidal black man who had repeatedly attempted to enter the wrong door of a local barbecue place at high noon on Saturday until outraged Anglos finally beat him to death.[87]

Sheriffs tried their best to keep this sort of thing from happening; they disliked trouble in general and racial trouble most of all. Violent racial attacks by Anglos on minorities often proved unpunishable in local circumstances, since grand juries refused to indict or trial juries to convict, and racial attacks by minorities on Anglos threatened to trigger something even more embarrassing to the sheriff, the ferocious mob response of lynching.

Sheriffs hated and feared racial "incidents." Consequently, had the sheriff been summoned in time at Lockhart, he probably would have taken the black man into custody and saved his life. Likewise, should black "field hands" have dared to show up at Navasota with fine white Stetson hats or silk shirts on, the sheriff or his deputy might have sent them home to reattire themselves in racially appropriate overalls and straw hats, thus preventing trouble. By long-standing tradition, black males wearing upscale clothing on the streets of Navasota invited swift and violent attack. One man recalled: "You go there with a silk shirt on, they'd tear it off and spit on it—tear that shirt off you! You couldn't wear a silk shirt to Navasota, and you couldn't wear nothing during the week but blue duckings or khakis and straw hat. You get out with a white Stetson on and you'd come back with it all flopped down round your head."[88]

As every sheriff knew, white Stetsons and other trivial violations of racial norms might cause drastic violence. African American servicemen returning to their home towns often got in trouble when they proved reluctant to reassume customary subservience. For example, in Wharton County during 1946, an Anglo customer at a filling station became irritated with the loud conversation of two blacks, one a serviceman and one a returned veteran. He walked over and told one of the black men to tuck in his shirt-tail, but the man refused, noting that "he was wearing the shirt." At that point the white armed himself with a length of pipe and called the sheriff's office. Two deputies arrived to talk to the black men, who had moved across the street to avoid trouble. An argument ensued, then a fight, and then a deputy shot the black veteran to death.[89]

Clothing made a statement, especially on the back of a minority person, and a sheriff might fear the social consequences of this. Zoot-suit-clad Hispanics, with long-tailed coats and pegged pants, sometimes arrived at bus stops at Wharton, Carthage, and elsewhere during the late 1940s and early 1950s, and sheriffs Buck Lane and Corbett Akins gave them their attention and soon had them back on the buses and departing to somewhere else. Sheriffs personally disapproved of the zoot-suiters, but they also ran them out of town for their own protection. To a rural sheriff in a conservative county seat, a zoot-suiter looked like a racial incident about to happen. At Carthage, Sheriff Corbett Akins's preparation for banishment of a zoot-suiter itself approached the level of a racial atrocity. Akins jerked out the young man's "Hitler moustache and goatee" with pliers and sent him off to the bus stop in his underwear.[90]

Zoot-suiters (and town blacks in silk shirts) obviously failed to contribute to the cotton harvest—one of the things sheriffs held against them. About 1950, sheriffs in cotton-growing counties still played an informal role in motivating black and Hispanic labor. Especially during the harvest season, editors of weekly papers commonly wrote about the need for more cotton pickers and the disgusting lethargy of "town blacks" and "Meskins" who refused to get out into the fields and work. Pressure mounted on sheriffs to do something about this, and many of them acquiesced. At more than a few places sheriffs arrested black men on the streets for vagrancy and forced them to pick cotton.[91] Citizens often complained to Sheriff Buck Lane about idle blacks and Hispanics loitering about the Wharton streets, and Lane evoked the vagrancy law to harass them into agricultural labor. For example, in February 1945, Lane rousted a "pool hall full" of young Hispanics into employment, and in July 1945 he forced six young black women to go to work.[92] As cotton-harvest season neared during 1945, Lane wrote in his column: "Beginning immediately, we, the officers, are going to encourage the local idlers and street-setters to begin helping out with the harvest of the large cotton and rice crops in the county, and we hope that those that are not working will realize these crops must be gathered, and will do their part to help feed America and clothe the world."[93]

Periodically during the year, Anglo landowners called sheriffs like Buck Lane and asked them to help collect debts owed by blacks. Civil suits and writs of sequestration offered a formal route for accomplishing this, but landowners often had no documentary proof for their loans and hoped to use the intimidating sheriff to force blacks to "work it out" on their farms. This might have been the old way of doing things, but Texas's antipeonage laws made it illegal, and Lane repeatedly informed readers of his column that his office was not a debt collection agency. After discussing the matter at length with Sheriff Lane, journalist Wesley Stout explained: "There is more here than meets the eye; it is an old Southern custom for a Negro to borrow from a white in an emergency, promising to chop cotton or otherwise work the debt off. In former days, if the negro failed to pay off, the white man complained to the sheriff, who impounded the debtor. The peonage law made this a crime, though a lot of the old-timers haven't heard the news yet."[94]

Blacks and Hispanics had their own perspective on the county sheriff, for whom they might or might not have been able to vote. They evaluated him in terms of how fairly he enforced the law across racial boundaries and—above all—by how effectively he protected them from the social, economic, and sexual aggressions of the dominant race. In rural Texas during the first four decades of the twentieth century, minority persons remained almost helpless in the face of Anglo exploitation. To physically fight back invited lynching, local courts refused to decide in their favor, and a minority person could not dispute an Anglo's word. Only certain informal rules of apartheid protected them from Anglo aggressions, and then only if the Anglos involved voluntarily recognized the rules or the sheriff intervened in their behalf.

Before the return of the minority vote, political realities did not encourage such interventions, but some sheriffs patrolled the boundaries between races in a more even-handed way and insisted on at least minimal racial justice. When Henderson county landowners hired blacks as share-croppers, allowed them to bring crops to near harvest, then accused them of "half working" their fields and evicted them, the blacks appealed to Sheriff Jess Sweeten. After checking the fields and finding "good clean tomatoes and watermelons and peas and corn and cotton," Sweeten told the landowner, "'You're not gonna run him off. If you run him off, you're gonna pay him for his crop.' Now, believe you me, you talk about politics, that was darn bad politics! That nigger couldn't even go to the polls and vote, and he was getting a raw deal, and I just wasn't gonna stand for it."[95] Likewise, Sheriff Buck Lane for years forced sexually adventurous Anglos to stay out of the Wharton "quarter" of Oxblood, a policy that Lane also freely admitted was bad politics. Lane wrote in his newspaper column: "It is no place to play around, that section of Wharton belongs to the colored people, it is their section of town, and they don't like it when the white man comes there and makes advances at the colored women."[96]

In Caldwell County, Sheriff Walter Ellison served from 1915 to 1940, and some local black people called Ellison "Limpin' Jesus," though not to his face. In truth, Sheriff Ellison had one leg shorter than the other, and, after twenty years in office, the comparison to the Lord did not seem entirely inappropriate. Ellison was nearly colorblind as far as enforcing the law was concerned. He once jailed his father for public drunkenness, forcing his own brother to bail him out. African American Nelson Jones worked for Sheriff Ellison for years and knew him well, and Nelson—outspoken in later life about local whites—had little ill to say of the old sheriff. "He was a good sheriff," Jones told an interviewer. "He'd pull a white man's leg as quick as he would a colored, just a pretty straight man. He just gonna do what he need do. The white, oh, he'd just eat him up, do him worse than he would a nigger."[97]

With an appreciation for small favors, Caldwell County blacks approved a sheriff who approached race relations in this way. As Nelson Jones recalled from personal experience, the county had a history of racial harassments, and worse. When Jones was growing up, Anglos commonly shot into black houses at night, blocked their doors with wagons, and threw black people into the ice house swimming pool to sink or swim. "They'd do most anything to a colored man," Jones admitted, "and you had to treat them with a spoon, just like if they had feathers on them and the wind was high." In this context, Sheriff Ellison did the best he could to insist on safety and respect for minority citizens. Once, after a black minister complained of harassment by white troublemakers during Sunday morning services, the sheriff stationed himself on the church steps with a .30-30 carbine and touched off a few warning shots when the Anglo youths showed up.[98] When Ellison approached retirement during the late 1930s, minority citizens probably felt something like "Old Henry Butler, age 84," who told Sheriff Dan Saunders of Martin County in 1964, "Mr. Dan, I just don't know what the colored people will do if you ever decide to leave Stanton."[99]

Sheriffs' interventions in minority disputes often had a high-handed, paternalistic quality about them, even if well- intentioned, and so did sheriffs' enforcement of the law in minority communities. Buck Lane and Jess Sweeten both told of stepping in to settle bitter disputes in black church congregations. Sheriff Sweeten visited a Henderson County church where the war between minister and deacons had escalated until worshipers brought ice picks and straight razors with them to church services. A black minister from Athens accompanied Sweeten, and the minister instructed warring factions about proper Baptist procedures and compelled a vote to settle their dispute. Then Sweeten played the role of enforcer, telling the congregation: "This decision is going to stick. If anyone of you cause any trouble, I'll knock the back end of the jail out with you!"[100]

"High-sheriff" behaviors dominated some officers' dealings with minority perpetrators—behaviors they probably would never have used with Anglos. After a woman complained to Sheriff Roy Herrington about her husband's "jumping on her and beating her up," Herrington visited the couple in their home and presided, pistol on hip, while the woman administered just retribution to the husband with a bed slat until she broke the slat. After that, Herrington warned the man not to retaliate or "I'm gonna be back and lock you up." On another occasion, Sheriff Herrington allowed two hostile female jail prisoners to work out their mutual hostility in a minimally supervised, hand-to-hand combat at the jail, then turned them loose. "I told 'em, I said, 'Y'all got it out of your system, both of you get gone.'"[101]

Sheriff Corbett Akins sometimes felt himself too busy to intervene in black disputes, and on other occasions he intervened in a drastic manner. After being informed by a man that another black man was stealing his pulp wood, Akins told him to "go shoot the son-of-a-bitch," and the man did just that. According to Akins, another such "license to kill" came over a one-dollar debt and resulted in a death by butcher knife. Lane recalled:

"The grand jury called me and asked me did I tell that nigger to kill that nigger. I said, 'I did, but I was just joking with him.' Well, they didn't indict him."[102] Sheriffs like Akins sometimes seemed to find it too much trouble to apply full bureaucratic procedures of law enforcement to solve black problems or arrest black outlaws. Only slightly less high-handed than Akins's licenses to kill was Buck Lane's resolution of a stabbing incident between a black man and his former girlfriend. After a jealous argument over the woman's riding her new boyfriends around in the car, once communal property, the woman turned to flee, and "George accidentally stabbed her in the back when she turned to run and he reached to grab her." Lane explained to Wharton County citizens in his newspaper column: "I talked fairness to George that we had an agreement, if I'd let him off this time, he would not stab Josephine any more. I believe George, and I did not make George pay a fine."[103]

Sheriffs' arrests of minority perpetrators more commonly were accompanied by informal punishments administered in the field, and the subsequent interrogations of minority persons more commonly involved threats, tricks, and physical coercions than did the cases of Anglos. Sheriff Tom Brown of Caldwell County once solved a case of a dead baby by checking the breasts of all the Hispanic women on a cotton farm until he found the guilty lactating mother, and (as noted previously) he frightened a jailed black man into confessing by imitating the voice of his murdered wife.[104] Angry after repeated failed attempts to catch a black deserter, Sheriff Corbett Akins waded through muddy fields at night to apprehend the culprit at his farmhouse, then mounted the black man's back and forced him to crawl on all fours several hundred yards to Akins's patrol car—this by way of informal punishment.[105] On one occasion, Sheriff Lester Gunn invited a TDC dog captain and his pack to help him catch a black car thief, and after the man became trapped under a concrete bridge, the officers "turned old Blue loose" to chew on him a little and break him from stealing cars. "Old Blue did a very good job on this nigger," the sheriff recalled, "We like to let him chew too long."[106]

The failures, trials, and tribulations of minority citizens of Wharton County played a major role in Sheriff Buck Lane's newspaper columns of the 1940s and early 1950s. The sheriff depicted local blacks and Hispanics as childlike, emotionally unstable, prone to violence, stupid, and often ridiculous. For example, Lane's column of July 5, 1946, told of a black couple visited by a Hispanic man who soon evicted them from their own house. Asked why they let him do it, the black man replied, "Mr. Buck, you know a Mexican is sho-nuff fast with them knives." Lane also noted in his column that a black woman had called to tell the sheriff that a dog had bitten her little boy, asking, "Do he need to take them teethrumus shots?"

Even deadly violence lent itself to amusing interpretations in the sheriff's column. On July 12, 1946, Lane noted that three black men and one woman, "negroes of El Campo, got into a big fight. Nearly every one of them had to go to the doctor to be sewed up." The fight had broken out over a debt of fifty-five cents, "That is what you call not self control." Furthermore, a black barber at Wharton reading a newspaper in his barber chair, had been set upon by an irate husband. "Out of the blue sky, another negro steps in and starts to whittle on him. He did some fancy whittling too, before the barber could get untangled from his paper. The whittler said nothing, just did his whittling and left as he came." Later, this man turned himself in to the sheriff, telling him, "I cut up on so-and-so, it was about my wife." However, Sheriff Lane's tone turned suddenly serious for one minority-related news item reported on July 12, 1946. A drunken black former soldier tried to get into the same seat as an Anglo lady on the bus, prompting two white men to attack him. Lane reported that he had been jailed, and: "It is a pity that some of our Wharton County better negroes were not on that bus so they could have knocked him in the head and stopped him in the beginning. Just such business as this is no good for either race."

Although black-on-black violence lent itself to amusing stories, inter-racial violence—and any social changes that seemed to make it more likely—deeply troubled Sheriff Lane. On October 11, 1946, he wrote very seriously of "a good and respected old negro citizen" who had come to show him an NAACP brochure and to ask Lane's opinion about the black community's organizing a local chapter. Lane thought it a very bad idea and that such an attempt might start trouble.

> Why the negro people of Wharton County need this I cannot say, for I can name to you many negro people of this county who have advanced not by the efforts of any association, but simply by merit. They used their heads, and they worked, and they earned their advancement. I can say that if there is an association for the advance-ment of the white man, I have never heard of it. Believe you me, any man regardless of color or creed in Wharton County has the same

chance to advance. I will discourage any such organization, for I
think it would not be good for the people.[107]

Two years later, in his column of March 5, 1948, Lane again turned
deadly serious about interracial matters. After pointing out how he had
defended the black community by discouraging "the promiscuous
prowling of white men in the negro section of Wharton," he discussed the
current problem, blacks walking ten blocks through the white neighborhood to attend black basketball games scheduled in the white high school
gym. "The negroes are coming into the white section at night after the
basketball games are over," and white citizens have complained. The
sheriff told his readers that he feared that "ambitious or drunk" young
black men "might use the blind of attending the basketball game in the
white section of Wharton to attack some white lady, or some white man
may resent the negroes being in his neighborhood and start something."
Nothing had happened yet, but it was time for Wharton to build a black
gym. Sheriff Lane feared mob actions, "lynchings, race riots," and whites
going on the rampage in the black community.

Few sheriffs besides the irrepressible Buck Lane would have dared to
discuss sexual line crossers, lynchings, and race riots in their local newspaper, but the little sheriff's fears were not unreasonable. In 1948, many
minority and Anglo citizens of Wharton County had seen, or had heard
eyewitness accounts of, violent racial assaults of almost unbelievable
horror. Nobody, and least of all Sheriff Buck Lane, thought that such things
could not happen again. For example, thirteen years before, on November
12, 1935, just across the county line in Colorado County, a lynch mob of
several hundred men and women had seized two teenaged blacks from
the county jail and had hung them from a tree. The Colorado County
sheriff either assisted the mob or got out of its way while it indulged itself
in this ultimate "county tradition." After the deed was done, County
Attorney O. P. Moore of Colorado County defended this traditional violence,
stating that "I do not call the citizens who executed the negroes a mob, I
consider their action an expression of the will of the people." Likewise, the
Colorado County judge noted: "I am strongly opposed to mob violence
and favor orderly process of the law. The fact that the negroes that brutally
murdered Miss Kolman could not be adequately punished by the law
because of their ages prevents me from condemning those citizens who
meted out justice to the ravishing murderers last night."[108]

By 1935, Texas lynch mobs such as the one in Colorado County had withdrawn into the cover of darkness to do their work, but earlier mobs had tortured, mutilated, burned, and hanged black men before large crowds in the broad light of day, with sheriffs often failing to prevent these atrocities. Such full-blown expressions of "the lynching ritual" had ended by World War II, although rural sheriffs certainly did not know that.[109] Fearing this last and most horrific "county tradition" above all other local traditions of violence, sheriffs such as Buck Lane promoted racial harmony and the status quo by stringent enforcement of the laws and customs of racial segregation.

CHAPTER FOUR

A FRIEND AT THE COURTHOUSE

For several decades at midcentury, Sheriff Malin Owen of Hardeman County placed a sign above his door which read, "Sheriff's Office, Tell Your Troubles Here," and many county residents did just that.[1] Few sheriffs posted such signs, but people lined up to talk to them just the same. Gaston Boykin recalled of his circumstances in rural Comanche County, population 15,461, in 1950: "Every day they took every minute of your time. Lots of times there were more people than you could talk to, and most of 'em wanted to see the sheriff—didn't want to talk to a deputy, wanted to see the sheriff. There wasn't anything they didn't ask, I was out all the time. But a good officer cares, you know; time don't mean nothing if you got it in you."[2] At San Augustine County in "deep East Texas," Sheriff Nathan Tindall's phone rang and rang, and people stood in line at his door. "In San Augustine, if you're out of water, the sheriff's supposed to being it to you," Tindall's wife, Willie Earl, told a researcher. "If your car breaks down, the sheriff is supposed to carry you home. If your lights go out, and you can't call the electric company, it's the sheriff's job to bring you a flashlight."[3] The researcher commented, "In the end, the rural sheriff, for all his autonomy and local power, is in a service profession, and the parameters of his job description had a tendency to expand indefinitely."[4]

In their responses to a questionnaire study conducted by political scientist James Dickson in the late 1970s, Texas sheriffs estimated that one-tenth to three-fourths of their work days were taken up with personal requests having nothing whatsoever to do with enforcement of the law. Dickson observed in *The Politics of the Texas Sheriff: From Frontier to Bureaucracy:*

A basic assumption of any appraisal of the politics of the Texas sheriff is that the office is uniquely affected by the imperatives of electoral democracy. The sheriff is the principal "good old boy" of the county, with an extensive knowledge of the voters' needs, priorities, and peculiarities; he is the number one "Mr. Fixit" and universal *pater familias* of the county. The personal service aspects of the sheriff's tasks intrude upon impartial and professional law enforcement with significant impact on getting elected and staying in office—shaping the sheriff as a social and professional institution.[5]

Dickson's research established what every old-time sheriff knew before he entered the office, or found out soon after he went in: voters evaluated the rural sheriff first and foremost not for his technical law enforcement standards but for how well and frequently and cheerfully he performed this personal-service aspect of the role. He indeed served as "resident good old boy" of the county, the "Mr. Fixit," and as time went on the "Mr. Insider" as well, the master of everybody's secrets. Calls came in to the sheriff's office all day long and very often, and as in the case of the elderly woman who visited Frank Brunt in Cherokee County, the deputies were "too light," and only the high sheriff would do. The personal phone calls pursued the officer to his home at night, for his job went on twenty-four hours a day, and rather often troubled citizens concluded that the phone did not provide close enough contact. As at other places, every morning, even into the late 1980s, a line of persons waited to see Sheriff Rufe Jordan of Gray County at his Pampa office—citizens who believed they needed "to talk to the old sheriff" face-to-face.[6]

When asked about what sorts of personal services they had been asked to perform, sheriffs invariably answered, "Anything, you name it." Besides removing sexually aroused dogs from under houses (as H. F. Fenton did on his first call), sheriffs told of being asked to evict skunks and armadillos from crawl spaces; execute mad dogs; rescue cats from trees; investigate strange lights and noises; mediate neighborhood disputes over barking dogs, animal trespasses, fencelines, and rights-of-way; find lost children and runaway sons and daughters; provide emergency medical services; deliver death notices; offer stern counsel (or even give a good thrashing) to rebellious youths; mediate marital squabbles; tell how much rain had fallen or who had won the high school football game; give business and legal advice; and do many, many other things. In Gray County, one elderly lady made numerous personal requests for advice and assistance to Sheriff Jordan over several decades, calling him perhaps ten times a year on the average. Finally, as she lay on her deathbed at age ninety-three, she made one last request of the high sheriff, as Jordan recalled to a historian:

> I got out there, it was in the evening, she was very ill. Her daughter was there from the state of Pennsylvania and maybe another relative. She had one of these small, slick dogs, I think it was a Mexican Chihuahua. She said, "Rufe, I'm not long for this world, and I'm ready to go. My people do not live here. Butch, that's the little dog, I want you to be responsible for this little dog. I'm not asking for you to keep him, but you see that he has a good home, somewhere. I want to pass that on to you." I said, "That's fine, that is fine, my dear. I'll surely do that."[7]

During the 1950s, most rural counties had little or no "social net" beneath their citizens to aid bedridden old ladies, battered wives, abused children, dysfunctional families, insane or suicidal persons, the desperate poor, or even accident or heart attack victims, and sheriffs' offices did the best they could to help such needy citizens. Sheriff "Big Ed" Darnell's motto was, "A kind word and a helping hand," but on some occasions the kind word was all Darnell could supply, so overburdened did his office become with personal requests.[8] In Wharton County, Buck Lane's newspaper columns often encouraged citizens to come to the sheriff's office with their problems, but sometimes in other columns Lane warned readers not to expect too much when they did. Lane's resources were limited, he could not go beyond (or too far beyond) his formal legal powers, and he lacked the wisdom of Solomon. To convey this message, in his column of September 10, 1948, Sheriff Lane briefly described the personal requests made of him during a single day in the previous week. A black woman had left her child with relatives several years before when she had been sick and experiencing personal problems. Now she wanted the child back, but the relatives refused. Would Lane make them return her child? Next, an Anglo man came in to talk to Lane about troubles with his wife. What did the sheriff suggest he should do? Next, a black woman entered Lane's office to tell of her difficulties in compelling the company employing her truck driver husband to pay medical expenses for his injuries sustained in the line of duty. Would Lane please call the company and persuade it to right this wrong? Next, a Hispanic woman came in to report a lost brother, and no sooner had she passed out the door than an Anglo lady entered to report a daughter who had run away from home two months before and had not gotten in touch. Would Lane's office please launch a missing-persons search for the wayward child? Finally, an Anglo lady from outside the county came to Lane's door—unannounced, as usual—to ask for help with her elderly brother. He lived a reclusive existence in a "dirty shack" far out in the Wharton County countryside, and his physical and mental health were on the decline, but he refused his sister's help. Would Sheriff Lane please visit this man and persuade him to come live with her?[9]

Buck Lane did not inform his readers how he answered these people's requests, but to a remarkable degree some sheriffs paid the Good Samaritan role for desperate people who came to them for help. Rather commonly, tramps, stranded servicemen, and wandering youths turned up at the sheriff's door asking for a place to spend the night and were given an unlocked cell in the jail. Sheriff Perry St. Clair of Comanche County, for example, often found room in the jail for hitchhiking servicemen during World War II years. An editor noted: "The fame of the Comanche jail spread until it was not unusual to hear the knock of a weary G.I. Joe on the jail door. Always the door swung ajar and the soldiers were welcomed."[10] Buck Lane disliked panhandlers and tramps, but if they approached him properly, he gave them free lodging in his jail. One Sunday evening while Lane was writing his column, a Hispanic boy knocked on the jail door and told the sheriff, "I'm cold and I'm scared and I live out in the country. Can you let me sleep here tonight?" Lane noted: "The boy was very promptly let in, and he was given a clean and warm bunk, and it makes me feel good this boy felt that way about the jail house."[11]

Outsiders passing through a county often turned to the sheriff, and he usually responded to these nonvoters' requests. If people ran out of gas or money or their car broke down in Frank Brunt's Cherokee County, he helped to get them fuel, food, car repairs, and on their way.[12] At remote and sparsely populated Terrell County, Sheriff Bill Cooksey regularly patrolled the roads with emergency food, water, gasoline, and repair tools to aid stranded motorists. Sheriff Cooksey carried "enough tools to fix flats on any commercial car. In a county as remote as we are, most things come to the sheriff's office. I feel, and most of our citizens feel, that we've got an obligation to people passing through here."[13] Sheriffs always had been the desperate traveler's last resort. In Karnes County just after 1900, a

Bexar County sheriff Jim Stevens and courthouse shoeshine boy, 1925. (Institute of Texan Cultures, San Antonio)

prankster stole the pants of 325-pound newspaperman Pink Gresham at a Kenedy hotel, and the sheriff shopped local mercantile stores until he found a pair of overalls big enough to fit Gresham.[14] Such helping hands had their limits, however, and the out-of-county drunks who telephoned the Fannin County sheriff's office and told the dispatcher, "I want Sheriff Hoyt Ivy to come out and fix this flat," instead ended up in jail.[15]

Sheriffs' direct personal philanthropies were not uncommon. In Ochiltree County during World War I, cowboy J. S. "Sid" Talley bought groceries for remote families whose husbands had gone off to war. As Rufe Jordan told the story, "Later on he ran for sheriff and no one even ran against him." During the Great Depression, Talley often paid taxes for Ochiltree County families who could not pay them and would otherwise have lost their homes in sheriff's tax sales. Just before Talley's defeat in office at age seventy-six, Jordan tactfully tried to talk his old friend out of running, but Talley said: "Why, Rufe, I don't know what I'd do. I been down there ministering to these people for years and years and years."[16]

In Kleberg County, Sheriff Jim Scarborough III inherited a number of philanthropic relationships from his father. An elderly black man received thirty dollars a month, an elderly Hispanic woman got twenty-five dollars monthly (or her water bill paid), and a "shoeshine boy" received a five-dollar tip with each weekly shine. Furthermore, an old couple received complimentary transport to their family reunion at Edna each year.[17] In San Augustine County, Nathan Tindall presided as a rare millionaire sheriff with a private fortune from businesses on the side, including a truck dealership, a fleet of logging trucks, and a sawmill. A friend of the sheriff recalled: "The sheriff's office used to look like a bank. People actually stood in line to borrow money from Nathan. Some paid him back, but my impression was that most never did." Sheriff Tindall gave money away to the county's poor black families, commonly paying their hospital bills, mortgage payments, and birthing fees. Tindall told a reporter: "Hell, I paid for over fifty babies to be born. Everybody, black or white, knew that if a baby was coming and there was no money you just had to call the high sheriff."[18] In Martin County, Sheriff Dan Saunders lacked Tindall's financial resources, but he helped people so commonly that he wrote in his journal: "I am running a welfare office. Domingo ———— came to my office today to borrow some money. He said all the Mexicans call me 'The Salvation Army Man.' I have done without and my family has done without to loan money to needy families." Saunders also paid many fines for destitute people in justice of the peace court and many towing fees to recover cars from storage. These were all for individuals "who had no one else to go to. What else as a Christian could I do?"[19]

Even before "deinstitutionalization" of the insane during the 1970s, many mentally unstable individuals lived in sheriffs' counties. Requests for assistance from them, or about them, often funneled in to the sheriff, and such persons became his personal concern. Although a man named Felix once attacked Sheriff Dan Saunders while under transport to the Big Spring Hospital, "Years later I was the only person in Stanton that would help or look after Felix. I was the only one to buy him groceries or have his prescriptions filled or take him to the doctor."[20] Some strange requests came from mentally unstable persons such as Felix, "walking wounded" who fixated on their county sheriff. One bitterly cold night, Saunders went out to a remote farmhouse near Ackerly because a "man said there were little men living under his house and kept saying, 'Can't you hear them!?'" The man insisted that Sheriff Saunders crawl under his house, and "that was the only way I could ever get back home for the rest of the night. I crawled under the house and his old dog crawled under there with me. I got to laughing to myself, thinking 'I'm the one that's crazy. He's up there nice and warm by the fire and I am the one that's crawling under this cold house with an old dog looking for little men.'"[21]

Ordinary citizens sometimes saw things as strange as "little men" in their pastures and side yards and the night sky, and they often reported these weird occurrences to the sheriff's office. If a Volkswagen struck and killed a "500-pound alligator" on a Chambers County river bridge, the sheriff's office was sure to hear about it, and if Wharton County's "black panther" made yet another appearance, Buck Lane got the call.[22] Lane never found the black panther, although he confirmed that some big predator had been attacking local livestock, and he politely discounted repeated calls about strange lights in the sky until Saturday, July 17, 1947, when a man from Hungerford called Lane at about 9 P.M. and told him to look towards the northeast. "I did with double time," Lane said, "everybody else in the jail did, too, we saw a number of lights moving about in the sky, they would move in one direction for a while, then fade out, in a minute or more or less the lights would show up moving back again. This went on for some time, then all disappeared."[23]

Many such reports came from concerned citizens who had seen strange shapes in the field or heard something go bump in the night, and the sheriff had to investigate such calls. The frightened voters calling in these phenomena invariably became furious if he did not. After an elderly lady reported her little dog barking frantically at a strange object in the dark Wharton street in front of her house, Lane said, "I'll be there in a jiffy, lady," only to find a newly fallen tree limb.[24] A report of a strange creature crouched in the woods watching a Smithville farm likewise did not check out for Bastrop County sheriff Nig Hoskins, who went out three times in one night. "Don't you see him yonder? Right yonder, look, right under that cedar tree!" the farm woman said, but Hoskins never saw anything.[25] Sometimes sheriffs successfully dispelled the apparition. After a man frantically reported an "80-foot dragon swimming on Lake Comanche," Gaston Boykin rowed him out in the middle of the lake to investigate and found a flock of ducks "swimming in formation."[26]

Monster, wild man, and sorcery calls invariably came in to the sheriff. At Panola County, Sheriff Corbett Akins launched his man-hound pack after a hairy, naked "wild man" in the woods—a phenomenon often reported from other counties.[27] Galveston County officers sometimes took calls about sorcery involving "spook dust" placed in and around people's houses, and a local woman reported that two men had smoked a "mystery cigarette" whose fumes had penetrated her screen door and developed evil spirits in her house.[28] Officers went out on sorcery calls, too, since if they did not, the next call might be to report a killing. H. F. Fenton, Truman Maddox, and other sheriffs puzzled about the phenomenon of livestock dead in the field with strange surgical incisions of the eyes, tongue, and genitalia. These things got on Sheriff Fenton's nerves, and he walked concentric circles around the carcasses trying to "cut tracks or find sign," summoned local vets to examine the animals, and even skinned some carcasses to look for bullet holes or needle marks. Fenton never discovered anything and finally accepted the theory that some sort of strange cult was doing this.[29] The other theory was, as Truman Maddox sarcastically reported, "little green men from space." However, "being a country boy," Maddox never could accept the extraterrestrial explanation, and late one evening he bought a calf, killed it, took it to an area that had several recent reports of strange animal deaths and dissections, and prepared to see what might come to the carcass. He watched it with binoculars until dark, then returned the next day before daylight to resume observation. In the early morning, turkey vultures, black vultures, and caracaras arrived and began making strange, precise surgical incisions with their sharp beaks at the dead calf's anus, eyes, and genitalia.[30]

However, as in the case of Buck Lane's flying saucers, not all the sheriff's calls about outside-the-paradigm phenomena could be explained away so neatly. In Dallas County, Sheriff Smoot Schmid and Chief Deputy Bill Decker became the last resort for a family troubled with an outbreak of spirit forces at their house. After several visits to the house to find nothing going on, Bill Decker finally stationed a deputy there to spend the night, but this show of force did little good. The next day the deputy called in to report that chairs, vases, and other objects had indeed banged about during the night, that carefully locked doors had unlocked themselves, and that a full-sized bed with a thirteen-year-old boy on it had risen into the air. What did Bill Decker want him to do now?[31]

Personal requests to the sheriff varied from the ridiculous to the life-threatening. On February 30, 1948, a farmer called Sheriff Lane to ask his advice about the best way to birth a sow, and on November 11, 1949, a black woman called to report a dead dog rotting under her house. True to form, Lane dispatched a reluctant deputy to remove the dog. Then, perhaps to affirm that his department remained ready for anything, even dead dogs, Lane again wrote, "Folks, don't you hesitate to call us night or day."[32] Local people took him at his word. Unlike many rural counties, Wharton County had a primitive ambulance service by 1950, but many people still called the sheriff's office with life-or-death emergencies, and Lane always responded. In his column of February 16, 1951, for example, Buck Lane reported that he had just rushed to Hungerford to pick up a black baby that had consumed kerosene, then had driven the baby to the Wharton hospital. Likewise, in nearby Fayette County in June 1954, a child got something stuck in its throat that local doctors had no tool to remove, and Sheriff Jim Flournoy put the boy and his father in a patrol car and rushed him to Houston's Herman Hospital at speeds topping one hundred miles per hour, with the Columbus County sheriff clearing roads up ahead.[33] In Martin County, Sheriff Dan Saunders drove ambulances of the two Stanton funeral homes to heart attack and accident calls, though patients often succumbed during his hour's run to the nearest hospitals at Midland or Big Spring. These ambulances "never had good equipment and had nothing in the way of emergency use but a small oxygen bottle and lots of times it was empty."[34] Saunders often dealt with less serious medical emergencies himself, as on the memorable night in August 1975 when he ministered to a "bleeding hemorrhoids case" in the countryside east of Lenorah. "When I got there it was the darndest sight I ever had seen. The 'old woman' had the 'old man' over the edge of the bed on his stomach. She had a thick rubber glove on (the kind used to wash dishes with) and was trying to put his hemorrhoids back which were bleeding and protruding badly. Well, I got the other glove and between the two of us we got the hemorrhoids back in. It's a wonder he lived, but he did."[35]

Later, Saunders led this man's funeral to his grave. Like many other rural sheriffs, Saunders also accompanied the primitive ambulances/ hearses to local funerals, leading all in-county funerals and escorting those of county residents buried out of the county. By January of 1989, Saunders estimated that over several decades he had attended 2,860 funerals as "the last respect you can show for and to the family."[36] Attendance at funerals was good politics for the sheriff, but for Saunders and many other men it took on much deeper meaning over the years. At Burnet County, as his son recalled, Wallace Riddell participated in "every funeral he could get to. That became a tradition with him, he truly wanted to pay his respects."[37]

Some complaint calls to the sheriff presaged neighborly violence, and he did his best to keep this from happening. A woman once called Buck Lane saying that a neighbor had just told her that she had the high sheriff's formal permission to kill the woman anytime she liked—a license to kill—and was this true? "No!," said the sheriff, arguing strongly against a preemptive strike.[38] A man called Sheriff Dan Saunders to warn him that he planned to kill his neighbor's dog, a "very, very large Great Dane." Saunders lectured the man: "If you are going to kill a dog, don't you tell me, God in Heaven, or anyone else. You are fixing to get in trouble." However, the man killed the dog anyway, and "the next morning two of the brothers met the shooter when he came to the court house and beat the 'hound' out of him on the court house lawn."[39] Dog matters commonly caused major trouble among rural Texans. People often complained to Buckshot Lane about their neighbors' loose dogs or overaggressive dogs, and—conversely—dog owners complained about the neighbors who shot or poisoned their animals. Please do not let your dogs run loose, Lane pled over and over again in his columns; "killings" might result. When the complaints were about dog poisoning, the illegal corrective for loose dogs, Lane tried various approaches in his column to convince the perpetrators to stop. He threatened them with use of the full force of the law, he warned them of hostile dog owners in a killing rage, and he appealed to their better instincts. "Have you good folks ever watched these little boys and girls, how they love and admire their little pet dogs?" he wrote in his column of July 23, 1948. "Have you ever watched the little shavers, how the tears come out of their eyes when one of those little pet dogs get killed or died? Friday in Wharton it was a sad day for a number of these little chaps."[40]

When citizens complained about other citizens in property disputes, sheriffs rushed out to try to calm the troubled waters before blood was spilled upon them. In an armed society, property quarrels rapidly escalated to serious violence. Consequently, Sheriff C. C. Maxie of McLennan County immediately got in his car after neighbors complained of their neighbor's horse, which had a "vicious hatred of all chickens" and perhaps had killed as many as seventy-five. The horse often waited until farmers' "yard chickens" wandered a good distance from their property lines, then ran them down and trampled them to death. Maxie arrived on the scene to commiserate with the angry chicken owners, to politely inform them that there was no law to enforce about this, and—by his presence—to post a silent warning to the owner of the chicken-killing horse.[41] Property complaint calls had to be answered and the circumstances defused, or else, and sheriffs constantly mediated property disputes from the lowest to the highest levels of rural society. After a young Hispanic man complained about an old black man's running him out of the Wharton dump, Buck Lane checked it out. "Manse," the elderly black man, served as the informal keeper of the Wharton town dump. He kept the fires burning and scavenged cardboard and other things to sell. The young Mexican, not understanding the situation, had tried to take some of Manse's hoard of pasteboard boxes to line the walls of his home for the winter, Manse angrily had stopped him, and both men had pulled their guns and threatened each other. "I explained the situation to them both, and they decided it was all a mistake," Lane wrote, "and each one could just gather all the pasteboard boxes they needed and wanted, so they shook hands and started all over, a fuss about nothing."[42] However, the next Wharton County killing had been only a twitch of the trigger finger away.

Another large group of property calls involved complaints about wandering stock in the fields and on the highways and the complaints of stock owners about neighbors who had taken matters into their own hands. Many east and south central Texas counties did not have a comprehensive stock law for cattle and hogs until the 1950s, or even later, and by local custom a family's earmarked stock animals mixed and merged with other people's animals across an unfenced "open range." Gradually, from the mid-1950s into the early 1970s, counties and commissioners' precincts voted in stock laws, and private landowners erected perimeter fences to contain their animals and keep out the hogs and cattle of other persons. Traditionalists hated this, cut neighbors' fences, and let their animals wander far and wide—especially the semiferal razorback hogs, for which barbed-wire fences presented no obstacle at all. Sheriffs' offices fielded all the complaints of traditionalists and modernists during this prolonged grassroots conflict over "closing the woods," and though officers often procrastinated and looked the other way for a time, they ultimately had to enforce the new stock laws.[43]

Calls about broken fences, stock on the highway, and lost animals galvanized the sheriff into action, since local property owners were—as usual—very angry before they called the sheriff.[44] If a man complained about illegal stock on the county road, and the animals still menaced traffic there a week later, he might well shoot them, thus launching a local feud.[45] If hogs violated a man's property and the owner refused to get them out, the aggrieved landowner might become mad enough to kill the swine raiser, as a young man did to an elderly man in Buck Lane's Wharton County in 1947.[46] At some point, most southeastern Texas counties hired a special "stock deputy" to deal with these conflicts and to tactfully help keep people's animals off the highways and behind fences.

When stock was finally properly kept behind fences, it was a relief for the sheriffs, who had received many complaints of stolen animals during free-range days. Wandering stock tempted thieves and caused much social trouble in earlier times, and many sheriffs' jail logs list "hog theft," "cattle theft," and "turkey theft" beside the names of inmates. Sometimes stock deputies went out on calls about disputed ownership. After two men got into a fistfight about ownership of a hog, someone summoned Wharton County deputy Busek. "After arguing and explaining and trying his best to straighten them out," Buck Lane wrote, "he gave up and said, 'How much will you take for the hog and be satisfied?' They told him, so he just paid them, and he got the hog, and they made up and split the difference."[47]

Property line disputes also triggered many calls to the sheriff, and once again he felt obligated to go out to mediate the squabbles, which were almost always between immediate neighbors. If rural Texans became angry during disputes about wandering stock and "movable property," they became homicidal when "real property"—"grandaddy's fence line"—became involved. At the root of the trouble was the often imprecise relationship between actual land boundaries and rural fencelines. Sheriff Aubrey Cole estimated that perhaps three-fourths of all fencelines in Jasper County were off the actual land boundaries, thus setting the stage for endless trouble. When, for whatever reason, a landowner had his property line surveyed and found a neighbor's ancient fence a few feet over onto his land, conflict often followed.[48]

A land-line survey, then action in the civil courts, was the legal avenue for settling such conflicts, but some people did not wish to pay for surveyors and instead preferred the free services of the high sheriff. In San Saba County, landowners often called Sheriff Brantley Barker to mediate property line disputes. On one occasion, two neighbors wished to build a fence between them and were engaged in a prolonged argument about where within a two-foot disputed area the fence should go. A surveyor might have settled the matter, but neither man wished to pay for him, and besides, the landowner might not like what the surveyor had to say. Barker examined the disputed property boundary and sat down in a plowed field to talk it over with the two neighbors, who the sheriff judged were nearly mad enough to kill each other. Finally, the neighbors asked Barker to settle the property line, and the high sheriff placed it exactly down the middle of the two-foot zone of contention.[49] As Brantley Barker well knew, fence-line disputes could break out even when neither neighbor contested the property line. If one neighbor wanted to build a fence, and the other neighbor refused to share the costs, the first man might build what Sheriff Joe Goodson called a "son-of-a-bitch fence," two or three feet back from his property line. This punished his chinchy neighbor by forcing him to build another parallel fence a few feet away to keep his stock from trespassing on the first fence builder's land.[50]

Sometimes rural sheriffs received calls to mediate property disputes between private citizens and county or state agencies when no one else had the clear authority to do this. Sheriff Dan Saunders counseled violent disputes between a farmer and a county road maintenance man and between a farmer and a seismograph crew, as well as similar squabbles. He recorded in his journal: "Have been refereeing a squabble between the Maintenance Foreman of the Texas Highway Department and four farmers up on Knott Highway. This not really my job but there is no one else to do it."[51]

Calls to pacify or mediate "domestic squabbles" also were not formally part of the sheriff's job, but he expended much effort on such matters. Sheriffs well knew that when citizens' closest human relationships went wrong, calls about domestic trouble often turned into calls about beatings, cuttings, and killings. Buck Lane sometimes seemed to complain about how much of his time was spent mediating domestic troubles, but on April 20, 1945, he told his reading public that "if for any reason you or your wife and your friend and neighbor have troubles, makes no matter how small they may seem, I want you to know that this department stands ready to help you in any way humanly possible." Lane continued: "Often times a stitch in time saves nine, you call us we will come, and certainly we will do all in our power to help you. You can depend on us to keep to ourselves what you may care to divulge to us."[52] At Lee County, however, Sheriff J. R. Goodson disliked his frequent late-night calls to referee domestic conflicts, and Goodson used his newspaper column in the Giddings paper to reduce such calls. His son explained: "He was getting so many calls at night, that he started publishing the calls in the paper. He wouldn't put the names in, but he would say, 'So-and-so from Birdsong community, where he and his wife were in a tussle last night.' They knew who they were, and the neighbors knew who they were, that slowed the night calls quite a bit."[53]

Most sheriffs reported numerous interventions into private affairs, and some found this the most satisfying part of their job. Frank Brunt told of solving a young couple's marital problems in his office at the Cherokee County jail. "I sat 'em down there, and I let him tell his story," Brunt recalled, "and she just rared and pitched over there, and cried. I listened to 'em a few minutes, I said, 'Now, what you'll need to do—I know you're in love, you just both got married—you need to cool off. You ought to kiss her, make love to her, go on and sleep real close to her tonight, and love her.' And directly, I got 'em to kiss and they left there arm in arm."[54] Sheriff Brantley Barker of San Saba County reported: "What makes me feel good is to go to a family fuss, and they was ready to separate and divide up all the furniture, and I talk to 'em awhile. They'd go back together, and then I get a letter from 'em telling me how they appreciated me sitting there talking to 'em that night."[55]

Sometimes the sheriff's intervention was not so simple. Sheriff Ed Darnell once turned back a divorce case with child custody battle right at the courtroom door. Darnell asked the judge for five minutes' conversation with wife, husband, and the husband's mother and aunt, who were deeply involved in the marital squabble. Darnell told the mother and aunt, "Ya'll are breaking up this family. I'm gonna give you about five minutes to get out of this courthouse. You're not gonna interfere with those kids. Why don't you go home and leave 'em alone?" Having banished the in-laws, Sheriff Darnell then took the warring couple into a small room and ordered them to stay away from the husband's in-laws and to drop the divorce, which they agreed to do, thus saving their marriage.[56]

Many such interventions were not as successful. As Dan Saunders observed from long experience: "The worst situation that a peace officer can get into is a family squabble. Couples are mad, vindictive, scared, vengeful, wanting attention and sympathy and usually one or both parties are drunk."[57] After pacifying many family disturbances, Saunders went out on one too many and found himself in a kill-or-be-killed confrontation with a drunken, homicidal father, whom he shot to death. Kendall County sheriff Douglass Kueber handled family trouble calls for nearly two decades until the early morning hours of September 28, 1971, when he approached the door of a house and died in a blast of buckshot before saying a word to the domestic combatants.[58]

Bizarre behaviors were commonplace in family disturbances, but over long years of service sheriffs heard and saw so much at such affairs that their memories blurred, with one remarkable scene blotting out another. Sheriff Dan Saunders, however, kept a daily journal, recording some remarkable happenings for the historian of law enforcement. For one thing, Saunders's log often showed recurrent calls to the same home on the same night, with domestic conflagrations damping down at the sheriff's presence, then springing up again after his departure, sometimes requiring the sheriff to go back and forth from his home to some distant farmhouse all night long. Saunders began his daily journal in 1969, two decades into his career, but his accounts had a timeless quality.

On January 5, 1977, Saunders noted, "A young girl came by the office and told me she was pregnant and was extremely afraid to go tell her father so I went to his house and told him."[59] On June 20, 1977, a man getting a divorce from his wife called Saunders to his house to look at something. "Someone had a bowel movement on top of his neatly stacked steaks in a large chest-type deep-freeze. He insisted that it was his estranged wife and demanded that a sample be taken of the deposit and analyzed by the DPS lab at Midland. Well, I collected a sample in an envelope but I didn't take it to the lab."[60] On June 18, 1978, Saunders went out on a family squabble call in the Brown community. The husband's father lived with the couple, and "he hated his daughter-in-law and every time he would pass where she was sitting he would pass gas. I ordered him to quit 'blowing off.'"[61]

On October 4, 1978, an irate Hispanic man visited Saunders in his office, complaining that another man had stolen his daughter's "flower." Saunders for a time honestly believed this to be a report of a flour theft, but his offer to buy the young lady "another sack of flour" made the father even more furious.[62] On October 25, 1978, a man angry at another man for insulting his mother asked the sheriff's permission to give the mother insulter "one lick," the insulter having agreed to absorb it. The one-lick retribution was staged on a remote road, with the sheriff presiding, and Saunders wrote, "Well, as the Bible says, 'An eye for an eye,' everyone was happy." Then he noted, as a postscript to this affair: "You can't always go by the book or straight down the line on squabbles. If I did I would have J.P. Court, County Court, and District Court swamped. I tried to work these squabbles out myself and usually I did without the County or District Attorney ever having knowledge of them. I never got sued in forty years and didn't get the county sued either."[63] On November 12, 1978, for example, Saunders again issued a sheriff's permit for two people to fight it out, this time two warring sisters-in-law.[64]

On January 18, 1980, Saunders finished a lengthy intervention in the personal affairs of a local couple who would quarrel, file for divorce, reconcile, quarrel, and go through the whole process over again, repeatedly involving their mutual friend, the sheriff. On this date the courthouse reconciliation seemed genuine, and later that day Saunders got a call to visit them at their home. He walked in to see them both naked in their bedroom. "They wanted me to watch them consummate their coming back together, so I could report back to the judge. Did I watch? No one will ever know."[65] On February 26, 1980, Saunders got a call from an elderly woman who had been fighting with her husband for more than a month. "Last night it was extra cold and the old man had slipped up to the old woman's house (they are in their seventies) and nailed the front and back door solidly shut and cut her butane off. When she woke up this morning she was about to freeze. Fortunately her phone was still working and she called me. I took a claw hammer and pulled the nails out of the doors and turned her butane back on."[66]

Sometimes Saunders had nothing even remotely amusing to report in his log. On June 3, 1980, neighboring sheriff Bud Gregory called Saunders on the phone to inform him that he was about to kill his wife and himself, and Saunders had begun to try to persuade Gregory not to do it when Gregory hung up. "Before I could get my clothes on and get out of the house, the dispatcher from Andrews called me and said Bud had killed Biddy and then himself. Such a waste of talent and life."[67]

Then, as usual, dark comedy followed black tragedy in Sheriff Saunders's remarkable log. On June 16, 1980, he wrote: "Got another call from the old couple that live in the northeast part of town and have had so much trouble. She claimed that ——— was peeing in her front yard. When I got there, sure enough he was and she had a hammer trying to whack his 'thing' with it. I ordered them both to put up their 'tools.'"[68] On December 16, 1980, Saunders stayed up thirty-two hours straight working on a family squabble at Tarzan. He spent the night at the house, then "this morning at 5:00 AM, the man started his airplane and started 'dive bombing' his house. I was in the house with his wife and three kids. I thought he was going to kill himself and the rest of us. I guess, as Mama used to say, that God looks after fools and idiots."[69]

Over time, Sheriff Dan Saunders came to know about too many secrets and too many situations he could not do anything about, such as the two Martin County families where incest had become part of the domestic round. Sheriffs commonly traveled alone when they administered to local secrets, and on January 19, 1984, Saunders wrote: "A Sheriff's job is the most lonesome in the world. I have lots and lots of friends but no real buddy to ride around and confide to. You can't get real close to anyone in this job."[70]

The sheriff served as every citizen's "friend at the courthouse," but this aspect of the sheriff's job had another side to it. Over the years, as the numbers of citizens who had come to this public official with their very private problems accumulated, the sheriff became a man who knew too much, the county's Mr. Insider, the keeper of everyone's darkest secrets. The man whose daughter finally had been located in the motel just over the county line, the outstanding citizen who had been saved from the embarrassing consequences of his public drunkenness, the Kleberg County socialite who had once been on the staff of the Chicken Ranch brothel near La Grange, all these became part of that body of private knowledge that the sheriff could never divulge. Jim Scarborough II carried the identity of the Chicken Ranch veteran to his grave, along with the rest of his secrets, but at times people must have looked at him in the same manner described by Jim Scarborough III:

> Some of these personal calls are worse than that, especially about doper kids, pregnant girls that have to get sent off, things like that. They've come to me and said, "Where is a good place for my daughter to go to have this child?" I don't even tell my wife. I've been that way, my father was that way, my grandfather was that way. Some of those people now resent me because they know I know their family secrets, and I feel uncomfortable about it, because when I say hello to 'em they give me that jaundiced look, like, "I wonder who he's told?" Yet, they call me knowing that I won't tell anybody.[71]

Kleberg County sheriff J. S. Scarborough III. (Author's collection)

Not surprisingly, the rural sheriff's commitment to serve as everyone's friend at the courthouse strongly affected his enforcement of the law. Sheriffs often let voters off with a warning or two, for such illegal traditions of the county as gambling, public drunkenness, or fighting, before finally hauling the repeat offenders off to jail. As Gaston Boykin said, "A sheriff never handles any two cases alike."[72] When Frank Brunt of Cherokee County caught bootleggers on the county roads transporting recreational liquor for the county's Friday night football games, his treatment of them was calibrated to the social circumstances. Sometimes Sheriff Brunt took them to jail and had rough conversations with them on the courthouse elevator. Sometimes he just took them to jail and notified their families. Sometimes he merely bade them stand and observe him while he took target practice on their gallon bottles of expensive bonded whiskey with his service revolver, then let them go. The manner of enforcing the law was made to fit the crime and took into consideration who they were, who their families were, who they were bootlegging for, how many times they had been caught in the past, and a variety of other things.[73] Many old-time sheriffs were especially lenient with juvenile offenders, going well out of their way to keep the youths' records clean and to devise strategies of punishment and reform short of the full formalities of the law.

The first few minutes after the sheriff caught the perpetrator often determined much of what happened next. Sheriffs had two aspects; was the wrongdoer in the hands of the "mean sheriff" or the "voters' friend"? An officer looked closely to determine if he knew the law violator personally and whether this individual was a county resident or an outsider, a youth or a mature adult, and a habitual violator or a first-timer. Sheriff Jess Sweeten had a clear distinction in his mind between ordinary transgressors against the law and innate, unreformable "born criminals," and persons Sweeten placed in the latter category were in trouble. Likewise, Buck Lane made an immediate distinction of "sheep" or "goats" among lawbreakers. "I believed there was 'accidentals' and there was 'habituals,'" Lane explained, "and if an accidental gets into trouble, you should be happy to help, if it's a habitual, put him in jail."[74] Sometimes the high sheriff added a moral test to these early sheep-or-goat judgments to help determine the fate of wrongdoers. After a Colorado County sheriff caught a farmhouse full of gamblers, he asked each in turn what he had been doing at the house. As each man lied, the sheriff marched him upstairs to spend a long night in jail. Finally, one man admitted he had been gambling with family grocery money, and the sheriff bought him a sack of flour and sent him home.[75]

On some occasions the "mean sheriff" and the "voter's friend" followed successively in an officer's relationship with a perpetrator. Buck Lane struck a stock poacher to make him confess, sent him to the pen, then helped find him a job with the county.[76] Sheriff Lewis A. Latch, former sheriff of Upshur County, told a reporter, looking back over his long career: "I haven't an enemy in the world, so far as I know. One of the few men I ever had to shoot while I was in office came to me as soon as he had finished his prison term and stayed at my house until he could get his feet on the ground and start life over."[77]

Many "accidentals" captured in the act received informal field reprieves from the sheriff and never reached the sheriff's jail records. On other occasions, sheriffs intervened with their county or district attorneys on behalf of jail prisoners awaiting trial. Sheriffs' racist beliefs about the ignorance and emotional instability of minority citizens sometimes led them to plead for their special treatment, as when Deputy Tom Brown successfully intervened with his district attorney for the "old ignorant Mexican woman" whose dead baby had been found under a washtub at a Caldwell County cotton farm. The woman escaped with a suspended sentence, subsequently rewarding Brown with the gift of a hog and a sack of pecans.[78] Sheriff Buck Lane also tried to help two migrant cotton pickers accused of attacking another Hispanic man after a quarrel about who would sleep on a farmhouse porch. Lane wrote in his newspaper column on September 23, 1949: "So, in they came [to the jail], like wild deer. As it looks now, the man butchered up so bad is going to live and be all right, and we hope so for several reasons, hate to see any man killed and too would hate to prosecute that old very, very ignorant half-Indian and his son for murder, when all their life in Mexico they have had to live by their wits and strength."[79]

Interventions on behalf of wayward youths seemed far more common, however, and many sheriffs proudly recalled such things as the most positive experiences of their professional career (and as vindications of the "old way" of law enforcement). After Buck Lane caught a precocious Anglo youth of fourteen writing hot checks, Lane talked to him a long time, then made him a deal. He would not be charged but must return home, apologize to his mother and father for hot checks, stay on the farm and pick cotton (a hated task), and report to a mutual friend on a weekly basis. Having thus proved himself, the boy would "be taken in as a Junior Deputy

Sheriff, and he will join the team of Law Enforcement Officers so he can help prevent other boys from getting in trouble."[80] Looking back over his long career as sheriff, Jack Marshall told a reporter that "what I liked about it back then was if you caught someone in a bind, a good officer could help them more than a preacher, or a lawyer, or a judge." Then he offered an example of what he meant. After catching a young man who had stolen a valuable piece of rice farming equipment and sold it for scrap metal in Houston, Marshall made the man buy the equipment back, supervised him while he returned it to the farmer and welded it back together, then talked the farmer and the district attorney into dropping all charges. Marshall explained: "We had done our job, you see, but hadn't ruined him. We kept him from getting that [prison] number and saved the taxpayer's money."[81]

Some sheriffs even proved willing to challenge their district attorneys in such interventions. In Henderson County, Jess Sweeten arrested three teenaged boys from outside the county for robbing three local stores. Finding out that all three came from "broken homes," and that all three had signed up to enter military service, Sweeten decided to help them. Even a suspended sentence would keep them out of the service, so Sweeten pleaded with store owners and his district attorney not to prosecute—a request they refused. During the trial, however, Sheriff Sweeten had a chance to address the jury to explain the situation, and as a result the boys were acquitted. Of the political consequences of this, Sweeten told a historian: "Sure, the store owners, they got mad as the devil, and believe you me, they vote. But I didn't care about that, that's not the point. The point is to try to help these boys to be good men. And they did, and I've been proud of it ever since. I never was scared to be in the right."[82]

According to his son, Sheriff Wallace Riddel often made not one but several attempts to reform each wayward Burnet County youth and keep him out of jail, with the last one being a reluctant ultimatum: join the military service in ten days or go to jail.[83] Many sheriffs followed similar policies. In Milam County, Sheriff Carl Black's practice regarding youthful lawbreakers was first chance, second chance, then banishment. After a third transgression, Black advised, "Son, I think you've been in Cameron long enough."[84] Such a banishment was an expedient and merciful act, the sheriff believed. It was good for the county, good for the sheriff's politics, and good for the wayward youth, since his sheriff finally had lost patience with him.

Many sheriffs saw their jails as the places to befriend local outlaws and to show them the error of their ways, and some men explicitly tried to operate their jails in terms of the Golden Rule. After a minister told Dan Saunders, following a visit with a pregnant female murderer, "If it was in my power I would take that girl home with me," Saunders immediately unlocked the woman's cell door. Saunders recalled, "He looked shocked but do you know he took her home with him and he and his wife looked after her until she had her baby and then he brought her back to jail after letting her folks have the baby."[85] At Liberty County, Sheriff W. P. "Red" Rose told an editor that he liked living in the jail because "I want to know my prisoners and try to understand their problems—you'll be surprised how many people you can steer back to the straight and narrow if you have the patience to give them a boost."[86] Wallace Riddel explained to a reporter: "I told myself my first day in office in 1939 that I was sheriff of Burnet County to help people, not to put a lot of 'em in jail. They've been a bunch in my jail, but I didn't put them in unless I had to. There never was a man or woman who went in that jail and need help that I didn't give it to them if they were entitled to it. A few went out [of the jail] who wasn't my friends, but they wouldn't let me be."[87]

Most sheriffs went into office; performed their strange, complicated job more or less adequately for a term or two; gradually eroded their political bases by arresting voters and revealing their impatience with the wearing, relentless, personal demands of citizens; and were voted out or quit. Some sheriffs, however, served their counties selflessly for long decades and put down their wonderful burden only when their health broke or they died in office. Invariably, these "thirty-year men" regarded themselves, first and foremost, as everyone's friend at the courthouse. In a tribute to his father, sheriff of Kleberg County for almost forty years, Jim Scarborough III told a historian:

> My dad was considered a personal sheriff. Everybody in this county felt like he was their sheriff. He earned that. He'd throw great barbecues, Thanksgiving dinners, with a dance following it. He'd dance with the eighty-year-old grandmas and all the women in between, things like that. He knew every child and grandchild in sight by name. He knew everybody in this county, and he made it his business if a new person came to town to know him. He'd personally drive out and tell em who he was, give em his phone number, tell em: "If you ever need anything done for you, if you're in trouble, you just let us know."[88]

Kleberg County sheriff J. S. Scarborough II. (Author's collection)

A wave of shock passed through a rural county when a thirty-year man like Jim Scarborough II, Rufe Jordan, Truman Maddox, Nathan Tindall, Dan Saunders, or Wallace Riddel left office, and for a time citizens felt disturbed and unmanned, as if they had lost both an ancient county tradition and their own stern and generous grandfather. After Sheriff Riddel died in office on February 11, 1978, thousands of people came to his funeral at the Burnet High School auditorium. A newsman spoke at his eulogy: "He was the big man in Burnet County for everyone from the little kids to the oldtimers. They all knew and trusted him. He did many things for people simply because he liked almost everybody and had a big heart. Maybe that's why they are burying him on Valentine's Day." A minister said: "Sheriff Riddel's greatest characteristic was his open hand. He extended his right hand, his gun hand, to everyone, regardless of their station in life." Finally, the editor of the *Burnet County Bulletin* wrote of Wallace Riddel: "With him died in a sense the office of Burnet County sheriff and the concept of what represented the law in Burnet County for nearly forty years. For those who were born and raised in Burnet County, the words 'Sheriff Wallace Riddel' rolled off our tongues and fell on our ears with a familiarity of 'mother,' 'father,' and 'flag.' No matter whose name fills the blank after 'sheriff' in the future, Burnet County citizens will be saying 'sheriff' and thinking Wallace Riddel for many years to come."[89]

LAST DAYS OF THE HIGH SHERIFF

In 1977, former Caldwell County sheriff Tom Brown told a historian that he had no wish to seek the office once again. Too much had changed, and the high sheriff had lost much of his power. "Back in those days," Brown said, "the sheriff he was law! And I couldn't be sheriff now, no—nowhere in the world, nowhere in the world. Cause I'd want to do it the old way."[1]

The chapters above attempt to describe Tom Brown's "old way" of the Texas sheriff during the last decades before the sheriff's power became increasingly circumscribed by federal courts, federal investigations, and two state regulatory agencies focused on law enforcement, the Texas Commission on Law Enforcement Officer Standards and Education and the Texas Jail Standards Commission. Even into the 1990s, however, the rural sheriff's problem was that citizens assumed the old way still operated and felt free to make old-time requests. In Sheriff Joe Goodson's Lee County in 1998, elderly county residents still showed up unannounced on his doorstep at first light, expecting private audiences with the high sheriff, then asked him to intervene in property disputes, neighborhood quarrels, domestic squabbles, and other private matters. Sheriff Goodson always listened to their troubles and their requests, then—more often than not—tried to explain why he could not help.[2]

For good legal reasons, Ed Darnell's "kind word and helping hand" had shrunken to only the kind word, but sheriffs still did not like to say no to a voter. Texas rural society had turned litigious by 1998, and sheriffs could no longer safely accost private citizens in their homes without legal papers in hand. Even the sheriff's direct helping hand had become restricted. After a bedridden elderly woman requested a Jasper County deputy to buy groceries for her during the 1980s, the deputy had to ask Sheriff Aubrey Cole for his permission to do this, and Sheriff Cole had to consider the possibility of a charge of improper use of a county vehicle before telling the deputy to go ahead.[3]

By 1990, however, nothing so rapidly led to trouble for the sheriff as his use of force, and sheriffs accustomed to the old way often strained to control themselves. Only the TDC fielded packs of man-hounds by this late date, since, as Rufe Jordan dryly observed, "one little nip and you'd be in a lawsuit."[4] Nor could sheriffs use direct physical force without risking harassing lawsuits. In 1986, for example, Sheriff Nig Hoskins faced a major civil rights lawsuit for striking a prisoner with his billy club to stop him from pounding the head of an unconscious deputy against the concrete floor of the Bastrop jail. The prisoner was African American, but so was the deputy. Hoskins had been in office since a time when citizens expected him (as he said) "to go out here and just grab one, far as that goes, and just work him over," but now his hands were tied.[5]

During the early 1980s, H. F. Fenton of Coleman County became quite explicit in explaining to *Texas Monthly* reporter Dick Reavis just what he thought about this great change in allowable behavior: "If a suspect walks up here and calls you a son-of-a-bitch, and you haul off and hit him in the mouth, then he'll file on you for his civil rights, then sue you in federal court. Back when law was law, well, you could knock his damn head off, go put him in jail, and file on him for calling you a son-of-a-bitch. But I still don't let none of them call me a son-of-a-bitch. I'll knock their damn heads off and let them go get a lawyer, that's what I'll do."[6]

Much of the old way of the Texas sheriff had eroded by the mid-1970s, though, with ever increasing risks, some sheriffs still adhered to older ways of doing things. Just below the surface of the traditional role lay the effective use of physical force. Voters expected their sheriff to maintain proper authority, brook no insults, lose no fights, and do whatever he needed to do to accomplish this, even including the use of deadly force. Old-way sheriffs had considerable tacit leeway from the citizenry to use force—even, if circumstances demanded it, permission to kill. Even in very suspicious circumstances, local grand juries customarily no-billed their sheriffs. As Buck Lane said, if a criminal came into serious conflict with the sheriff, "he got killed" and "we were not tried."[7]

Even the friendly old "personal sheriffs" often had a pair of knucks in their back pocket, as did Jim Scarborough II, or a mysterious "loaded arm," as did Nathan Tindall, so that when one of them hit a criminal, he could not easily get up. Tindall never carried a gun and rarely used force, but, like an old master of the martial arts, he was rarely challenged. A general public belief in, and acceptance of, the sheriff's ability to be effectively violent, to "get rough," lay just below the surface of the old way of the Texas sheriff—a traditional way of doing things that included the sheriff's complete control of his jail and everyone in it, his use of interrogation to break cases, and his banishment of troublesome individuals beyond the county line. Even when the sheriff donned his robe of Good Samaritan and went forth to mediate property line disputes and domestic quarrels, his proven ability to be effectively violent lurked in combatants' minds, no matter how angry they were at each other; the sheriff's very presence implied a physical threat. As his son explained, after a fighting family exhausted Wallace Riddel's arguments and patience and his performance as a peacemaker failed to pacify the combatants, Riddel "literally beat the hell out of them."[8]

As Sheriff Vail Ennis's violent career demonstrated, before the rise of civil rights litigation during the 1950s, sheriffs rarely got into legal trouble over their use of excessive force, but fiscal matters—charges of "extortionate collection of fees of office," misappropriation of public funds, and bribery—sometimes brought them down, especially if local political enemies got on their trail. During the Depression, sheriffs in "fee counties" often came under attack for discrepancies in their collection of fees, and even minor errors received heavy punishment. During the first months of 1932, for example, state courts sentenced five sheriffs to two- and three-year terms in the penitentiary, one for an excess charge of $3.40 and one for $5.00.[9] Likewise, a weak sheriff with strong local enemies did well to watch every penny in his departmental budget lest a fine misdirected for departmental operating money end in a felony charge of misappropriation of public funds. Big-money bribery offers tempted almost every sheriff; some gave in to the temptations, and some of them got caught. Sheriff John J. Reeves, for example, "could not withstand charges of conspiracy and protection of bootleggers during Prohibition,"[10] and in 1950 a jury convicted Sheriff "Doc" Scholl of Comal County of accepting a $2,500.00 bribe to avoid giving testimony in the trial of a cattle thief.[11]

Occasionally a sheriff took public money and ran away with it, as did sheriff and tax-assessor/collector Paul Bone of Somervell County in 1964. After Bone suddenly disappeared, officials at Glen Rose discovered that twenty-two thousand dollars was missing from Bone's tax accounts, stolen in his joint public role of sheriff and tax collector. Somervell County had something of a tradition of this sort of thing, since a sheriff had absconded with thirteen thousand dollars of county money in 1913, another sheriff with forty-three thousand dollars in 1929, a county judge with forty-one thousand dollars in 1938, and a deputy with eight thousand dollars in 1955. After a few weeks Sheriff Bone returned to inform authorities that he had only visited Mexico for a while to think about his problems, but a local jury sent him to the penitentiary nonetheless.[12]

Occasionally sheriffs used their great formal and informal powers of office to build formidable political machines and to coopt entire counties into corruption and outlawry. Several Texas counties became major moonshine whiskey producers during national prohibition, with their sheriffs invariably playing central roles as protectors of the whiskey outlaws, and in "North County" during the 1920s and 1930s and in San Jacinto County during the 1970s and 1980s, "Sheriff Cameron" and Sheriff S. C. Parker demonstrated the outer limits of official corruption and abuse of office.

"North County," its county seat of "North Town, and the sheriff, "Mr. Cameron," are all pseudonyms for a Texas county, courthouse town and sheriff studied in depth by political anthropologist Douglas Foley and his colleagues and students. Sheriff Cameron had served from 1920 to 1948, and by the early 1970s retired politicians and minority citizens of North Town were willing to talk about Cameron's long reign as political boss. Tall, handsome, flamboyant, fluent in Spanish, and a good fighter, Cameron had dominated his county by a mixture of charisma and violence. A "political entrepreneur," as Foley termed him, the son of a small landowner, Cameron controlled North Town and North County for a quarter of a century. Making sure that little or no records were kept documenting his activities, the sheriff/tax collector made money by underreporting tax collections and pocketing a percentage. He also made sure that some Mexican property owners did not get their tax notices, did not pay their taxes, and so had their property seized and sold for back taxes, with Cameron getting his cut. Another money-making tactic of Sheriff Cameron's was to skim off a percentage of county funds paid for the frequent burials of "fake Mexican indigents." Cameron also loaned money to Mexicans at extremely high rates of interest and forced both legal cantina owners and illegal bootleggers to pay protection money to be allowed to operate in North County.

By various favors, intimidations, and small business deals, Sheriff Cameron built up a following in "Mexican Town." Anglos often said approvingly of Cameron that "'He ruled the Mexicans with an iron fist,' which meant he frequently beat up drunks at the casinos, slept with Mexican women, and inflicted severe pistol whippings in public," becoming, as Foley noted, "the archetype of the rough, racist South Texas lawman of this era." Foley continued: "Mr. Cameron actually ruled through what was a common style among sheriffs, that is, to 'go native' with the Mexicanos and drink and brawl in the *cantinas*. Mr. Cameron was feared, but he was also admired for his manliness and his brutality. He was as one old Mexicano put it, 'muy hombre.' He made the Mexicans laugh and could enjoy the manly pursuits of drinking and fighting. He also gave them favors like extra jobs and 'breaks' when they broke the law as he defined it."[13]

Cameron functioned as a boundary keeper between minority and Anglo societies, and to play this role he kept a foot in both camps. Law enforcement at North County had a minority focus, and Spanish surnames filled the sheriff's jail logs and the records of local courts. Cameron's main job seems to have been keeping Hispanics in line, in their place, and under control—and while doing this making all the money for himself that he could. Foley explained: "This was a very common way that the rough, sometimes brutal, law authorities were able to control the Mexicanos. They controlled them through being 'a good ole boy' and drinking and socializing with them. They gave them favors as well as occasional beatings."[14]

Although Sheriff Cameron's political power declined somewhat in his last years in office, and some people dared to circulate rumors about fiscal wrongdoing, Cameron grew old in office and retired with no formal charges ever having been brought against him.

Sheriff S. C. "Humpy" Parker of San Jacinto County, however, operated forty years later and in the end paid a severe price for his official corruptions. Earlier sheriffs often had laid highway traps for long-range bootleggers, outside outlaws whose capture brought welcome fines and confiscated property into county coffers, but Sheriff Parker modernized the process, linked it to the fashionable "war on drugs," and turned it into a major industry. Poor, rural San Jacinto County needed financial help, since a majority of its land was tied up in the untaxable Sam Houston National Forest. Soon after taking office in the mid-1970s, Sheriff Parker found a way to help his county make ends meet while supplementing his official salary. Parker devised an elaborate drug-trap operation on the fifteen miles of Highway 59 passing through the south part of the county.

Eventually, many San Jacinto County public officials and citizens became involved in the sheriff's operations. Humpy Parker (nicknamed for a bird dog of his youth) had five regular deputies, one of them his son; twenty or so "reserve deputies"; and an indeterminate number of "honorary deputies," some of whom took part in the action on Highway 59. Probably all regular deputies and reserve deputies became involved in the "highway robbery," as federal investigators later termed it. One very active reserve deputy had been recruited out of the San Jacinto County jail.

Especially on weekend nights, deputies, many of them in unmarked cars, took up positions near the Trinity River bridge just inside the eastern county line on Highway 59 and carefully scrutinized oncoming traffic. In accordance with Humpy's instructions, their "profile" for stopping and searching cars included out-of-county and out-of-state license plates, youths at the wheel, long-haired males and males wearing headbands, multiple young people in the car, blacks or other minorities in the car, vans, old cars, and vehicles with rock station bumper stickers (especially Houston's K-101). Having chosen a victim, deputies stopped the car, made vague allegations about irregular driving or defective tail lights, then launched a thorough search of driver, passengers, and the car itself. The least trace of illegal drugs triggered an arrest, and victims later alleged that they had been frightened, abused, humiliated, sexually molested, and falsely accused, with drugs sometimes planted by searchers.

After the stop and the score, speed became the key, since the "catcher" deputies wanted to hand the captured party off and go after additional quarry. Tow-truck men rapidly hooked up to tow the car, and "runner" deputies motored handcuffed prisoners to county jail at breakneck speed so they could swiftly return to the action. At the jail in the county seat of Coldspring, a strange team of bail bondsmen and jail trusties processed prisoners, since all available deputies were out on the hunt. Bail was set by the bondsmen or trusties, fees were charged to file guilty pleas in the next court, and towing fees and other fees also were charged. Trusties in jail-house white coveralls read prisoners their rights and took their bonds and money. Drugs, liquor, weapons, and other valuable items were confiscated and soon disappeared—in one instance, seven thousand dollars' worth of new stereo equipment, in another, nine ounces of cocaine. Usually a person captured in Humpy Parker's Highway 59 drug trap paid from two hundred dollars to five hundred dollars in bond money to escape San Jacinto County that night or the next day. No records were kept, no further contacts were made (despite promises about receipts in the mail, notification about trial dates, etc.), and few people ever came to trial. Probable cause for the stop, if given at all, was usually a problem with a taillight or license plate light. Sometimes when a person returned to his car to escape San Jacinto County, he found a taillight kicked out and the shattered plastic lying beneath it on the courthouse parking lot. As the person thankfully entered his car, he usually saw tow trucks roaring up with other captured vehicles. Humpy's drug trap did a high-volume business, with up to fifty vehicles and their occupants processed on a good Saturday night. In 1981, San Jacinto County reported 1,124 drug arrests, second only to Harris County (Houston) with 1,172, and many of Sheriff Parker's arrests went unrecorded.

After several years, a few citizens dared to complain about Humpy Parker's operations, and in 1978 six FBI agents set up a temporary office at the Coldspring bank and advertised in the local newspaper for people to come forward with information. The glass-fronted sheriff's office lay just across the street, however, and the bank's president also functioned as Parker's chief bail bondsman in the drug trap, so citizens made few if any visits to the FBI. Gregg McGee, a former deputy, told a reporter, "The feeling was that if you walked through that door, you would be signing your death warrant." Soon, the FBI dropped the case and departed, leaving locals even more convinced that Sheriff Parker was invulnerable. Many citizens shared in the drug-capture industry, and most others were intimidated. Sheriff's office, volunteer deputies, county judge, county attorney, county commissioners, bank president, bail bondsmen, and tow-truck operators all cooperated to one degree or another in the enterprise. Parker's drug trap assured the county of a great deal of operating money, with a lot left over for all participants, and confiscated drugs and property soon disappeared from the county's walk-in property vault.

Beginning during 1982, however, Sheriff Parker's little outlaw fiefdom began to fall apart. Investigative reporters from Austin got on the sheriff's trail, the *Austin American-Statesman* published a series of articles, and the FBI and the Texas Rangers returned to San Jacinto County in force. This time they met with local citizens in secrecy, wherever the citizens wished, and people began to talk. As the investigation progressed, one of Parker's deputies decided to testify against him. Soon, district and county grand juries indicted Parker, his son, and several deputies, and by early 1984 the former sheriff stood convicted of torturing prisoners, violating civil rights, extorting bond money, stopping cars without probable cause, and illegally seizing property. Both Humpy Parker and his son, Gary, received lengthy prison sentences.[15]

At midcentury the rural sheriff still possessed—or could develop—social and political power beyond the formal definitions of office. Many sheriffs used that traditional power in selfless public service for the good of the people, and a few used it for self-indulgent violence and personal gain. It had always been so, but S. C. Parker had become an anachronism by the 1980s, a time when Texas sheriffs had become circumscribed by many new restraints. The "lord of the county line" was lord no more, but a man constantly monitored by critical authorities from outside his juris-diction: Texas Rangers, federal courts, and regulatory stage agencies. The district Texas Ranger, helpmate and professional observer of local sheriffs, was an old friend and antagonist. Sheriffs often worked closely with their district Rangers to break cases, using the Rangers' professional expertise and their impressive crime-solving resources at Texas Department of Public Safety headquarters in Austin. However, sheriffs remained wary; Rangers were appointed law officers with a very different perspective than that of an elected sheriff. If, as they sometimes did, voters wished to continue a tradition of an "open county," with lax enforcement of gambling, vice, and liquor laws, they might elect a sheriff to maintain that tradition. Then, however, the sheriff had to deal with his district Ranger, who usually had little sympathy with illegal local traditions.

The prolonged scuffle between Texas Ranger captain Clint Peoples and McLennan County sheriff C. C. Maxey during the 1960s typified this recur-rent situation. Maxey denied the existence of gambling, prostitution, and liquor-law violations in his county until Ranger Peoples brought proof, then Maxey promised to clean up the problems but did nothing. Finally, in 1961, Rangers and the Waco police raided the local Elks Club and the Rinky-Dink Club, a black roadhouse, arresting large numbers of gamblers at both locations. Two years later, Ranger Peoples worked closely with two irate grand juries in a prolonged investigation into McLennan County's chaotic jail, local gambling and vice, bribery of officers, irregular legal processes, and other illegalities long allowed under Maxey. Several of Sheriff Maxey's deputies were indicted, and the sheriff said publicly, "We've been humiliated, some deputies are now ashamed to be seen in a marked sheriff's department car." In their final reports, the grand juries strongly criticized Sheriff Maxey for his lax and incompetent operation of the sheriff's office, and Maxey apologized and took full responsibility for the circumstances. Finally, in November, the Waco Junior Chamber of Commerce added insult to injury by electing Ranger Clint Peoples as "McLennan County's Law Enforcement Officer of 1963."[16] Then, however, something rather typical happened, probably because most people wanted it to: Waco and environs gradually slid back into an open county, and approving voters continued to elect C. C. Maxey as their sheriff.

The practitioner of Tom Brown's old way of the Texas sheriff did not like outside officers operating without his knowledge or his permission in his county. Sheriffs such as Buck Lane of Wharton County viewed the arrival of DPS highway patrolmen after World War II with ambivalence. Having someone assume part of the burden of traffic control and accident investigation was a relief, but Lane distrusted the state troopers, suspected them of serving as informants for the district Ranger, and disliked the arrogant and unpolitical way that troopers enforced the law. Lane at first officially praised the DPS highway patrolmen in his column, but years later he told a historian that he had complained about their behavior to DPS head Homer Garrison, telling him, "They don't know the difference between right and wrong." Lane called the DPS troopers stationed in Wharton County in to a meeting and said, "Now, fellows, let's have an understanding, I'm the predominant officer." Lane then told the troopers in no uncertain terms to stick to their business and stay out of his and the county judge's business. However, "They didn't do that, they kept on telling the judges what to fine a man. I couldn't stand that, I run 'em out. I was writing stories about what the Highway Patrol was doing, and it wasn't long till they got out [of Wharton County]. I told 'em, 'Now, when I need a Ranger, I'll send for him.'"[17]

Officers of the Texas Liquor Control Board, established in 1935, also sometimes intruded on the sheriff's turf, and he usually resented this. In 1949, Buck Lane recorded in his column in an uncharacteristically terse note that "Tuesday in Wharton, State Liquor Men, better known as 'L-Men', came to Wharton and swooped down on a local liquor store and the jail is now the depository of the liquor store."[18] This was, of course, a liquor store Sheriff Lane had allowed to operate, and he clearly regarded the "swooping" of the "L-Men" as an insult to his authority and mentioned it in his column only because everybody knew about the incident. Increasing

LCB activism continued to plague county sheriffs, and unannounced raids by Rangers, L-Men, the FBI, and other officers would be on the increase. During 1959, for example, the LCB supervisor of fourteen northeastern Texas counties lost patience with Smith County sheriff Ross C. Turner and raided the American Legion Hall at Tyler, the Troup Country Club, and other high-status wet spots without notifying Turner in advance. Furious, Sheriff Turner said of the LCB supervisor, "Every time I turn my back he puts a knife in it."[19] By a decade later, intrusions into sheriffs' fiefdoms had increased, and the knife-in-the-back sensation had become commonplace.

Beginning about 1950, the old way of the Texas sheriff began to result in civil rights cases brought in federal courts, and FBI agents now occasionally arrived at the sheriff's county asking questions and investigating. Month after month the *Sheriffs' Association of Texas Magazine* dutifully reported the bad news about sheriffs' ever-increasing legal difficulties, though for many years the editor continued to print "civil rights" and "police brutality" bracketed in quotes, as if these concepts were of dubious reality. Allegations about rough treatment of prisoners in county jails occasioned many federal civil rights cases, as in Smith County in 1947, Rockwall County in 1950, and other places.[20] Punishments for civil rights violations generally were light during the 1950s. For example, the court fined Sheriff Jack Pullin of Rockwall County $7.50 and sentenced him to one day in jail after Pullin pled guilty to depriving R. D. Andrews of his constitutional rights by jailing him for a $15.00 debt owed the sheriff.[21]

By the late 1950s, prisoners began to use threats of civil rights lawsuits to curb sheriffs' power over their jails, and sheriffs bitterly resented these attacks at the citadels of their local power. Plagued by repeated food riots in his Bexar County jail during 1957, Sheriff Owen Kilday proclaimed that he had "his dander up" and informed reporters:

> I may get in trouble with the FBI, but those men are going to respect authority over there at the jail. I was never so sick of anything in my life as I am of civil rights. Every thief, burglar, and killer over there may not know anything else, but he knows all about civil rights, and defies anyone to touch him or order him about or exercise any kind of control. The next man who refuses to obey a jailer, guard, or me, I will take out of there and work him over. If I have to, I'll use a rubber hose. I don't want to, but I will.[22]

Nevertheless, sheriffs such as Kilday began to be more careful about interrogation of prisoners and other things that went on in their jails, and deputies who could not curb their behavior often got fired. For example, in Harrison County in 1959, Sheriff Earl Franklin forced his veteran chief deputy to resign after a court indicted him for beating a black prisoner "to induce a confession"—the last in a series of violent incidents involving this deputy.[23]

During the Kennedy and Johnson presidencies, the U.S. Civil Rights Commission increased pressure on state and local governments to enforce civil rights.[24] By the mid-1960s many more cases were brought, and federal courts sometimes punished sheriffs with large fines and penitentiary sentences, as much of the old way of the Texas sheriff came under legal attack. When Montgomery County sheriff Gene Reeves ordered a man out of his county, the man refused to go and threatened a lawsuit.[25] After former Sheriffs' Association of Texas president Sheriff John E. Tittle of Franklin County thrashed a prisoner with his fists, the prisoner complained and Tittle eventually pled *nolo condendere* in federal court to the charge of depriving the prisoner of his civil rights.[26] The federal judge at Texarkana stated his personal sympathy for Sheriff Tittle, but not so the federal judge and jury that harshly punished Glasscock County sheriff Sam F. "Buster" Cox in 1964 for tying a horse thief to a fencepost and torturing him with an electric cattle prod.[27]

FBI investigations of civil rights complaints became common during the 1960s, though sheriffs often claimed that Hoover's men for long seemed less than zealous about these matters. The FBI agents who set up at the epicenter of Sheriff S. C. Parker's "highway robbery" operations in 1978 chose a suspiciously poor location to solicit complaints from concerned citizens. An anonymous former president of the Sheriffs' Association of Texas recalled a visit of the FBI to a South Texas county to interview a prisoner who had complained of jail beatings. Agents walked through the door, shook the sheriff's hand, briefly interviewed the prisoner, photographed his suspicious bruises and contusions, and left the county, and nothing ever came of the matter. Only later did the sheriff notice that the FBI photos showed a rubber hose, used to discipline prisoners, hanging on the wall; someone had forgotten to remove it. An anonymous East Texas sheriff told a historian: "I had the FBI to investigate me sixteen times the fourteen years I was sheriff. I never was even charged with any violation— never was even called before a federal grand jury, far as that goes."

By the late 1970s, however, Texas sheriffs had entered the era of the harassing lawsuit, usually brought in federal district court, and a sheriff was lucky indeed if he did not have one or more long, tedious, and costly court cases to think about. As in Williamson County and Wharton County in 1976, if the sheriff allowed a prisoner to die in his jail or shot a deranged gunman in a roadhouse, lawsuits often followed,[28] and by 1978 every issue of *Texas Lawman* began with a long list of sheriffs sued, indicted, and otherwise in trouble in the courts.[29] By 1980 a sheriff had to be very, very careful about everything he did and said. Maintaining the jail, serving civil writs, and mediating private disputes now offered fertile grounds for the growth of harassing lawsuits.

Likewise did the steady expansion of prisoners' constitutional rights brought about by landmark decisions of the U.S. Supreme Court. In *Mallory* v. *U.S.* (1957), *Mapp* v. *Ohio* (1961), *Gideon* v. *Wainwright* (1963), *Escobedo* v. *Illinois* (1964), and *Miranda* v. *Arizona* (1966), the Supreme Court virtually eliminated sheriffs' ability to solve cases by prolonged unrestricted interrogations in their jails, a mainstay technique of the old way of the Texas sheriff. After 1966, as Sheriff Lon Evans told a reporter, "Most crimes will have to be solved in witnesses' statements and evidence." In the past, lawmen used their local knowledge and informants to come up with a suspect, made an arrest, interrogated the suspect until they obtained a confession, then used what the suspect told them to gather supporting evidence. Now, however, "they must gather such evidence through investigative means" before arresting a suspect, and any departure from the proper procedures would lead to cases dismissed and charges brought against them in federal court. For example, in 1966 the Tarrant County district attorney dismissed over five hundred pending felony cases as "untryable in court under the new code of criminal procedure."[30]

Sheriff Lon Evans also believed that the new intricacies of law enforcement required a new sort of officer—better trained, better educated, and more professional—and the Texas state legislature, pressured by the federal government, agreed. Established on paper by the legislature in 1965, the Texas Commission on Law Enforcement Officer Standards and Education by 1967 functioned as one of twenty-three such state commissions throughout the United States. By 1970 the regulatory agency, known as TCLOS, had established a mandatory program of standardized law enforcement training required of sheriffs' deputies and every other law officer in the state. Besides successful completion of the mandated training program, law officers had to be high school graduates or have a GED, be nineteen years old or older, be able to pass a physical exam, have corrected 20-20 vision, and have no felonies, convictions for driving while intoxicated, or crimes of "moral turpitude" on their record.[31] By the mid-1980s, sheriffs themselves were required to become TCLOS-certified officers by two years into their first four-year term.

If traditional sheriffs smarted at this interference by a state agency in their selection of deputies, worse was to come with the establishment of the Texas Jail Standards Commission (TJSC) in 1975. Texas jails had been entirely unregulated until 1957, then were loosely supervised by a division of the Texas State Health Department, which lacked true regulatory teeth. By 1975, however, Texas jails were under assault by federal grand juries and federal courts for conditions that violated prisoners' civil rights, and the Texas legislature empowered the new commission with full regulatory authority.

In 1977, the TJSC set physical and operating standards for county jails, and in 1978 it announced the results of its first round of jail inspections. Sixty county jails needed only minor improvements to attain compliance with the new jail code, but the rest required major overhauls or replacement with new jails. Sheriffs, who had brooked no interference in their jail procedures, now had such matters spelled out for them in great detail, with jail inspectors looking over their shoulders. County commissioners, who had once begrudged small sums for jail upkeep, now found themselves forced to raise county taxes to build state-of-the-art, modern jails.[32]

Gaston Boykin and a good many other long-term sheriffs retired at the end of 1977, just before the TJSC's detailed requirements for jail construction and jail management slammed into place. Traditional sheriffs disliked the new TCLOS requirements for deputies and jailers, but the TJSC intruded on something far more basic; the lord's last citadel had been breached. In 1986, Boykin remarked about the then incumbent sheriff of Comanche County: "They all tell him exactly how to run the jail—he don't run it, he's just a tool unto them. He's a good boy, but he's running it for the jail commission. The man that comes by to inspect the jail also has the authority to close it. That chain link fence around the jail? He come here and told 'em where to put the posts!"[33] In truth, the TJSC's physical requirements could be extremely specific; for example, hand pulls on jail windows were mandated to be exactly seven inches in length.[34]

Sheriff H. F. Fenton of Coleman County, a contemporary of Gaston Boykin, chose to remain in office and succeeded in having his old jail certified in the first round of jail certifications, but a decade into the TJSC's new era, Fenton had bitter things to say to a visiting historian:

> I've been there 23 years in the jail, and it's more of a problem now than it's ever been. You got to keep more paperwork, you got to keep records on every little thing that happens to that prisoner from the time he goes in to the time he goes out. You got to take care of them prisoners just like they was babies. Most of them old prisoners have been in and out of jail so much that they know more about that jail-house law than anybody else does, and if you don't abide by it and take care of 'em like you should, they'll throw a writ on you right quick. Or, they'll be hollering to the jail commission, and then they'll be down investigating you or be filing federal suits. I've got a federal civil suit for $80,000 on file on me now, filed in federal court in San Angelo.[35]

The prisoner who filed this lawsuit alleged ten mistreatments while in Sheriff H. F. Fenton's care, among them a lack of privacy in his cell, poor mail delivery, and that Fenton's son Sean had been slipping a *Playboy* magazine to other prisoners in his section of the jail.

From the 1950s into the 1970s, many older sheriffs saw the great changes on the way and left office, and some who stayed around followed the old ways of doing things too long and got into trouble. Jess Sweeten quit twice, once to join the circus as a trick shot performer in 1947 and then for good in 1954. "I didn't run in 1954," Sweeten said. "I went with Mobil Oil Company as an investigator. I didn't want any part of it anymore. You were just screwed down too tight."[36] Buck Lane of Wharton County quit in the early 1950s to run for a seat in the U.S. House, but Lane also had other reasons. "I'll tell you the truth," he informed a historian, "one reason I quit was because they was sending a bunch of sheriffs up for violating civil liberties, and I knew they were after me. I said, 'I'm quitting before they get me,' and I did."[37] For other traditional sheriffs, the new complexities of law enforcement had simply taken the zest out of the game. Sheriff W. B. "Blackie" McNerlin retired as Ward County sheriff in 1968, and McNerlin told the *Texas Lawman* editor: "There have been so many changes in these past 29 years. It used to be that we could spend a little time with a suspect and get him to admit his crime. Within a few weeks, he would be tried, convicted, and start paying his dept to society. Now, we have to be so careful about what we say and do while making an arrest, and it is so long before the suspect is tried and convicted and gone through all the appeal courts, that all the fun has gone out of it."[38]

Waves of sheriffs departed at about the time TCLOS went into operation just after 1970 and again when TJSC assumed full authority in 1978. From that time on, veteran sheriffs had to change their ways of doing things, and new sheriffs needed to be quick learners. Slings and snares abounded for the county sheriff as the 1980s progressed, and a lot of them besides S. C. Parker got into trouble. In August 1988, as the fall elections approached, reporter Karen Potter of the *Fort Worth Star-Telegram* surveyed Texas sheriffs to find that 11 of 254 had been indicted, convicted, or forced out of office since the last election and that an additional 6 were under investigation for aiding and abetting drug trafficking in their counties. Furthermore, 32 sheriffs were retiring, the largest number in recent memory, according to Gordon Johnson, executive director of the Sheriffs' Association of Texas, and an additional 46 incumbents had been defeated in primary elections.[39]

By the 1990s the elected sheriff seemed an anomaly among an ever increasing assemblage of appointed, trained, standardized officers, which now included the sheriff's own deputies and jailers. Sheriffs themselves had to submit to standardization—to formal TCLOS training and certification by the end of their second year in office. For critics of the elected officer, such as historian and law enforcement professional Frank Prassel, the change could not have come too soon,[40] but some long-term sheriffs were not so sure. As J. R. Sessions said, "A good sheriff is a buffer from other law enforcement, a good sheriff's gonna protect his people from abuse," and sometimes "mechanical" officers did commit abuses.[41] The sheriff could offer a kinder, gentler mode of law enforcement for rural Texans awash in a rising tide of urbanization. As political scientist Jim Dickson wrote, he could "use his unusual brand of discretion in law enforcement to provide the citizens of his county a cushion of time to decide how much of their old ways can be preserved within a facade of compliance with inevitable and unavoidable adjustments."[42]

Even in the 1990s it was good to have a friend at the courthouse when you got in trouble, someone with "discretion in law enforcement" to discreetly negotiate a subtler justice from the rigid requirements of the law. In

Chief Deputy Tom Brown of Caldwell County during the late 1930s. At that time Brown served under Sheriff Walter Ellison. (Author's collection)

Martin County, Sheriff Dan Saunders refused to fingerprint persons until their formal prosecution, and he had a good reason. "I've seen officers fingerprint four boys and sent their fingerprint cards to the FBI and DPS," Saunders wrote in his journal. "The next morning the county attorney wouldn't take but one complaint and that would be on the driver. There you have three boys with a 'possession' charge on their rap sheet for the rest of their lives."[43]

During research for her 1988 essay on Texas sheriffs in trouble, Karen Potter elicited a telling comment from Bill Pruitt, chief of the DPS Criminal

Law Enforcement division. The ballot box was a sufficient check on the power of sheriffs, Pruitt believed. "You have to recognize an elected position reporting directly to the voter has many safeguards that wouldn't be there if we required certificates of training."[44] Dan Saunders wrote: "A sheriff is the ONLY officer that the public has any say-so about who serves them. FBI agents, U.S. marshals, Liquor Board agents, Texas Rangers, Highway Patrolmen, Game Wardens, and City Police are all appointed. The Sheriff is directly responsible to the people who elect him, and the public doesn't give you much room for error. I think that is the way it should be. It makes a better officer out of you."[45]

NOTES

INTRODUCTION

1. Frank Brunt, taped interview with Thad Sitton, February 20, 1986, Center for American History, Austin, Texas.

2. Paul Recer, "Bill Decker," *Texas Lawman* 34, no. 9 (December 1965): 66.

3. Kent Biffle, "The Men Behind the Star," *Dallas Morning News,* August 28, 1983, 27.

4. Ibid.

5. James G. Dickson, *The Politics of the Texas Sheriff: From Frontier to Bureaucracy,* 2.

6. Ibid.

7. Ibid., 3.

8. Walter H. Anderson, *A Treatise on the Law of Sheriffs, Coroners, and Constables,* 6.

9. Thad Sitton, *Texas High Sheriffs,* 3.

10. Frank Richard Prassel, *The Western Peace Officer,* 119.

11. Davis, "Legal Aspects of the Sheriff's Office," 66–70; F. W. Chatfield and S. M. Sewell, *Texas and the Nation: Civil Government,* 35.

12. Biffle, "The Men Behind the Star," 29.

13. James Buckner Barry, *Buck Barry, Texas Ranger and Frontiersman,* 64.

14. Ralph Semmes Jackson, *Home on the Double Bayou: Memories of an East Texas Ranch,* 23–24.

15. Frank Brunt interview, February 20, 1986.

16. Ibid.

17. Chuck Parsons, *James Madison Brown: Texas Sheriff and Texas Turfman,* 21–56.

18. William Ransom Hogan, *The Texas Republic: A Social and Economic History,* 260–75.

19. C. L. Sonnichsen, *I'll Die Before I'll Run: The Story of the Great Feuds of Texas,* 6.

20. Parsons, *James Madison Brown*, 39.

21. Ibid., 37.

22. Flora G. Bowles, "The History of Trinity County" (master's thesis, University of Texas at Austin, 1928), 53.

23. Sonnichsen, "Feuds," in *The New Handbook of Texas* 2:988.

24. Ibid.

25. Sonnichsen, *I'll Die Before I'll Run*, 7.

26. Ibid., 6.

27. Bowles, "History of Trinity County," 94.

28. Harold Preece, *Lone Star Man: Ira Aten, Last of the Old Texas Rangers*, 199.

29. Ibid., 188–97.

30. Joseph H. Combs, *Gunsmoke in the Redlands*, 3.

31. Ibid., 3–201.

32. William Finnegan, "Deep East Texas," *The New Yorker* 70, no. 26 (August 22 and 29, 1994): 72–80.

33. Steve Cherry, "A History of the Sheriffs of Caldwell County," *Sheriffs' Association of Texas Magazine* 2, no. 1 (First Quarter 1982): 11.

34. T. Brantley Barker, taped interview with Thad Sitton, March 10, 1986, Center for American History, Austin, Texas.

35. H. F. Fenton, taped interview with Thad Sitton, March 13, 1986, Center for American History, Austin, Texas.

36. Truman Maddox, taped interview with Thad Sitton, March 25, 1986, Center for American History, Austin, Texas.

37. Ibid.

38. Ibid.

CHAPTER ONE

1. Truman Maddox interview, March 25, 1986.

2. Ibid.

3. Ed Darnell, taped interview with James G. Dickenson, 1979, James G. Dickenson personal collection.

4. Leon Jones, taped interview with Thad Sitton, February 14, 1986, author's personal collection.

5. H. F. Fenton interview, March 13, 1986.

6. Aubrey Cole, taped interview with Thad Sitton, August 14, 1995, Center for American History, Austin, Texas.

7. Quoted in S. K. Bardwell, "Sheriff Recalls Good Ol' Days," *Waco Tribune-Herald*, May 27, 1985.

8. Ibid.

9. Bob Gladney, taped interview with Thad Sitton, October 17, 1986, Center for American History, Austin, Texas.

10. T. W. Lane, taped interview with Thad Sitton, October 3, 1986, Center for American History, Austin, Texas.

11. H. F. Fenton interview, March 13, 1986.

12. Gaston Boykin, taped interview with Thad Sitton, Center for American History, Austin, Texas.

13. Leon Jones interview, February 14, 1986.

14. I. R. Hoskins, taped interview with Thad Sitton, March 27, 1986, Center for American History, Austin, Texas.

15. Aubrey Cole interview, August 14, 1995.

16. Chuck Parsons, *James Madison Brown: Texas Sheriff and Texas Turfman*, 56.

17. Jim Scarborough, taped interview with Thad Sitton, April 28, 1986, Center for American History, Austin.

18. Frank Richard Prassel, *The Western Peace Officer*, 51.

19. H. Gordon Frost and John H. Jenkins, *"I'm Frank Hamer": The Life of a Texas Peace Officer*, 84.

20. Jess Sweeten, taped interview with James G. Dickenson, 1979, James G. Dickenson personal collection.

21. Prassel, *Western Peace Officer*, 111.

22. Quoted in Albert Bigelow Payne, *Captain Bill McDonald, Texas Ranger: A Story of Frontier Reform*, 235–36.

23. Carl Busch, "The Incredible Mr. Busch," *Chinquapin* 2, no. 5 (1980): 51.

24. Ibid., 52.

25. Ibid., 55.

26. Lee Simmons, *Assignment Huntsville: Memoirs of a Texas Prison Official*, 18.

27. Quoted in *Sheriff's Association of Texas Magazine* 25, no. 7 (September 1951): 68.

28. William W. Sterling, *Trails and Trials of a Texas Ranger*, 225.

29. Gaston Boykin, taped interview with Thad Sitton, February 26, 1986, Center for American History, Austin, Texas.

30. J. R. Sessions, taped interview with Thad Sitton, November 6, 1997, Center for American History, Austin, Texas.

31. *Sheriffs' Association of Texas Magazine* 19, no. 11 (February 1951): 89.

32. Gaston Boykin, taped interview with Thad Sitton, February 10, 1986, Center for American History, Austin, Texas.

33. Jim Scarborough interview, April 28, 1986.

34. Gaston Boykin interview, February 10, 1986.

35. Corbett Akins, taped interview with Thad Sitton, May 4, 1986, Center for American History, Austin, Texas.

36. Gaston Boykin interview, February 10, 1986.

37. H. F. Fenton interview, March 13, 1986; *Sheriffs' Association of Texas Magazine* 17, no. 3 (June 1948): 74.

38. Busch, "The Incredible Mr. Busch," 52.

39. *Sheriffs' Association of Texas Magazine* 1, no. 2 (March 1931): 7.

40. Jim Scarborough interview, April 28, 1986.

41. Quoted in "Wallace Riddell," *Burnet County Bulletin,* August 10, 1974.

42. I. R. Hoskins interview, July 21, 1986.

43. H. F. Fenton interview, March 13, 1986.

44. Roy A. Herrington, taped interview with Thad Sitton, March 8, 1986, Center for American History, Austin, Texas.

45. George Dolan, "Haskell County Sheriff Has Eyes for the Job," *Fort Worth Star-Telegram,* May 8, 1961.

46. Wesley W. Stout, "The Law According to Buckshot Lane," *Saturday Evening Post,* July 14, 1951, 36.

47. Dan Saunders, *Trails and Trials of a Small Town Sheriff,* 42.

48. Ibid.

49. I. R. Hoskins interview, July 21, 1986.

50. Ibid.

51. H. F. Fenton interview, March 13, 1986.

52. Leon Jones interview, February 14, 1986.

53. Corbett Akins interview, May 4, 1986.

54. Gaston Boykin interview, February 10, 1986.

55. Corbett Akins interview, May 4, 1986.

56. James M. Day, *Captain Clint Peoples,* 60.

57. Quoted in Thad Sitton and James H. Conrad, *Nameless Towns: Texas Sawmill Communities, 1880–1942,* 125.

58. Peggy Walker, *George Humphreys 6666: Cowboy and Lawman,* 19.

59. Quoted in Tanner Lane, "Veteran West Texas Lawman Sees Many Changes in Law Enforcement," *Lubbock Avalanche-Journal,* September 24, 1961.

60. Day, *Captain Clint Peoples,* 57; Jim Scarborough interview, June 25, 1986.

61. Ibid.

62. William Finnegan, "Deep East Texas," *The New Yorker* 70, no. 26 (August 22 and 29, 1994): 74.

63. Frank Brunt interview, February 20, 1986.

64. H. F. Fenton interview, March 13, 1986.

65. T. Brantley Barker interview, March 10, 1986.

66. *Sheriffs' Association of Texas Magazine* 17, no. 4 (July 1948): 15.

67. Wallace Patton Riddell, personal communication, January 20, 1998.

68. Loretta Fenton, taped interview with Thad Sitton, June 2, 1986.

69. Leona Bannister Bruce, *Four Years in a Coleman Jail: Daughter of Two Sheriffs,* 170.

70. *Sheriffs' Association of Texas Magazine* 10, no. 4 (June 1944): 72.

71. Ibid., 17, no. 9 (December 1948): 21.

72. Lon Evans, *The Purple Lawman: From Horned Frog to High Sheriff,* 74–78.

73. Bob Gladney interview, October, 17, 1986.

74. H. F. Fenton interview, March 13, 1986.

75. I. R. Hoskins interview, March 27, 1986.

76. Leon Jones interview, March 15, 1986.

77. Quoted in Bardwell, "Sheriff Recalls Good Ol' Days."

78. Day, *Captain Clint Peoples*, 15.

79. Quoted in Tom Brown, taped interview with Jim Lutz, 1977, Center for American History, Austin, Texas.

80. Aubrey Cole interview, August 14, 1995.

81. John Moulder, "Best Civil Deputy Retires from Duty," *San Angelo Standard-Times*, December 15, 1961.

82. Tom Brown interview, 1977.

83. Truman Maddox interview, March 25, 1986.

84. Gaston Boykin interview, February 10, 1986.

85. Saunders, *Trails and Trials of a Small Town Sheriff*, 60.

86. Quoted in Riddell, personal communication, January 20, 1998.

87. *Sheriffs' Association of Texas Magazine* 15, no. 11 (February 1947): 105.

88. Holly W. Osborne, "Long Time Colorado County Deputy Still Going Strong," *Texas Lawman* 46, no. 2 (May 1977): 40.

89. *Sheriffs' Association of Texas Magazine* 27, no. 1 (March 1958): 10.

90. E. A. "Dogie" Wright, self-interview, undated, E. A. "Dogie" Wright Collection, Center for American History, Austin, Texas.

91. Jim Scarborough interview, June 25, 1986.

92. Gaston Boykin interview, February 10, 1986.

93. Charlie Munson, *Mr. Charlie: Memoir of a Texas Lawman, 1902–1910*, 44; Bill Duncan, "'Cap' Kennedy, Veteran Lawman, Retires," *Corpus Christi Caller-Times*, April 18, 1962.

94. Saunders, *Trails and Trials of a Small Town Sheriff*, 50.

95. Ibid., 47.

96. T. Brantley Barker interview, March 10, 1986.

97. Jess Sweeten interview, 1979.

98. Riddell, personal communication, January 20, 1998.

99. T. W. Lane, "The Inimitable Style of Sheriff T. W. Lane," *Wharton Spectator*, January 30, 1950.

100. Truman Maddox interview, "March 25, 1986.

101. I. W. Hoskins interview, March 27, 1986.

102. William Lester Gunn, taped interview with Thad Sitton, October 23, 1986, Center for American History, Austin, Texas.

103. Gaston Boykin interview, February 10, 1986.

104. Cherry, "Sheriffs of Caldwell County," 9.

105. Frank Brunt interview, February 20, 1986.

106. *Texas Lawman* 29, no. 11 (February 1961): 34.

107. William Lester Gunn interview, October 23, 1986.

108. Jess Sweeten interview, 1979.

109. Quoted in Tom Brown interview, 1977.

110. Truman Maddox interview, March 25, 1986.

111. H. F. Fenton interview, March 13, 1986.

112. *Sheriffs' Association of Texas Magazine* 24, no. 2 (April 1955): 2; 27, no. 10 (January 1959): 16.

113. Quoted in Saunders, *Trails and Trials of a Small Town Sheriff*, 51.

114. H. F. Fenton interview, March 13, 1986.

115. Corbett Akins interview, May 4, 1986.

116. Quoted in Day, *Captain Clint Peoples*, 31.

117. *Sheriffs' Association of Texas Magzine* 12, no. 9 (December 1943): 31.

118. H. F. Fenton interview, March 13, 1986.

119. Lane, "Inimitable Style," January 5, 1951.

120. *Texas Lawman* 40, no. 8 (November 1971): 64.

121. Lewis C. Rigler and Judyth Wagner Rigler, *Reflections of a Texas Ranger Private*, 48; *Sheriffs' Association of Texas Magazine* 17, no. 10 (January 1949): 17.

122. Roy Herrington interview, March 8, 1986.

123. Day, *Captain Clint Peoples*, 120.

124. Brownson Malsch, *Captain M. T. Gonzaullas: Lone Wolf*, 107; Frost and Jenkins, *"I'm Frank Hamer,"* 268.

125. Carlos Vidal Greth, "The Legend of Joaquin Jackson," *Austin American-Statesman*, August 10, 1986.

126. Roy L. Wade, "Money Mad Mechanic Poisons Wife," *Sheriffs' Association of Texas Magazine* 11, no. 4 (July 1942): 18–20.

127. Ibid., 10, no. 7 (September 1941): 61.

128. J. R. Sessions interview, November 6, 1997.

129. John R. Lightfoot, taped interview with Thad Sitton, December 23, 1993, Center for American History, Austin, Texas.

130. Roy Herrington interview, March 8, 1986.

131. Billy Platt, taped interview with Thad Sitton, November 14, 1992, Center for East Texas Studies, Stephen F. Austin State University, Nacogdoches; John R. Lightfoot interview, December 23, 1993.

132. *Sheriffs' Association of Texas Magazine* 19, no. 4 (July 1950): 12; 26, no. 9 (May 1957): 29.

133. Quoted in Joe G. Goodson, taped interview with Thad Sitton, October 28, 1997, Center for American History, Austin, Texas.

134. Lane, "Inimitable Style," September 1, 1950.

135. *Sheriffs' Association of Texas Magazine* 23, no. 5 (August 1954): 96.

136. Gaston Boykin interview, Febuary 26, 1986.

137. Payne, *Captain Bill McDonald*, 31.

138. John Lightfoot interview, December 23, 1993; Ed Darnell interview, 1979.

139. Gaston Boykin interview, Febuary 26, 1986.

140. Day, *Captain Clint Peoples*, 35; *Texas Lawman* 33, no. 6 (September 1964): 24.

141. *Texas Lawman* 31, no. 9 (December 1962): 46.

142. *Sheriffs' Association of Texas Magazine* 15, no. 1 (April 1946): 51.

143. *Texas Lawman* 31, no. 7 (October 1962): 12.

144. Henry Billingsley, unpublished memoir, Lufkin Public Library, Lufkin, Texas, n.d.

145. *Sheriffs' Association of Texas Magazine* 18, no. 1 (April 1949): 96; 18, no. 8 (November 1949): 9.

146. Roy Herrington interview, March 8, 1986.

147. James G. Dickson, "Communication Without Understanding: The Informal Interplay of Politics in Texas County Government," in *The Challenge of Texas Politics: Texts and Readings*, ed. Earnest Crain, Charles Deeton, and William Earl Maxwell, 350.

148. Evans, *The Purple Lawman*, 31.

149. Jess Sweeten interview, 1979.

150. Ed Darnell interview, 1979.

151. T. W. Lane interview, December 15, 1986.

152. Busch, "The Incredible Mr. Busch," 52.

153. *Sheriffs' Association of Texs Magazine* 15, no. 2 (May 1946): 47.

154. Ibid., 24, no. 2 (April 1955): 87.

155. *Texas Lawman* 32, no. 11 (April 1963): 33.

156. *Sheriffs' Association of Texas Magazine* 13, no. 8 (November 1944): 15.

157. Ibid., 22, no. 9 (September 1953): 100.

158. Ibid., 13, no. 8 (August 1944): 7.

159. Ibid., 24, no. 7 (September 1955): 14.

160. Saunders, *Trails and Trials of a Small Town Sheriff*, 48.

161. Joe Goodson interview, October 28, 1997.

162. Saunders, *Trails and Trials of a Small Town Sheriff*, 48; *Texas Lawman* 30, no. 3 (June 1961): 8.

163. *Sheriffs' Association of Texas Magazine* 18, no. 6 (September 49): 40; 28, no. 3 (June 1959): 37.

164. Lane, "Inimitable Style," January 20, 1950.

165. *Sheriffs' Association of Texas Magazine* 25, no. 12 (February 1957): 21.

166. Ibid., 20, no. 8 (November 1951): 97.

167. Ibid., 25, no. 10 (January 1957): 8.

168. Ibid., 24, no. 5 (July 1955): 43.

169. Truman Maddox interview, March 25, 1986.

170. *Sheriffs' Association of Texas Magazine* 28, no. 2 (May 1959): 80.

171. Tom Brown interview, 1977.

172. Busch, "The Incredible Mr. Busch," 50; Joe Goodson interview, October 28, 1997.

173. *Sheriffs' Association of Texas Magazine* 17, no. 10 (January 1949): 3.

174. *Texas Lawman* 30, no. 8 (November 1961): 7.

175. Ibid., 34, no. 11 (February 1966): 7.

176. Ibid., 46, no. 1 (April 1977): 7.

177. Ibid., 29, no. 3 (June 1960): 11.

178. Frank Brunt interview, February 21, 1986.

179. Quoted in *Texas Lawman* 32, no. 12 (March 1964): 7.

180. Ed Darnell interview, 1979.

181. Quoted in Selden Hayle, "Ten Commandments and Common Sense Guide Sheriff Rufe Jordan," *Amarillo Daily News*, October 29, 1964.

182. Dick J. Reavis, "Howdy Son, I'm the Law In This County: Texas Sheriffs in All Their Glory," *Texas Monthly* 12, no. 11 (1984): 152.

183. Quoted in Finnegan, "Deep East Texas," 77.

184. Ibid., 196.

185. Gaston Boykin interview, February 10, 1986.

186. T. W. Lane interview, October 3, 1986.

187. Stout, "The Law According to Buckshot Lane," 34.

188. Lane, "Inimitable Style," August 5, 1949.

189. Ibid., October 28, 1949.

190. Ibid., December 5, 1947.

CHAPTER TWO

1. Wallace Patton "Pat" Riddell, personal communication to Thad Sitton, January 20, 1998.

2. Leona Bannister Bruce, *Four Years in a Coleman Jail: Daughter of Two Sheriffs*, 39.

3. Ibid., 96.

4. Loretta Fenton interview, June 2, 1986.

5. E. A. "Dogie" Wright self-interview, undated.

6. Ibid.

7. Jim Scarborough interview, April 28, 1986.

8. Quoted in Loretta Fenton interview, June 2, 1986.

9. E. A. Wright self-interview, undated.

10. Loretta Fenton interview, June 2, 1986.

11. H. F. Fenton interview, March 13, 1986.

12. Ibid.

13. T. W. Lane, "The Inimitable Style of T. W. Lane," *Wharton Spectator*, August 19, 1949.

14. Nat Henderson, "Burnet County Sheriff Wallace Riddell," *Austin American-Statesman*, August 7, 1974.

15. Quoted in "Sheriff Wallace Riddell and Family," *Marble Falls Highlander*, June 29, 1972.

16. Riddell, personal communication, January 20, 1998.

17. "Sheriff Wallace Riddell and Family," *Marble Falls Highlander*, June 29, 1972.

18. Bruce, *Four Years in a Coleman Jail*, 34.

19. Ibid., 38.

20. Gaston Boykin interview, February 26, 1986.

21. *Sheriffs' Association of Texas Magazine* 15, no. 12 (March 1947): 8.

22. Bruce Smith, *Rural Crime Control*, 53.

23. Gaston Boykin interview, February 26, 1986.

24. *Sheriffs' Association of Texas Magazine* 10, no. 3 (May 1941): 9; 21, no. 2 (May 1952): 80.

25. Gaston Boykin interview, February 26, 1986.

26. Joe Goodson interview, October 28, 1987.

27. Riddell, personal communication, January 20, 1998.

28. Loretta Fenton interview, June 2, 1986.

29. G. W. Blanton, "Trials and Tribulations of the Jail," *Denison Herald*, February 7, 1963.

30. *Sheriffs' Association of Texas Magazine* 21, no. 8 (November 1952): 42.

31. Lane, "Inimitable Style," December 9, 23, 1949.

32. I. R. Hoskins interview, March 27, 1986.

33. William Finnegan, "Deep East Texas," *The New Yorker* 70, no. 26 (August 22 and 29, 1994): 76.

34. Quoted in Martha Spinks, "Sheriff and Mrs. Bill Eddins Move after Twenty Years," *Winkler County News*, May 29, 1967.

35. Riddell, personal communication, January 20, 1998.

36. Dan Saunders, *Trails and Trials of a Small Town Sheriff*, 107.

37. Ibid., 70.

38. Ibid., 108.

39. Quoted in Dick J. Reavis, "Howdy, Son. I'm the Law in This County: Texas Sheriffs in All Their Glory," *Texas Monthly* 12, no. 11 (1984): 154.

40. William E. Stone, "The Suicide Problem in Texas Jails," *Texas Lawman* 53, no. 6 (June 1984): 5.

41. Saunders, *Trails and Trials of a Small Town Sheriff*, 132.

42. Lane, "Inimitable Style," May 5, 1948.

43. Saunders, *Trails and Trials of a Small Town Sheriff*, 132.

44. *Sheriffs' Association of Texas Magazine* 15, no. 1 (April 1946): 56.

45. Ibid., 21, no. 9 (December 1952): 1.

46. Lane, "Inimitable Style," November 4, 1947.

47. Ibid., January 27, June 16, 1950; January 5, 1951.

48. Lane, "Inimitable Style," January 27, 1950.

49. H. F. Fenton interview, March 13, 1986.

50. Ibid.

51. *Sheriffs' Association of Texas Magazine* 25, no. 12 (March 1956): 62.

52. *Texas Lawman* 31, no. 5 (August 1962): 48.

53. Ibid., 36, no. 1 (August 1962): 48.

54. *Sheriffs' Association of Texas Magazine* 26, no. 12 (February 1958): 28.

55. *Texas Lawman* 30, no. 4 (July 1961): 71.

56. Clarke Keyes, "Problems Confront Hopkins County Sheriff's Department," *Sulfur Springs News-Telegram*, September 16, 1962.

57. Roy Herrington interview, March 8, 1986.

58. *Sheriffs' Association of Texas Magazine* 18, no. 5 (August 1949): 23.

59. Ibid., 15, no. 5 (August 1946): 39.

60. Ibid., 25, no. 1 (March 1956): 36.

61. *Texas Lawman* 31, no. 6 (September 1962): 9; *Sheriffs' Association of Texas Magazine* 20, no. 8 (November 1951): 26.

62. Lane, "Inimitable Style," July 15, 1949.

63. *Texas Lawman* 33, no. 6 (September 1964): 24.

64. Ibid., 33, no. 1 (February 1965): 19.

65. Lon Evans, taped interview with James G. Dickenson, 1979, James G. Dickenson personal collection.

66. Lane, "Inimitable Style," August 5, 1949.

67. Tom Brown interview, 1977.

68. I. R. Hoskins interview, March 27, 1986.

69. Frank Richard Prassel, *The Western Peace Officer*, 123.

70. *Sheriffs' Association of Texas Magazine* 13, no. 12 (March 1945): 42.

71. *Texas Lawman* 30, no. 4 (July 1961): 5.

72. Tom Brown interview, 1977.

73. Lon Evans interview, 1979.

74. H. F. Fenton interview, March 13, 1986.

75. Truman Maddox interview, April 2, 1986.

76. T. W. Lane interview, December 15, 1986.

77. Finnegan, "Deep East Texas," 79.

78. Quoted in ibid., 76.

79. Quoted in ibid., 80.

80. J. R. Sessions interview, November 6, 1997.

81. Leon Jones interview, February 14, 1986.

82. Lewis C. Rigler and Judyth Wagner Rigler, *Reflections of a Texas Ranger Private*, 79.

83. Aubrey Cole interview, August 14, 1995.

84. Jess Sweeten interview, 1979.

85. Frank Brunt interview, February 20, 1986.

86. Jess Sweeten interview, 1979.

87. *Sheriffs' Association of Texas Magazine* 16, no. 8 (November 1947): 14.

88. Gaston Boykin interview, February 26, 1986.

89. Saunders, *Trails and Trials of a Small Town Sheriff*, 61.

90. Jim Scarborough interview, June 25, 1986.

91. B. Rufus Jordan, taped interview with Thad Sitton, April 18, 1986, Center for American History, Austin, Texas.

92. *Sheriffs' Association of Texas Magazine* 8, no. 3 (May 1939): 35.

93. Jim Byrd, "Beer Can Boulevard," *Sheriffs' Association of Texas Magazine* 21, no. 1 (April 1952): 84.

94. Frank Brunt interview, February 20, 1986.

95. I. R. Hoskins interview, March 27, 1986.

96. Charlie Harber interview, February 21, 1992.

97. Joe Goodson interview, October 28, 1997.

98. Saunders, *Trails and Trials of a Small Town Sheriff*, 66.

99. Ibid., 92.

100. Finnegan, "Deep East Texas," 76.

101. Truman Maddox interview, March 25, 1986.

102. Frank Brunt interview, February 21, 1986.

103. Truman Maddox interview, March 25, 1986.

104. Jim Scarborough interview, April 28, 1986.

105. Frank Brunt interview, February 20, 1986.

106. Truman Maddox interview, March 25, 1986.

107. Walter Fellers, taped interview with Thad Sitton, February 28, 1986, Center for American History, Austin, Texas.

108. Gaston Boykin interview, February 10, 1986.

109. Brantley Barker interview, March 10, 1986.

110. H. F. Fenton interview, March 13, 1986.

111. Christopher Long, "Jess Sweeten," in *The New Handbook of Texas* 6:172.

112. Allan Sigvard Lindquist, *Jess Sweeten, Texas Lawman*, 73–120.

113. T. W. Lane interview, October 3, 1986.

114. Ibid.; *Sheriffs' Association of Texas Magazine* 21, no. 7 (October 1952): 75.

115. Corbett Akins interview, May 4, 1986.

116. T. W. Lane interview, October 3, 1986; Roy Herrington interview, March 8, 1986.

117. Peggy Walker, *George Humphreys 6666: Cowboy and Lawman*, 29.

118. Bill Douthat, "Sheriff's Tyranny Echoes through Tiny Realm," *Austin American-Statesman*, August 6, 1985.

119. *Sheriffs' Association of Texas Magazine* 14, no. 5 (August 1945): 67.

120. Tom Brown interview, 1977.

121. Henry Billingsley, unpublished memoir, Lufkin Public Library, Lufkin, Texas, n.d.; Henry C. Fuller, "*A Texas Sheriff*," 84.

122. *Sheriffs' Association of Texas Magazine* 2, no. 4 (February 1933): 8.

123. Aubrey Cole interview, August 14, 1995.

124. Frank Brunt interview, February 21, 1986.

125. Jess Sweeten interview, 1979.

126. This sheriff wished to remain anonymous.

127. Corbett Akins interview, May 4, 1986.

128. T. W. Lane interview, October 3, 1986.

129. Ibid.

130. Ibid.

131. Lane, "Inimitable Style," November 25, 1949.

132. Ibid., June 13, 1947.

133. Ibid., June 27, 1942; February 20, 1951.

134. Ibid., March 19, 1948.

135. Ibid., May 30, 1947; February 23, 1951.

136. Ibid., May 13, 1949.

137. Ibid., May 14, 1948.

138. Quoted in Reavis, "Howdy, Son. I'm the Law in This County," 156; Leon Jones interview, February 14, 1986.

139. *Sheriffs' Association of Texas Magazine* 20, no. 10 (March 1952): 12.

140. E. A. Wright self-interview, undated.

141. Loretta Fenton interview, June 2, 1986.

142. Tom Brown interview, 1977.

143. Ibid.

144. Saunders, *Trails and Trials of a Small Town Sheriff,* 126.

145. Truman Maddox interview, April 2, 1986.

146. Jim Scarborough interview, April 28, 1986.

147. Riddell, personal communication, January 20, 1998.

148. Fuller, *"A Texas Sheriff,"* 63.

149. James D. Allred and David Allred, "Imprints in Sidewalk Recall Colorful Sheriff," *Corpus Christi Caller-Times,* July 15, 1956.

150. Jim Scarborough interview, April 28, 1986.

151. John Lightfoot interview, December 23, 1993.

152. *Sheriffs' Association of Texas Magazine* 18, no. 6 (September 1949): 5.

153. Ibid., 22, no. 4 (July 1953): 56.

154. Ibid., 23, no. 5 (August 1954): 18.

155. Ibid., 24, no. 2 (May 1955): 12.

156. Wesley W. Stout, "The Law According to Buckshot Lane," *Saturday Evening Post,* July 14, 1951, 34.

157. Bernard Brister, "Frank Hunt of San Patricio County Had Varied Career," *Sheriffs' Association of Texas Magazine* 10, no. 2 (April 1941): 10.

158. Saunders, *Trails and Trials of a Small Town Sheriff,* 49.

159. Ibid., 63.

160. Frank Brunt interview, February 21, 1986.

161. Quoted in Thad Sitton and James H. Conrad, *Nameless Towns: Texas Sawmill Communities, 1880–1942,* 98.

162. *Sheriffs' Association of Texas Magazine* 18, no. 4 (July 1949): 70.

163. Ibid., 9, no. 9 (November 1940): 36.

164. Ibid., 15, no. 10 (January 1947): 23.

165. Jess Sweeten interview, 1979.

166. Long, "Jess Sweeten," 172.

167. *Texas Lawman* 30, no. 3 (June 1961): 2–3.

168. Jim Scarborough interview, April 28, 1986; Stan Redding, "Living Legends of the Law," *Houston Chronicle,* March 5, 1972; Corbett Akins interview, May 4, 1986.

169. Gaston Boykin interview, February 10, 1986.

170. Billingsley, unpublished memoir, undated.

171. Frank Brunt interview, February 21, 1986.

172. Jess Sweeten interview, 1979.

173. Carl Busch, "The Incredible Mr. Busch," *Chinquapin* 2, no. 5 (1980): 55.

174. Jim Scarborough interview, June 25, 1986.

175. Quoted in *Sheriffs' Association of Texas Magazine* 20, no. 12 (March 1952): 27.

176. Quoted in "Candidate Retires from Sheriff's Race," *Bee Picayune,* May 15, 1952.

177. Jim Scarborough interview, April 28, 1986.

178. *Texas Lawman* 38, no. 10 (January 1970): 8–9.

179. Ted Hinton, *Ambush: The Real Story of Bonnie and Clyde,* 51.

180. *Sheriffs' Association of Texas Magazine* 4, no. 2 (February 1935): 6.

181. Ibid., 8, no. 2 (April 1939): 7.

182. *Texas Lawman* 29, no. 6 (September 1960): 58.

183. J. R. Sessions interview, November 6, 1997.

184. *Sheriffs' Association of Texas Magazine* 28, no. 3 (June 1959): 54.

185. Ibid., 17, no. 11 (February 1949): 37; 18, no. 2 (May 1949): 75.

186. Frank Brunt interview, February 20, 1986.

187. *Texas Lawman* 32, no. 7 (October 1963): 62.

188. Ibid., 31, no. 6 (September 1962): 26.

189. James M. Day, *Captain Clint Peoples,* 31.

190. *Texas Lawman* 38, no. 8 (November 1969): 6.

191. Gaston Boykin interview, February 26, 1986; *Sheriffs' Association of Texas Magazine* 26, no. 9 (November 1957): 6.

192. Jerry Turner, "Uncle Bud: A Texas Prison Legend," *Mexia Daily News,* October 24, 1997.

193. Riddell, personal communication, January 20, 1998.

194. William Lester Gunn interview, October 23, 1986.

195. Loretta Fenton interview, June 2, 1986.

CHAPTER THREE

1. Truman Maddox interview, March 25, 1986.

2. J. R. Sessions interview November 6, 1997.

3. James G. Dickson, *The Politics of the Texas Sheriff: From Frontier to Bureaucracy,* 5.

4. Walter H. Anderson, *A Treatise on the Law of Sheriffs, Coronors, and Constables,* 6.

5. Leona Bannister Bruce, *Four Years in a Coleman Jail: Daughter of Two Sheriffs,* 22.

6. H. F. Fenton interview, March 13, 1986.

7. *Sheriffs' Association of Texas Magazine* 15, no. 10 (January 1947): 61.

8. T. W. Lane, "The Inimitable Style of Sheriff T. W. Lane," *Wharton Spectator,* April 28, 1950.

9. Quoted in Thad Sitton and James H. Conrad, *Nameless Towns: Texas Sawmill Communities, 1880–1942,* 98.

10. Quoted in Thad Sitton and Dan K. Utley, *From Can See to Can't: Texas Cotton Farmers on the Southern Prairies,* 244.

11. Henry Billingsley, unpublished memoir, Lufkin Public Library, Lufkin, Texas, n.d.

12. T. W. Lane interview, October 3, 1986.

13. Lane, "Inimitable Style," July 30, 1948.

14. Ibid., July 18, 1947.

15. *Sheriffs' Association of Texas Magazine* 18, no. 3 (June 1949): 90.

16. Ibid., 19, no. 2 (May 1950): 37.

17. Ibid., 20, no. 6 (September 1951): 97.

18. Billingsley, unpublished memoir.

19. Lane, "Inimitable Style," August 19, 1949.

20. Ibid., July 15, 1949.

21. *Sheriffs' Association of Texas Magazine* 11, no. 2 (May 1942): 13.

22. Ibid., 26, no. 6 (August 1957): 22.

23. Aubrey Cole interview, August 14, 1995.

24. Lewis C. Rigler and Judyth Wagner Rigler, *Reflections of a Texas Ranger Private*, 80.

25. James M. Day, *Captain Clint Peoples*, 157.

26. Quoted in "Authorities Close Chicken Ranch," *El Paso Times*, August 2, 1973.

27. Quoted in ibid.

28. Gary Cartwright, *Galveston: A History of the Island*, 242.

29. Ibid.

30. Ibid., 244.

31. Day, *Captain Clint Peoples*, 85.

32. Cartwright, *Galveston*, 245.

33. *Sheriffs' Association of Texas Magazine* 25, no. 7 (September 1956): 58.

34. Joe Sharp, "Liquor Control in Texas," ibid., 8, no. 7 (September 1939): 17–18.

35. Ibid., 10, no. 3 (May 1941): 14; 20, no. 1 (April 1951): 82.

36. Leon Jones interview, March 15, 1986.

37. Wallace Patton Riddell, personal communication to Thad Sitton, January 20, 1998.

38. Leon Jones interview, March 15, 1986.

39. Billingsley, unpublished memoir.

40. Quoted in Thad Sitton, *Backwoodsmen*, 126.

41. Quoted in ibid., 131–32.

42. R. E. McWilliams, "Observations on Crime," *Sheriffs' Association of Texas Magazine* 1, no. 3 (July 1931): 5; *Sheriffs' Association of Texas Magazine* 10, no. 1 (August 1932): 8.

43. Sitton, *Backwoodsmen*, 128.

44. *Sheriffs' Association of Texas Magazine* 10, no. 5 (July 1941): 8.

45. Quoted in Sitton, *Backwoodsmen*, 128.

46. Quoted in ibid.

47. Roy Herrington interview, March 8, 1986.

48. Day, *Captain Clint Peoples*, 26.

49. Sitton, *Backwoodsmen*, 130.

50. Quoted in ibid., 131.

51. Ibid.

52. Brownson Malsch, *Captain M. T. Gonzaullas: Lone Wolf*, 17–23.

53. *Sheriffs' Association of Texas Magazine* 10, no. 7 (September 1941): 13.

54. Kent Biffle, "The Man Behind the Star," *Dallas Morning News*, August 28, 1983.

55. H. F. Fenton interview, March 13, 1986.

56. Frank Brunt interview, February 20, 1986.

57. Jess Sweeten interview, 1979; *Sheriffs' Association of Texas Magazine* 18, no. 9 (December 1949): 18; Frank Brunt interview, February 20, 1986.

58. Billingsley, unpublished memoir.

59. William Finnegan, "Deep East Texas," *The New Yorker* 70, no. 26 (August 22 and 29, 1994): 75.

60. Billngsley, unpublished memoir.

61. John Schoellkopf, "Veteran Dallas County Lawman Retires," *Dallas Times-Herald*, February 28, 1962.

62. *Sheriffs' Association of Texas Magazine* 12, no. 10 (January 1944): 7.

63. Ibid., 20, no. 1 (April 1951): 57.

64. Quoted in ibid., 21, no. 1 (April 1952): 70.

65. Porforio Flores, taped interview with Thad Sitton, June 27, 1986, Center for American History, Austin, Texas.

66. Quoted in Herman Kelly, "Texas Lawman," *Texas Highways* 20, no. 9 (September 1973): 4.

67. Quoted in Bob Ybarra, "Border Patrolmen Recall Many Gun Fights," *El Paso Herald-Post*, May 21, 1974.

68. Quoted in Georgie Meredith Hall, *Life of R. T. Hall*, 38.

69. William W. Sterling, *Trails and Trials of a Texas Ranger*, 66.

70. Quoted in Frank Richard Prassel, *The Western Peace Officer*, 60.

71. Carl Busch, "The Incredible Mr. Busch," *Chinquapin* 2, no. 5 (1980): 50.

72. Joe Goodson interview, October 28, 1997.

73. Sterling, *Trails and Trials of a Texas Ranger*, 60.

74. H. Gordan Frost and John H. Jenkins, *"I'm Frank Hamer": The Life of a Texas Peace Officer* 104.

75. Ibid., 143.

76. Ibid., 145.

77. Ibid., 148.

78. Quoted in Malsch, *Captain M. T. Gonzaullas*, 79.

79. Rufe Jordan interview, April 18, 1986.

80. Sterling, *Trails and Trials of a Texas Ranger*, 229.

81. *Sheriffs' Association of Texas Magazine* 6, no. 11 (November 1937): 1.

82. Day, *Captain Clint Peoples*, 17.

83. Quoted in *Texas Lawman* 36, no. 11 (February 1968): 26.

84. Tom Brown interview, 1977.

85. Grover Williams, taped interview with Dan Utley, 1991, Oral History Institute of Baylor University, Waco, Texas.

86. Quoted in Sitton and Conrad, *Nameless Towns*, 73.

87. A number of persons reported this story to researchers at the Caldwell County Historical Commission during the late 1970s.

88. Quoted in Sitton and Utley, *From Can See to Can't*, 52.

89. Lane, "Inimitable Style," March 1, 1946.

90. T. W. Lane interview, December 15, 1986; Corbett Akins interview, May 4, 1986.

91. Steven A. Reich, "Soldiers of Democracy: Black Texans and the Fight for Citizenship, 1917–1921," *Journal of American History* 82 (March 1996): 13; Troy C. Crenshaw, *Texas Blackland Heritage*, 85–86.

92. Lane, "Inimitable Style," February 2, 23, 1945; July 27, 1945.

93. Ibid., August 17, 1945.

94. Wesley W. Stout, "The Law According to Buckshot Lane," *Saturday Evening Post*, July 14, 1951, 36.

95. Jess Sweeten interview, 1979.

96. Lane, "Inimitable Style," June 3, 1949.

97. Quoted in Dee Azadian, ed., *Earth Has No Sorrows*, 84.

98. Ibid.

99. Dan Saunders, *Trails and Trials of a Small Town Sheriff*, 60.

100. Jess Sweeten interview, 1979.

101. Roy Herrington interview, March 8, 1986.

102. Corbett Akins interview, May 4, 1986.

103. Lane, "Inimitable Style," May 12, 1950.

104. Tom Brown interview, 1977.

105. Corbett Akins interview, May 4, 1986.

106. William Lester Gunn interview, October 23, 1986.

107. Lane, "Inimitable Style," October 11, 1946.

108. Quoted in Danalynn Recer, "Patroling the Borders of Race, Gender, and Class: The Lynching Ritual and Texas Nationalism" (master's thesis, University of Texas at Austin, 1994), 179.

109. David W. Livingston, "Lynching of Negroes in Texas, 1900–1925," (master's thesis, East Texas State University, 1972), 42. These generalizations about lynchings are based on the many case studies of Texas lynchings in David Livingston's master's thesis and the master's thesis of Danalynn Recer, "Patroling the Borders of Race, Gender, and Class."

CHAPTER FOUR

1. Ronnie Bookman, "Hardeman County Sheriff Malin Owen Offers Listening Ear to Those with Troubles," *Quanah Tribune-Chief*, July 20, 1961.

2. Gaston Boykin interview, February 10, 1986.

3. Quoted in William Finnegan, "Deep East Texas," *The New Yorker* 70, no. 26 (August 22 and 29, 1994): 77.

4. Ibid., 76.

5. James G. Dickson, *The Politics of the Texas Sheriff: From Frontier to Bureaucracy*, 34.

6. Rufe Jordan interview, April 18, 1986.

7. Ibid.

8. Ed Darnell interview, 1979.

9. T. W. Lane, "The Inimitable Style of Sheriff T. W. Lane," *Wharton Spectator,* September 10, 1948.

10. *Sheriffs' Association of Texas Magazine* 13, no. 9 (December 1944): 8.

11. Lane, "Inimitable Style," October 36, 1945.

12. Frank Brunt interview, February 20, 1986.

13. Paul Rowan, "Terrell County Sheriff Bill Cooksey," *San Angelo Standard-Times,* March 10, 1987.

14. *Sheriffs' Association of Texas Magazine* 1, no. 3 (July 1931): 15.

15. *Texas Lawman,* 32, no. 4 (October 1963): 96.

16. Rufe Jordan interview, April 18, 1986.

17. Jim Scarborough interview, April 28, 1986.

18. Quoted in Finnegan, "Deep East Texas," 77.

19. Dan Saunders, *Trails and Trials of a Small Town Sheriff,* 130.

20. Ibid., 83.

21. Ibid., 127.

22. *Texas Lawman* 35, no. 6 (September 1966): 93; Lane, "Inimitable Style," August 4, 1950.

23. Lane, "Inimitable Style," July 18, 1947.

24. Ibid., June 25, 1948.

25. I. R. Hoskins interview, July 21, 1986.

26. Gaston Boykin interview, February 10, 1986.

27. Corbett Akins interview, May 4, 1986.

28. *Sheriffs' Association of Texas Magazine* 13, no. 7 (October 1944): 35.

29. H. F. Fenton interview, March 13, 1986.

30. Truman Maddox interview, March 25, 1986.

31. *Sheriffs' Association of Texas Magazine* 12, no. 4 (July 1943): 31.

32. Lane, "Inimitable Style," February 30, 1948.

33. *Sheriffs' Association of Texas Magazine* 23, no. 3 (June 1954): 79–80.

34. Saunders, *Trails and Trials of a Small Town Sheriff,* 59.

35. Ibid., 85.

36. Ibid., 129.

37. Wallace Patton Riddel, personal communication to Thad Sitton, January 20, 1998.

38. Lane, "Inimitable Style," August 8, 1947.

39. Saunders, *Trails and Trials of a Small Town Sheriff,* 98.

40. Lane, "Inimitable Style," July 23, February 14, 1948; April 8, 29, 1949.

41. *Sheriffs' Association of Texas Magazine* 18, no. 1 (April 1949): 70.

42. Lane, "Inimitable Style," December 24, 1948.

43. Thad Sitton, *Backwoodsmen*, 233–56.

44. Aubrey Cole interview, August 14, 1995.

45. Joe Goodson interview, October 28, 1997.

46. Lane, "Inimitable Style," October 3, 1947.

47. Ibid., August 9, 1946.

48. Aubrey Cole interview, August 14, 1995.

49. Brantley Barker interview, March 10, 1986.

50. Joe Goodson interview, October 28, 1997.

51. Saunders, *Trails and Trials of a Small Town Sheriff*, 103, 109.

52. Lane, "Inimitable Style," April 20, 1945.

53. Joe Goodson interview, October 28, 1997.

54. Frank Brunt interview, February 21, 1986.

55. Brantley Barker interview, March 10, 1986.

56. Ed Darnell interview, 1979.

57. Saunders, *Trails and Trials of a Small Town Sheriff*, 54.

58. *Texas Lawman* 48, no. 4 (November 1971): 8.

59. Saunders, *Trails and Trials of a Small Town Sheriff*, 89.

60. Ibid.

61. Ibid., 91.

62. Ibid., 92.

63. Ibid.

64. Ibid.

65. Ibid., 98.

66. Ibid., 99.

67. Ibid., 100.

68. Ibid.

69. Ibid., 104.

70. Ibid., 84, 126.

71. Jim Scarborough interview, June 25, 1986.

72. Gaston Boykin interview, February 10, 1986.

73. Frank Brunt interview, February 20, 1986.

74. T. W. Lane interview, October 3, 1986.

75. Holly W. Osborne, "Long Time Colorado County Deputy Still Going Strong," *Texas Lawman* 46, no. 2 (May 1977): 40.

76. T. W. Lane interview, October 3, 1986.

77. Betty Staples, "L. A. Latch Settled in a Wilderness of Pines," *Lockhart Post Register*, January 24, 1935.

78. Tom Brown interview, 1977.

79. Lane, "Inimitable Style," September 23, 1949.

80. Ibid., August 4, 1950.

81. S. K. Bardwell, "Sheriff Recalls Good Ol' Days," *Waco Tribune-Herald*, May 27, 1985.

82. Jess Sweeten interview, 1979.

83. Riddel, personal communication, January 20, 1998.

84. Quoted in *Texas Lawman* 43, no. 7 (October 1974): 50.

85. Saunders, *Trails and Trials of a Small Town Sheriff*, 69.

86. Quoted in *Sheriffs' Association of Texas Magazine* 26, no. 12 (February 1958): 12.

87. Quoted in Nat Henderson, "Burnet County Sheriff Wallace Riddel, *Austin American-Statesman*, August 7, 1974.

88. Jim Scarborough interview, April 28, 1986.

89. "Sheriff Wallace Riddel" (special edition), *Burnet County Bulletin*, February 16, 1978.

EPILOGUE

1. Tom Brown interview, 1977.

2. Joe Goodson interview, October 28, 1997.

3. Aubrey Cole interview, August 14, 1995.

4. Rufe Jordan interview, April 18, 1986.

5. I. R. Hoskins interview, March 27, 1986.

6. Quoted in Dick J. Reavis, "Howdy Son, I'm the Law in This County: Texas Sheriffs in All Their Glory," *Texas Monthly* 12, no. 11 (1984): 154.

7. T. W. Lane interview, October 3, 1986.

8. Wallace Patton Riddel, personal communication to Thad Sitton, January 20, 1998.

9. *Sheriffs' Association of Texas Magazine* 1, no. 6 (April 1932): 1.

10. Frank Richard Prassel, *The Western Peace Officer*, 107.

11. *Sheriffs' Association of Texas Magazine* 18, no. 10 (January 1950): 31.

12. Ibid., 33, no. 2 (May 1964): 8; *Texas Lawman* 33, no. 3 (June 1964): 7.

13. Douglas E. Foley, Clarice Mota, Donald E. Post, and Ignacio Lozano, *From Peons to Politicos: Ethnic Relations in a South Texas Town, 1900 to 1977*, 24.

14. Ibid., 25.

15. Steve Sellers, *Terror On Highway 59*, 227–34.

16. James M. Day, *Captain Clint Peoples*, 143.

17. T. W. Lane interview, October 3, 1986.

18. T. W. Lane, "The Inimitable Style of Sheriff T. W. Lane," *Wharton Spectator*, December 2, 1949.

19. *Sheriffs' Association of Texas Magazine* 28, no. 2 (May 1959): 18.

20. Ibid., 17, no. 7 (October 1948): 3; 18, no. 12 (March 1950): 91.

21. Ibid., 18, no. 12 (March 1950): 91.

22. Quoted in ibid., 26, no. 8 (October 1957): 44.

23. Ibid., 27, no. 10 (January 1959): 9.

24. *Texas Lawman* 31, no. 2 (May 1962): 42.

25. Ibid., 33, no. 4 (May 1964): 22.

26. Ibid., 33, no. 12 (March 1965): 14.

27. Ibid., 33, no. 9 (December 1964): 6.

28. Ibid., 45, no. 8 (November 1976): 15.

29. For example, see ibid., 47, no. 4 (June 1978): 7.

30. Quoted in Eddie S. Hughes, "New Code Will Require More Law Enforcement Education Says Tarrant County Sheriff," *Dallas Morning News*, October 17, 1965.

31. *Texas Lawman* 39, no. 6 (September 1970): 22.

32. James G. Dickson, "State Role in Jail Standards Administration Becoming Greater, More Specific," *Texas Lawman* 45, no. 2 (May 1976): 45–61.

33. Gaston Boykin interview, Febuary 26, 1986.

34. Dickson, "State Role in Jail Standards Administration Becoming Greater, More Specific," 57.

35. H. F. Fenton interview, March 13, 1986.

36. Jess Sweeten interview, 1979.

37. T. W. Lane interview, December 15, 1986.

38. *Texas Lawman* 37, no. 8 (November 1968): 61.

39. Karen Potter, "Texas Sheriffs Tempted and Some Tainted," *Fort Worth Star-Telegram*, August 15, 1988.

40. Prassel, *The Western Police Officer*, 111–20.

41. J. R. Sessions interview, November 6, 1997.

42. James G. Dickson, *The Politics of the Texas Sheriff: From Frontier to Bureaucracy*, 51.

43. Saunders, *Trails and Trials of a Small Town Sheriff*, 130.

44. In Potter, "Texas Sheriffs Tempted."

45. Saunders, *Trails and Trials of a Small Town Sheriff*, 55.

BIBLIOGRAPHY

UNPUBLISHED SOURCES

Billingsley, Henry. Unpublished memoir. Lufkin Public Library, Lufkin, Texas, n.d.

Boon, Effie. "The History of Angelina County." Master's thesis, University of Texas at Austin, 1937.

Bowles, Flora G. "The History of Trinity County." Master's thesis, University of Texas at Austin, 1928.

Cowan, John. "E. A. 'Dogie' Wright: Experiences in Law Enforcement." Unpublished manuscript, E. A "Dogie" Wright Papers, File 2.325/M22, Center for American History, University of Texas at Austin.

Livingston, David W. "Lynching of Negroes in Texas, 1900–1925." Master's thesis, East Texas State University, 1972.

Mertz, James. "The Gregorio Cortes Case." Masters thesis, Texas A&I University, Kingsville, 1971.

Recer, Danalynn. "Patroling the Borders of Race, Gender, and Class: The Lynching Ritual and Texas Nationalism." Master's thesis, University of Texas at Austin, 1994.

Wright, E. A. "Dogie." E. A. "Dogie" Wright Collection, Center for American History, University of Texas at Austin.

BOOKS AND ARTICLES

Ahlgren, Frank. "El Paso County Sheriff's Deputies Set Impressive Record," *El Paso Herald-Post*, May 15, 1962.

Aiken, Bruce. Ballots, *Bullets, and Barking Dogs: Brownsville Yesteryears*. Brownsville, Texas: privately published, 1996.

Akins, Corbett. "Corbett Akins," *Loblolly* 8, no. 1 (Winter 1984): 3–44.

————. "The Sheriff's Column," *Panola Watchman*, 1951.

Allred, James D., and David Allred. "Imprints in Sidewalk Recall Colorful Sheriff," *Corpus Christi Caller-Times*, July 15, 1956.

Anderson, Walter H. *A Treatise on the Law of Sheriffs, Coroners, and Constables.* Buffalo, New York, 1941.

Ardery, Julie. "The People Just Won't Let Me Quit," *Bastrop County Times*, May 22, 1986.

Arnold, Claude R. "Runnels County Sheriff Don F. Adkins," *Abilene Reporter-News*, November 5, 1967.

Bardwell, S. K. "Sheriff Recalls Good Ol' Days," *Waco Tribune-Herald*, May 27, 1985.

Barry, James Buckner. *Buck Barry, Texas Ranger and Frontiersman.* Lincoln: University of Nebraska Press, 1978.

Bean, Covey. "Chief Civil Deputy Clyde Ray of Ector County," *Odessa American*, March 15, 1964.

Beckham, Bill. "Ellis Sommers, Former Sheriff of Winkler County," *Wink Bulletin*, October 30, 1975.

————. "Winkler County Sheriff (ret.) L. B. 'Bill' Eddins," *Winkler County News*, December 14, 1972.

Biffle, Kent. "The Men Behind the Star," *Dallas Morning News*, August 28, 1983.

————. "Wichita County Lawman Marks Half Century in Law Enforcement Work," *Texas Lawman* 27, no. 1 (March 1958): 68–69.

Bissonette, Bruce. "Hudspeth County Sheriff E. A. 'Dogie' Wright," *El Paso Times*, March 5, 1967.

Blanton G. W. "Trials and Tribulations of the Jail," *Denison Herald*, February 7, 1963.

Bookman, Ronnie. "Hardeman County Sheriff Malin Owen Offers Listening Ear to Those with Troubles," *Quanah Tribune-Chief*, July 20, 1961.

Bopp, William J., and Donald O. Schultz. *A Short History of American Law Enforcement.* Springfield, Illinois: Charles C. Thomas, 1972.

Brammer, Dana P., and James E. Hurley. *A Study of the Office of Sheriff in the United States: Southern Region.* University: University of Mississippi Press, 1968.

Brister, Bernard. "Frank Hunt of San Patricio County Had Varied Career," *Sheriffs' Association of Texas Magazine* 10, no. 2 (April 1941): 8, 10.

Broman, W. N. "Radio Systems for Small Departments," *Sheriffs' Association of Texas Magazine* 14, no. 8 (November 1945): 4, 35–36.

Bruce, Leona Bannister. *Four Years in a Coleman Jail: Daughter of Two Sheriffs.* Austin: Eakin, 1982.

Busch, Carl. "The Incredible Mr. Busch," *Chinquapin* 2, no. 5 (1980): 48–52.

Byrd, Jim. "Beer Can Boulevard," *Sheriffs' Association of Texas Magazine* 21, no. 1 (April 1952): 84.

Cardenas, Leo. "Anatomy of a Trouble Hot Spot," *San Antonio Express-News*, February 18, 1967.

Cartwright, Gary. *Galveston: A History of the Island.* New York: Atheneum, 1991.

Chatfield, F. W., and S. M. Sewell. *Texas and the Nation: Civil Government.* Richmond, Virginia: B. F. Johnson Publishing Co., 1904.

Cherry, Steve. "A History of the Sheriffs of Caldwell County," *Sheriffs' Association of Texas Magazine* 2, no. 1 (First Quarter 1982): 5–6, 8–15.

Combs, Joseph F. *Gunsmoke in the Redlands.* San Antonio: Naylor, 1968.

Conner, George M. "Smith County Deputy Fired, Indicted, in Fund Shortage," *Tyler Courier-Times-Telegraph,* March 16, 1962.

Cooper, Jim. "Deputy Sheriff Johnny Mellon," *Farmers Branch Suburban,* April 9, 1964.

Crenshaw, Troy C. *Texas Blackland Heritage.* Waco: Texian Press, 1983.

Cutbirth, Ruby Nichols. *Ed Nichols Rode a Horse.* Dallas: Texas Folklore Society, 1943.

Davis, J. C. "Legal Aspects of the Sheriff's Office," *Texas Lawman* 29, no. 10 (June 1961): 66–70.

Davis, Stewart. "Texas Commission on Law Enforcement Officer Standards and Education," *Dallas Morning News,* November 26, 1967.

Day, James M. *Captain Clint Peoples.* Waco: Texian Press, 1980.

Delony, Lewis S. *40 Years a Peace Officer.* N.p, n.d.

Denhardt, Robert M. *The Quarter Running Horse: America's Oldest Breed.* Norman: University of Oklahoma Press, 1979.

Dickson, James G. "Communication Without Understanding: The Informal Interplay of Politics in Texas County Government." In *The Challenge of Texas Politics: Texts and Readings,* pp. 347–55. Ed. Earnest Crain, Charles Deeton, and William Earl Maxwell. Saint Paul: West Publishing Company, 1980.

————. *The Politics of the Texas Sheriff: From Frontier to Bureaucracy.* Boston: American Press, 1983.

————. "Sheriffs, Jails, and Federal Courts: A Quandary of Administration," *Public Affairs Comment,* August 1977.

————. "State Role in Jail Standards Administration Becoming Greater, More Specific," *Texas Lawman* 45, no. 2 (May 1976): 45–61.

Dolan, George. "Haskell County Sheriff Has Eyes for the Job," *Fort Worth Star-Telegram,* May 8, 1961.

————. "Officers Prove Prowess with Firearms in Annual Rattlesnake Rodeo," *Texas Lawman* 26, no. 5 (May 1957): 28.

Douthat, Bill. "Sheriff's Tyranny Echoes through Tiny Realm," *Austin American-Statesman,* August 6, 1983.

Draper, Robert. "The Sheriff Who Went to Pot," *Texas Monthly* 22, no. 12 (December 1994): 130–33, 162–74.

Duncan, Bill. "'Cap' Kennedy, Veteran Lawman, Retires," *Corpus Christi Caller-Times,* April 18, 1962.

Edmondson, Gary. "Outcome of Jail Suit May Open Way to Many Others," *Corsicana Daily Sun,* October 27, 1974.

Esselstyn, T. C. "The Social Role of a County Sheriff," *Journal of Criminal Law, Criminology, and Police Science* 44 (July 1953): 177–84.

Evans, Lon. *The Purple Lawman: From Horned Frog to High Sheriff.* Fort Worth: The Summit Group, 1990.

Finnegan, William. "Deep East Texas," *The New Yorker* 70, no. 26 (August 22 and 29, 1994): 72–97.

Fisher, Norman. "Runnels County Sheriff Don Atkins of Ballinger Has Held the Office Since 1949," *Abilene Reporter-News*, September 18, 1963.

Foley, Douglas E.; Clarice Mota; Donald E. Post; and Ignacio Lozano. *From Peones to Politicos: Ethnic Relations in a South Texas Town, 1900 to 1977.* Center for Mexican American Studies of the University of Texas at Austin Monograph No. 3. Austin: The University of Texas, 1977.

Fox, Cris. "Know Thy Sheriff by the Jail He Keeps," *Sheriffs' Association of Texas Magazine* 9, no. 7 (December 1940): 29.

Frost, H. Gordan, and John H. Jenkins. *"I'm Frank Hamer": The Life of a Texas Peace Officer.* Austin: Pemberton Press, 1980.

Fuller, Henry C. *A Texas Sheriff.* Nacogdoches, 1931.

Gette, Tim. "Navarro County Sheriff Rufus Pevehouse," *Corsicana Daily Sun,* January 28, 1967.

Gettie, John. "Dallas County Sheriff Bill Decker," *Dallas Morning News,* January 28, 1967.

Gober, Jim. *Cowboy Justice: Tales of a Texas Lawman.* Lubbock: Texas Tech University Press, 1997.

Greth, Carlos Vidal. "The Legend of Joaquin Jackson," *Austin American-Statesman,* August 10, 1986.

———. "Today's Rangers: Modern Tradition," *Austin American-Statesman,* August 10, 1986.

Grote, Edith. "City Marshal is Third Generation Lawman," *Mason County News,* February 11, 1965.

Hale, Leon. "A Buckshot Lane Story: The Man Who Burned Kendleton Bridge," *Houston Post,* September 6, 1981.

Hayle, Selden. "Ten Commandments and Common Sense Guide Sheriff Rufe Jordan," *Amarillo Daily News,* October 29, 1964.

Hall, Georgie Meredith. *Life of R. T. Hall.* Carrizo Springs: Willems Press, 1980.

Henderson, Nat. "Burnet County Sheriff Wallace Riddel," *Austin American-Statesman,* August 7, 1974.

Hinojosa-Smith, Rolando. "River of Blood," *Texas Monthly* 14, no. 1 (January 1986): 196.

Hinton, Ted. *Ambush: The Real Story of Bonnie and Clyde.* Austin: Shoal Creek Press, 1979.

Hogan, William Ransom. *The Texas Republic: A Social and Economic History.* Norman: University of Oklahoma Press, 1946.

Hopping, R. C. *A Sheriff Ranger in Chuckwagon Days.* New York: Pageant Press, 1952.

Hoskins, I. R. "Nig". "Jail House Notes," *Smithville Times,* 1952–58.

Hughes, Eddie S. "New Code Will Require More Law Enforcement Education Says Tarrant County Sheriff," *Dallas Morning News,* October 17, 1965.

———. "Ousted Sheriff Paints Sorry Picture of His County," *Dallas Morning News,* June 7, 1964.

Jackson, Ralph Semmes. *Home on the Double Bayou: Memories of an East Texas Ranch.* Austin: University of Texas Press, 1961.

Jones, Nelson. "Nelson Jones." In *Earth Has No Sorrows,* pp. 79–85. Ed. Dee Azadian. Austin: Voluntary Action Center of Caldwell County, 1977.

Jordan, Mrs. R. H. "I Am the Wife of a Texas Law Enforcement Officer," *Texas Lawman* 27, no. 8 (October 1958): 10–11.

Kelly, Herman. "Texas Lawman," *Texas Highways* 20, no. 9 (September 1973): 4–6.

Keyes, Clarke. "Problems Confront Hopkins County Sheriff's Department," *Sulfur Springs News-Telegram,* September 16, 1962.

Kilpatrick, Joel. "Thirtieth Year in Law Enforcement Marked by the Man from Gunsight," *Galveston News-Tribune,* November 12, 1965.

Koethe, Jim. "Veteran Seymour Constable Recalls Days of Gallows Executions Locally Handled," *Texas Sheriff's Association Magazine* 23, no. 6 (September 1954): 14.

Lackey, Jerry F. "'Killed' Forty-five Years Ago, Former Kimble County Sheriff Still Spry at 84," *San Angelo Standard-Times,* August 18, 1963.

Landers, Clara. "Hearst Laws—'The Law in Dell City,'" *Texas Lawman* 42, no. 3 (June 1973): 78–79, 84.

Lane, Tanner. "Veteran West Texas Lawman Sees Many Changes in Law Enforcement," *Lubbock Avalanche-Journal,* September 24, 1961.

Lane, T. W. "The Inimitable Style of Sheriff T. W. Lane," *Wharton Spectator,* 1946–48.

Lee, Bill. "Urby Dyer Now Living in Barstow Recalls Long Colorful Career as Ward County Sheriff," *Texas Lawman* 27, no. 2 (April 1958): 67.

Lindquist, Allan Sigvard. *Jess Sweeten, Texas Lawman.* San Antonio: Naylor, 1961.

Long, Christopher. "Jess Sweeten." In *The New Handbook of Texas* 6:172. Austin: Texas State Historical Association, 1996.

Lunin, Fanchon. "Sheriff Joe Slater, Nolan County (Sweetwater)," *Abilene Reporter-News,* June 12, 1969.

McCormick, Harry. "Dallas County Jail, Sheriff, Draw Praise, Even from Melvin Belli," *Dallas Morning News,* November 8, 1964.

McWilliams, R. E. "Observations on Crime," *Sheriffs' Association of Texas Magazine* 1, no. 3 (July 1931): 5.

Malsch, Brownson. *Captain M. T. Gonzaullas: Lone Wolf.* Austin: Shoal Creek, 1980.

Martin, Jim. "Citizens Honor Former County Sheriff Charles Lovelace," *Amarillo Daily News,* January 27, 1966.

Matusik, David. "Williamson Jail Fix Ordered," *Austin American-Statesman* September 25, 1986.

Miles, Bob. "Frank T. Bailey of Ysleta," *El Paso Times,* August 29, 1965.

Miller, Bob. "Some of the Varied and Thrilling Experiences of Bob Miller," *Sheriffs' Association of Texas Magazine* 1, no. 2 (March 1931): 4–6.

Mills, Susie. *Legend in Bronze: Biography of E. J. Banks.* Dallas: privately printed, 1982.

Morgan, Earnest. "Nueces County Sheriff Gets Tired of Talking, Takes a Walk," *Corpus Christi Caller-Times*, June 12, 1962.

Moulder, John. "Best Civil Deputy Retires from Duty," *San Angelo Standard-Times*, December 15, 1961.

Mueck, Sue. "Ben D. Lee, Former Nueces County Sheriff, Was the Original 'Man Who Came to Dinner'," *Corpus Christi Caller-Times*, October 28, 1962.

Munson, Charlie. *Mr. Charlie: Memoir of a Texas Lawman, 1902–1910*. Austin: Madrona Press, 1975.

Neely, W. M. "Distinguished Ranger Captain Recounts Past," *Sheriffs' Association of Texas Magazine* 8, no. 5 (July 1939): 3–4.

O'Connell, Polly. "'Backbone' of Law Enforcement," *Daily Brazosport*, March 27, 1967.

Osborne, Holly W. "Long Time Colorado County Deputy Still Going Strong," *Texas Lawman* 46, no. 2 (May 1977): 40.

Parsons, Chuck. *James Madison Brown: Texas Sheriff and Texas Turfman*. Wolfe City: Henington Publishing Company, 1993.

Payne, Albert Bigelow. *Captain Bill McDonald, Texas Ranger: A Story of Frontier Reform*. New York: J. J. Little and Ives, 1909.

Pearson, Spencer: "Nueces County Sheriff Angry at Critics," *Corpus Christi Caller-Times*, February 20, 1975.

Pickett, Linda Jay. *Cast a Long Shadow*. Dallas: privately published, 1984.

Potter, Karen. "Texas Sheriffs Tempted and Some Tainted," *Fort Worth Star-Telegram*, August 15, 1988.

Prassel, Frank Richard. *The Western Peace Officer*. Norman: University of Oklahoma Press, 1972.

Preece, Harold. *Lone Star Man: Ira Aten, Last of the Old Texas Rangers*. New York: Hastings House, 1960.

Raymond, Dora Neill. *Captain Lee Hall of Texas*. Norman: University of Oklahoma Press, 1940.

Reavis, Dick J. "Howdy, Son. I'm the Law in This County: Texas Sheriffs in All Their Glory," *Texas Monthly* 12, no. 11 (1984): 150–61.

Recer, Paul. "Bill Decker," *Texas Lawman* 34, no. 9 (December 1965): 66.

Redding, Stan. "Living Legends of the Law," *Houston Chronicle*, March 5, 1972.

Reich, Steven A. "Soldiers of Democracy: Black Texans and the Fight for Citizenship, 1917–1921," *Journal of American History* 82 (March 1996): 1478–1504.

Rigler, Lewis C., and Judyth Wagner Rigler. *Reflections of a Texas Ranger Private*. Houston: Larksdale Press, 1984.

Ross, John D. "Lynching." In *The New Handbook of Texas* 4:346–47. Austin: Texas State Historical Association, 1996.

Rowan, Paul. "Terrell County Sheriff Bill Cooksey," *San Angelo Standard-Times*, March 10, 1967.

Salter, Bill. "Know Your Area Lawmen: Sheriff Bill M. Medlin, Guadalupe County (Sequin)," *San Antonio Express*, June 25, 1969.

———. "Know Your Area Lawmen: Sheriff H. D. Smith, Mason County (Mason)," *San Antonio Express*, October 8, 1969.

————. "Know Your Area Lawmen: Sheriff Jack L. Robinson, Bee County (Beeville)," *San Antonio Express*, September 2, 1969.

————. "Know Your Area Lawmen: Sheriff Kenneth Kelly, Uvalde County (Uvalde)," *San Antonio Express*, July 30, 1969.

————. "Know Your Area Lawmen: Sheriff Ronnie Dodds, Lavaca County (Halletsville)," *San Antonio Express*, June 11, 1969.

————. "Know Your Area Lawmen: Sheriff Vidal Garcia, Duval County (San Diego)," *San Antonio Express*, July 23, 1969.

————. "Know Your Area Lawmen: Sheriff Walter Fellers, Comal County (New Braunfels)," *San Antonio Express*, July 2, 1969.

Saunders, Dan. *Trails and Trials of a Small Town Sheriff.* Lubbock: Cotton Publishing Company, 1996.

Schoellkopf, John. "Veteran Dallas County Lawman Retires," *Dallas Times Herald*, February 28, 1962.

Sellers, Steve. *Terror On Highway 59*. Austin: Texas Monthly Press, 1984.

Sharp, Joe. "Liquor Control in Texas," *Sheriffs' Association of Texas Magazine* 8, no. 7 (September 1939): 17–18, 22.

Shapiro, Herbert. "Lynching." In *Encyclopedia of Southern History*, pp. 762–64. Ed. David C. Roller and Robert W. Twyman. Baton Rouge: Louisiana State University Press, 1979.

Shaver, Maryanne. "Wharton County Sheriff H. R. 'Mike' Flournoy," *Houston Post*, August 28, 1966.

Simmons, Lee. *Assignment Huntsville: Memoirs of a Texas Prison Official*. Austin: University of Texas Press, 1957.

Sinise, Jerry. *George Washington Arrington: Civil War Spy, Texas Ranger, Sheriff, and Rancher.* Burnet, Texas: Eakin, 1979.

Sitton, Thad. *Backwoodsmen.* Norman: University of Oklahoma Press, 1995.

————. *Texas High Sheriffs.* Austin: Texas Monthly Press, 1988.

————, and Dan K. Utley. *From Can See to Can't: Texas Cotton Farmers on the Southern Prairies* Austin: University of Texas Press, 1997.

————, and James H. Conrad. *Nameless Towns: Texas Sawmill Communities, 1880–1942.* Austin: University of Texas Press, 1998.

Smith, Bruce. *Rural Crime Control.* New York: Institute of Public Administration, Columbia University, 1933.

Smith, Doug. "Sheriff L. S. 'Slim' Johnson, Randall County," *Amarillo Globe-Times*, September 22, 1969.

Sonnichsen, C. L. "Feuds." In *The New Handbook of Texas* 2:988–990. Austin: Texas State Historical Association, 1996.

————. *I'll Die Before I'll Run: The Story of the Great Feuds of Texas.* New York: Devin-Adair, 1962.

Spinks, Martha. "Sheriff and Mrs. Bill Eddins Move after Twenty Years," *Winkler County News*, May 29, 1967.

Staples, Betty. "L. A. Latch Settled in a Wilderness of Pines," *Lockhart Post Register*, January 24, 1935.

Stephens, Robert W. *Walter Durbin: Texas Ranger and Sheriff.* Clarendon, Texas: Clarendon Press, 1971.

Sterling, William W. *Trails and Trials of a Texas Ranger.* N.p., privately published, 1959. Reprint, Norman: University of Oklahoma Press, 1979.

Stone, William E. "The Suicide Problem in Texas Jails," *Texas Lawman* 53, no. 6 (June 1984): 5–7.

Stout, Wesley W. "The Law According to Buckshot Lane," *Saturday Evening Post,* July 14, 1951, 32–38.

Thomason, Anna. "Moore County Sheriff John M. Easley," *Amarillo Daily News,* January 29, 1965.

Tolbert, Frank X. "Phil Medlin 'The Singing Sheriff' of Guadalupe County," *Dallas Morning News,* July 8, 1962.

———. "Tolbert's Texas: The Singing Sheriff," *Dallas Morning News,* March 5, 1967.

Travis, Marion. "Sheriff Carl C. Black, Milam County (Cameron)," *Waco Times-Herald,* August 22, 1969.

Trent, Bill, "He's an Expert on Jails," *Sheriffs' Association of Texas Magazine* 23, no. 8 (November 1954): 67–68.

Turner, Jerry. "Uncle Bud: A Texas Prison Legend," *Mexia Daily News,* October 24, 1997.

Turney, Thomas E. "Marvin 'Red' Burton," *Dallas Morning News,* February 6, 1965.

Wade, Roy L. "Money Mad Mechanic Poisons Wife," *Sheriffs' Association of Texas Magazine* 11, no. 4 (July 1942): 18–30.

Walker, Bob. "Montague County Sheriff's Department," *Nocona News,* June 16, 1966.

Walker, Peggy. *George Humphreys 6666: Cowboy and Lawman.* Burnet, Texas: Eakin, 1978.

Walton, Dale. "Former Pecos County Sheriff Recalls His Days of Service," *San Angelo Standard-Times,* October 31, 1961.

White, Ernest. "Martin County Sheriff Dan Saunders," *Stanton Reporter,* January 7, 1965.

Wood, Harry. "It Takes Five Hours to Answer a 'Dog Call'," *San Angelo Standard-Times,* September 12, 1967.

Worth, Robert M. "Andrew Jackson Spradley." In *The New Handbook of Texas* 6:40–41. Austin: Texas State Historical Association, 1996.

Ybarra, Bob. "Border Patrolmen Recall Many Gun Fights," *El Paso Herald-Post,* May 21, 1974.

INTERVIEWS AND PERSONAL COMMUNICATIONS

Akins, Corbett. Taped interview with Thad Sitton, 1986. Center for American History, Austin, Texas (hereafter, CAH).

Barker, T. Brantley. Taped interview with Thad Sitton, 1986. CAH.

Boykin, Gaston. Two taped interviews with Thad Sitton, 1986. CAH.

Brown, Earl D. Taped interview with James G. Dickenson, 1979. James G. Dickenson personal collection (hereafter, JD).

Brown, Tom. Taped interview with Jim Lutz, 1977. CAH.

Brunt, Frank. Two taped interviews with Thad Sitton, 1986. CAH.

Buckalew, F. M. Taped interview with James G. Dickenson, 1979. JD.

Cole, Aubrey. Taped interview with Thad Sitton, 1995. CAH.

Darnell, Ed. Taped interview with James G. Dickenson, 1979. JD.

Evans, Lon. Taped interview with James G. Dickenson, 1979. JD.

Fellers, Walter. Taped interview with Thad Sitton, 1986. CAH.

Fenton, H. F. Taped interview with Thad Sitton, 1986. CAH.

Fenton, Loretta. Taped interview with Thad Sitton, 1986. CAH.

Flores, Porforio. Taped interview with Thad Sitton, 1986. CAH.

Fox, Vonnie Riddel. Personal communication to Thad Sitton, January 20, 1998.

Gladney, Bob. Taped interview with Thad Sitton, 1986. CAH.

Goodson, Joe G. Taped interview with Thad Sitton, 1997. CAH.

Gunn, William Lester. Taped interview with Thad Sitton, 1986. CAH.

Harber, Charlie. Three taped interviews with Thad Sitton, 1992.

Heard, Jack. Taped interview with James G. Dickenson, 1979. JD.

Herrington, Roy A. Taped interview with Thad Sitton, 1986. CAH.

Hoskins, I. R. Two taped interviews with Thad Sitton, 1986. CAH.

Jones, Leon. Two taped interviews with Thad Sitton, 1986. Author's personal collection.

Jordan, B. Rufus. Taped interviews with Thad Sitton, 1986. CAH.

Kern, C. V. Taped interview with James G. Dickenson, 1979. JD.

Lane, T. W. Two taped interviews with Thad Sitton, 1986. CAH.

Lightfoot, John R. Taped interview with Thad Sitton, 1993. CAH.

Maddox, Truman. Two taped interviews with Thad Sitton, 1986. CAH.

McBride, Burl. Taped interview with James G. Dickenson, 1979. JD.

Platt, Billy. Taped interview with Thad Sitton, 1992. Center for East Texas Studies, Stephen F. Austin State University, Nacogdoches.

Riddell, Wallace Patton "Pat." Personal communication to Thad Sitton, January 20, 1998.

Scarborough, Jim. Two taped interviews with Thad Sitton, 1986. CAH.

Sessions, J. R. Taped interview with Thad Sitton, 1997. CAH.

Sweeten, Jess. Taped interview with James G. Dickenson, 1979. JD.

Williams, Grover. Taped interview with Dan Utley, 1991. Oral History Institute of Baylor University, Waco, Texas.

Wright, E. A. "Dogie." Self-interviews, tapes, and transcripts, undated. E. A. "Dogie" Wright Collection. CAH.

INDEX

Ackerly, Tex., 179

Adams, Walter, 61

African Americans, 25, 28, 36–37, 49, 70, 123, 138–39, 162–72, 175, 181. *See also* Sheriff

Akins, Corbett, 34, 38, 55, 111, 113–14, 126–27, 156–57, 165, 168–69, 180

Alcohol: and problems with law enforcement. *See* Sheriff

Alfred the Great (king of England), 4

Alguacil, 5

Allie, W. J., 94

Alto, Tex., 7

Anderson, E. T., 67

Anderson, Walter, 140

Anderson County, 36, 51, 62, 93, 152

Angelina County, 22, 25–26, 35, 43, 46, 53, 58, 62, 92, 102–103, 112, 120, 128, 141, 147–49

Antipeonage laws, 166

"Apartheid," 162–64

Apple Springs, Tex., 164

Armstrong, Bill, 74

Ash, "Knob," 102

Aten, Ira, 10–11

Athens, Tex., 51

Austin, Tex., 116, 143

Austin County, 16, 19–20, 51, 54, 143

Babb, Coleman, 68

Baker, Bill, 100

Bannister, John, 44, 76, 82, 140

Bannister, Leona, 44, 76, 82

Barber, F. L., 41

Barker, Brantley, 43, 50, 69, 108, 184–86

Barnes, Wylie, 56

Barrett, Howard, 152

Barrow, Buck, 135

Barrow, Clyde, 132

Barry, Buck, 6

Bastrop, Tex., 59

Bastrop County, 9, 26, 36–37, 46, 52, 87, 102

Beaumont, Tex., 143

Bee County, 83–84, 129–31

Bell County, 8, 52–53, 136

Bellville, Tex., 16, 19, 47

Belton, Tex., 53, 136

Bennett, Buck, 93

Bexar County, 67, 126, 136, 206–207

Biaggne, Frank L., 31, 69, 144–46, 150

Big Spring, Tex., 181

Billingsley, Henry C., 53, 55, 58, 62–63, 128, 141–42, 148, 150, 152, 156

Bishop, Beaver, 152

Black, Carl, 193

Blanton, G. W., 85

Bloodhounds, 45, 68, 92, 111, 115, 156, 163, 169, 198

Bone, Paul, 133, 199

Bootlegging. *See* Sheriff

Border, "Curg," 11–13

Border, George, 11

Border Patrol, U.S., 158

Borger, Tex., 159–62

Bowie County, 144

Boykin, Gaston, 25, 34, 47, 49, 52, 60, 70–71, 82–84, 101, 108, 110, 127–28, 134–35, 173, 180, 191, 209

Bracken, E. L., 96

Bradley's Corner, Tex., 155

Brantley, Houston, 123

Brazoria County, 23, 33, 45

Breckenridge, Tex., 159

Brenham, Tex., 142

Bribes. *See* Sheriff

Broocks, Ben, 12

Brown, Jim, 8, 27

Brown, Tom, 46–47, 68, 95–96, 111–12, 121, 163, 169, 192, 197, 205

Brunt, Bill, 7, 28, 42, 53

Brunt, Frank, 3, 7, 68–69, 100, 102, 105, 107, 113, 125–26, 134, 150, 155–56, 176, 186, 191

Buna, Tex., 26

Burleson County, 65

Burnet County, 35, 44, 51, 76–77, 80–82, 84, 87, 122, 136, 182, 193–96

Busch, Carl, 65, 128–29, 159

Butler, Henry, 168

Button, W. E., 157

Caldwell County, 46–47, 52, 95, 121, 163, 167–69, 192

Cameron, Tex., 193

Cameron County, 62–63, 101

Camp County, 93

Canton, Tex., 22

Carpenter, George, 152

Carthage, Tex., 134, 165

Casey, Homer, 65

Cass County, 157

Centerville, Tex., 92

Chambers County, 6–7, 179

Chambless, Rodney, 55, 96

Chandler, Ed, 128–29

Cherokee County, 3, 7, 28, 42, 53, 68–69, 100, 102, 105, 176, 186, 191

Chicken Ranch, 144, 189. *See also* Red light districts

Christian, Charlie, 60

Civil rights. *See* Fourteenth Amendment

Civil Rights Commission, U.S., 207

Coke County, 53

Coldspring, Tex., 201–204

Cole, Aubrey, 23, 26–27, 47, 59, 99–100, 112, 143, 150, 184, 196–97

Coleman, Tex., 142

Coleman County, 15–16, 23–25, 35–36, 38, 43–44, 76–77, 82, 120–21, 137, 140, 155–56, 198, 210

Collin County, 8, 157

Colorado County, 48, 171, 191–92

Columbus County, 181

Comal County, 88, 108, 199

Comanche County, 25, 33, 49, 52, 60, 70–71, 82–83, 101, 108, 127–28, 173, 176, 209

Commissioners court, county, 5, 44–45, 83, 132, 136, 142, 209

Conditt, J. D. ("Red"), 25–26, 43

Conroe, Tex., 142

Constable, 56, 58

Cooksey, Bill, 176

Cooper, Tex., 123

Corpus Christi, Tex., 141

Corrigan, W. J., 83–84

County attorney. *See* Sheriff

County judge. *See* Sheriff

County tax collector. *See* Sheriff

Cowart, R. Z., 143

Cox, Sam F. ("Buster"), 207

Crawford, Noble, 142

Crosby County, 66, 84

Crosbyton, Tex., 126
Cuero, Tex., 94

Dallas, Tex., 32–33
Dallas County, 6, 113, 132, 136, 157
Dancy, Oscar, 62
Danevang, Tex., 117
Darnell, "Big Ed," 22, 54, 64, 69, 175,
    186, 197
Deadly force, use of. *See* Sheriff
Decker, J. E. ("Bill"), 3, 45, 100,
    180–81
Delta County, 123
Denton, Tex., 56
Deputies, 12, 15–16, 29, 44–49, 204;
    black and Hispanic, 47; political
    considerations involved in selec-
    tion of, 47– 48; as potential political
    challengers for sheriff, 21, 23;
    sheriff's family used as unpaid,
    76–79; training of, 46–47, 208–209;
    varieties of, 48–49. *See also* Sheriff
De Witt County, 9, 94
Dickens County, 41
Dickson, James, 139, 173–74
Dibbel, Tiemann, 44
Dimmitt County, 57, 158
Dismuke, Jack, 61
District attorney. *See* Sheriff
Dodds, Ronnie, 135
Dunlap, Harry, 124
Duval County, 65

Eastland County, 142
Eddins, Bill, 87
El Campo, Tex., 73–74, 117, 170
Ellison, Walter, 46–47, 54, 167–68
Ennis, Vail, 129–31, 199
Erath County, 68
Evadale, Tex., 26
Evans, Lon, 45, 96, 208

Falls County, 149
Fannin County, 8, 177

Fayette County, 48–49, 89, 144, 181
Federal Bureau of Investigation (FBI),
    71, 100–101, 113, 140, 203, 206–207,
    212–13
Fellers, Walter, 88, 108
Fenton, H. F., 15–16, 24–25, 33, 36, 38,
    43–44, 46, 54–55, 77–78, 80, 84–85,
    90–91, 97, 108, 120–21, 137–38,
    155–56, 174, 180, 198, 210
Fenton, Mrs. H. F. (Loretta), 44, 77–78,
    80, 84–85, 90–91, 119, 137
Fenton, Sean, 79–80, 210
Feuds. *See* Sheriff
Flatonia, Tex., 48
Fleming, Boyington, 62, 101
Floresville, Tex., 78, 120
Flournoy, H. R. ("Mike"), 135
Flournoy, T. J. ("Big Jim"), 48–49, 144,
    181
Foley, Douglas, 200–201
Fort Bend County, 9–11, 143
Fort Hood, Tex. (army base), 53, 149
Fort Worth, Tex., 27, 32
Fourteenth Amendment, 111, 113
Franklin County, 94
Franks, J. H., 52
Free range, 183–84
Freestone County, 32, 133, 158–159
Franklin County, 49, 207

Galveston County, 27, 69
Gambling, 138–45
Game warden, 22, 58–59, 213
Gandy, C. W., 149
Garrett, Garth ("Tangle Eye"), 36
Garrison, Homer, Jr., 144, 146
Garvey, James ("King of the
    Woodpeckers"), 10
Garza, Tex., 96
Giddings, Tex., 8, 59, 104
Gladewater, Tex., 142
Gladney, Bob, 23, 45
Glasscock County, 207
Glen Rose, Tex., 32, 199

Gonzaullas, Manuel ("Lone Wolf"), 57,
    161–62, 116, 161–62
Good, Paul, 53
Goodson, Joe R., 59, 66, 77, 79, 84, 104,
    159, 185–86, 197
Grady, Tex., 104
Grand juries, 66–68, 150–60, 169
Gray County, 69, 102, 140, 161, 174–75
Grayson County, 8, 31, 85
Greaves, Raymond, 46
Gregg County, 67, 142, 162
Gregory, Bud, 188
Gresham, Pink, 177
Grimes County, 111
Groveton, Tex., 29–30, 57, 65, 129
Gunn, William Lester, 52, 53, 136, 169
Guthrie, Jeff, 140

Hackler, F. F., 93
Hale, David C., 68
Hall, Ron, 158
Hallettsville, Tex., 111
Hamer, Frank, 28, 55, 57, 132, 160–61
Hamilton, Raymond, 135
Hammondsville, Tex., 48
Hardeman County, 92, 124, 173
Hardin, John Wesley, 122–23
Hardin County, 163
Harker Heights, Tex., 53
Harris County, 136, 203
Harrison, Roy, 36
Harrison County, 5, 32, 67, 122, 149
Haskell County, 36
Hemphill County, 61
Henderson, Tex., 162
Henderson County, 28–29, 34, 50, 53,
    63–64, 100, 113, 126, 155–56, 167–68,
    193
Henigan, A. C., 134
Herrington, Roy, 56, 58, 62, 93, 111,
    152, 168
Hibbolt, Dallas, 16
Hicks, Ben, 46
Hillin, Roy, 84, 126

Hinton, Ted, 132
Hodges, W. O., 56
Hogg, James S., 60
Holbrook, J. E., 111
Holiday, R. D., 57
Hood County, 9
Hopkins, Paul, 31–32, 146
Hopkins County, 56, 93
Hoskins, I. R. ("Nig"), 26–27, 36–37,
    46, 52, 59, 87, 96, 102, 179–80, 198
Houston, Tex., 33, 65, 143, 153, 193, 203
Howard County, 65
Hudspeth County, 68
Humphreys, George, 41, 111
Hunt, Frank, 124
Hunt County, 8
Huntsville, Tex., 44, 135
Hutchinson County, 160–61

Immigration River Guards, 157
Informants. See Jail; Sheriff
Insane, 44, 56, 76, 81–82, 86, 89–90,
    178–79. See also Jail; Sheriff
Interrogation: of suspects, 97, 105–12,
    208
Ivy, Hoyt, 177

Jacksonville, Tex., 69
Jail, county: categories of prisoners in,
    6; custody of insane, 44, 76, 81–82,
    86, 89–90; escape attempts and riots
    in, 44, 85, 90–94, 96; food, 84–85;
    new sheriffs' problems with, 43–45;
    quarrels with county commis-
    sioners about, 63–65; and recruit-
    ment of informants, 96–99;
    regulated by Texas Jail Standards
    Commission, 209–10; sheriff's
    family in, 76–85; suicides in, 88–89;
    trustees, 80–81; used in solving
    crimes, 96–98, 208
Jasper, Tex., 26–27, 47
Jasper County, 23, 26, 61, 65, 99–100,
    112, 143, 149–50, 152, 184, 196–97

Jaybird-Woodpecker War, 9–10
"Jim Crow" laws, 139, 163
Johnson, Gerald ("The Dallas Kid"), 127
Johnson, Gordon, 211
Johnson, Harris, 57
Johnson, L. R., 23
Joiner, Dan, 162
Jones, Enoch, 22
Jones, Leon, 22, 46, 63, 92, 99, 115, 147–48
Jones, Nelson, 167
Jones, Paul Ray, 56
Jordan, B. Rufus ("Rufe"), 69, 102, 161, 174–75, 177–78, 196, 198

Karnes County, 176–77
Kenedy, Tex., 177
Kilday, Owen W., 67, 126, 206–207
Kilgore, Texas, 162
Killeen, Tex., 53, 136
King County, 41, 111
King Ranch, 49
Kirby, John Henry, 39, 126, 141
Kirby Lumber Company, 39
Kirbyville, Tex., 26
Kleberg County, 35, 41, 49, 80, 102, 107, 131, 178, 189–90, 194–95
Kountz, Tex., 163
Ku Klux Klan, 24

Ladd, William, 6
La Grange, Tex., 48
Lamar County, 62, 93–94, 102
Lamesa, Tex., 93
Lampasas County, 9, 92–93
Lane, T. W. ("Buckshot"), 24, 36–37, 49, 51, 56, 64, 67, 70– 75, 79–81, 85–86, 88–89, 94–95, 98, 100, 104, 111, 113, 115–20, 124, 126–27, 134, 140–43, 165–72, 175–76, 180–86, 191–93, 205, 210
Lane, Willie P., 62
Latch, Lewis A., 192

Lathan, Ed, 141
Lavaca County, 135
Lawrence, Wade, 79
Ledbetter, Huddie, 136
Lee County, 7–9, 27, 59, 66, 68, 77
Leon County, 92, 155
Lexington, Tex., 104
Liberty County, 61, 194
Lightfoot, John, 58–60, 69–70, 123
Limestone County, 124, 154–55, 160
Liquor Control Board (LCB), 58, 155, 140, 155, 205–206, 213
Loblolly, 115
Lockhart, Tex., 47, 111–12, 121, 163–64
Loessin, William, 89
Longview, Tex., 126
Lufkin, Tex., 99, 102–103, 120, 148
Luling, Tex., 47
Lynchings, 166, 171–72. *See also* Sheriff

McCamey, Tex., 104
McClennan County, 65, 182–83, 204–205
McDade, Tex., 26
McDonald, Bill, 29, 60
Maceo, Rose, 144
Maceo, Sam, 144, 146
McGee, Gregg, 203
McNerin, W. B. ("Blackie"), 210–11
Maddox, Truman, 16, 19, 20–21, 47, 51, 54, 70, 97–98, 105–108, 122, 134, 139, 180, 196
Madison County, 55, 96
Marion County, 120, 162
Markowsky, Ray, 94
Marshall, Jack, 23, 46
Martin County, 37, 66, 66, 68, 87–88, 104, 163, 168, 178–79, 181
Mason, John, 128
Mason, Tex., 57
Massey, John Wesley, 157
Massey, Willie, 164
Maydell, Tex., 42
Maxie, C. C., 182, 204–205

Media. *See* Sheriff
Menard County, 93
Mexia, Tex., 33, 158–60
Mexico, Republic of, 157
Midland, Tex., 181, 187
Midland County, 54
Milam County, 193
Miller, Charlie, 57
Mills County, 60, 135
Miranda warning, 95, 111, 208
Montgomery County, 39, 46, 55–56, 58, 61, 67, 135, 153, 207
Moody, Dan, 160–61
Moonshining, 148–57. *See also* Alcohol; Sheriff
Moore, J. F. ("Redbone"), 8
Moore, O. P., 171
Murray, Ben, 57

Nacogdoches, Tex., 58
Nacogdoches County, 36, 58, 69–70, 122, 134
National Association for the Advancement of Colored People (NAACP), 170–71
Navarro County, 6
Navasota, Tex., 28, 164
Neches, Tex., 56
Neff, Pat, 160
Newton County, 39
Noble, W. S. ("Sneed"), 13
Nixon, Thomas, 65
Nueces County, 123

Oatmeal, Tex., 134
Ochiltree County, 177–78
Oil booms, 33, 68, 115, 158–62. *See also* Sheriff
Owen, Malin, 124, 173
Ownby, Joe, 161

Pace, R. C., 112
Palestine, Tex., 58, 93
Palmer, Joe, 135

Pampa, Tex., 55, 161, 174
Panola County, 34, 38, 68, 111, 113–14, 132, 134, 157, 180
Parker, Bonnie, 132
Parker, J. C. ("Humpy"), 111, 200–204
Parker County, 155
Patton, George, 108
Peoples, Clint, 39, 41, 46, 55–56, 61, 124, 134, 146, 153, 204–205
Perry, Rufe, 122
Person, Luther B., 92
Player, Charles, 3
Police, municipal. *See* Sheriff
Populist Party, 9, 11, 24, 36
Port Arthur, Tex., 143
Posse comitatus (sheriff's posse), 5
Potter, Karen, 211
Prohibition, 9–10, 13, 29–33, 53, 62, 148–49, 157–58
Prostitution, 116, 139–45. *See also* Red light districts
Pruitt, Bill, 212
Pullin, Jack, 206

Quanah, Tex., 124

Radios, short-wave: used in law enforcement, 116, 120, 136–37
Ranger, Tex., 155, 159
Reavis, Dick, 198
Reconstruction, 8–11
Redfearn, Alvis, 68
Red light districts, 138, 143–44. *See also* Gambling; Prostitution; Sheriff
Red Rock, Tex., 26, 38, 102
Reeves, Gene, 207
Regulator-Moderator War (Shelby County War), 7–8
Richmond, Tex., 9, 105
Riddell, Essie, 81, 84
Riddell, Modina, 81
Riddell, Pat, 76, 99, 122, 148

Riddell, Wallace, 35, 41, 44–45, 48, 51, 69, 81, 87, 99, 121–22, 134, 136, 148, 182, 193–96, 199
Rigler, Lawrence, 99
Roberts, Noel, 12–14
Robey, George, 38
Rockwall County, 206
Rolston, Butler, 61–62, 148
Rose, W. P. ("Red"), 194
Round Top, Tex., 48
Rusk, Dave, 5, 69
Rusk, Tex., 42
Russell, Bud, 135–36

Safecrackers, 102, 117–19. See also Sheriff
St. Clair, Perry, 176
San Antonio, Tex., 32, 153
San Augustine, Tex., 11–14, 36, 42
San Augustine County, 11–15, 59, 70, 98–99, 102, 173, 178
San Jacinto County, 111, 201–204
San Patricio County, 124
San Saba, Tex., 50
San Saba County, 9, 43, 50, 184–86
Saunders, Dan, 37, 41, 47, 54, 66, 69, 87–88, 101–102, 121, 124–25, 163, 168, 178–79, 181–82, 185–89, 194, 212–13
Scarborough, Jim, I, 27, 102, 107, 126
Scarborough, Jim, II, 35, 41, 69, 121–23, 129, 189, 194–95, 198
Scarborough, Jim, III, 41, 79–80, 129, 131, 178, 189–90, 194–95
Schmid, Smoot, 180
Scholl, W. A. ("Doc"), 65, 199
Schulenberg, Tex., 48
Sealy, Tex., 16, 19–20, 47
Sessions, J. R., I, 32–33, 99, 133, 150
Sessions, J. R. ("Sonny"), II, 58, 69, 133, 139, 211
Shelby County, 7, 59–60
Sheriff: and alcohol law violations, 29–33, 52–53, 60, 62, 99, 102–103,
120–22, 128–29, 138–39, 146–58, 200; assassination (or attempted assassination) of, 11, 27, 31–32, 52; banishes undesirables from county, 97, 112–13, 116, 128; car chases by, 20, 131–34; corruption (or attempted corruption) of, 29, 33, 52–53, 61, 67, 140–46, 150–52, 199–205, 211–13; and county commissioners' court, 44, 63–66, 71, 73; and county and district attorneys, 60–61, 188, 193; and county jail, 43–45, 63–65, 76–98, 193–94; and county judge, 61–63; and criminals from outside the county, 104, 112–20; and dangers of prisoner car transport, 131, 134–36; and deadly force, use of, 55–56, 122–31; and deputies, 15–16, 23, 44–49; fiscal affairs of (salaries, fees, and budgets), 82–85; formal duties of, 5–6, 49–50, 79; and grand juries, 66–68, 142; influenced by powerful local economic interests, 39–41, 49, 144–46, 166; and illegal and extra-legal county traditions, 138–72; and informants, use of, 49, 96–100; and the insane, 56, 76, 81–82, 86, 89–90; and interrogation of suspects, 97, 105–12, 178–79, 207, 298; and joint role as tax-collector, 5, 50; and juvenile offenders, 191–93; limited equipment of, 15–16, 43, 64, 71, 73; and local criminals, 101–107, 120, 191–93; and local feuds, 7–17; and local media, 70–75; and minority citizens, 25, 28, 36–37, 47, 49, 70, 95, 111–12, 123, 138–39, 162–72, 175–76, 181, 192; and municipal police, 58–59, 69, 139; and neighboring sheriffs, 59–60; and oil booms, 33, 158–162; one-on-one physical challenges to, 6–7, 11, 13–14, 20, 28–29, 52, 54–55, 68, 121, 127–129; political

campaigns of, 20–42; and reform of
"wide open" county, 27–33, 67,
140–62; regulated by state commis-
sions, TCLOS, and TJSC, 208–11;
responds to private requests of
citizens, 3, 43, 49–51, 173–96; and
Texas Rangers, 29, 56–57, 32, 56–57,
79, 93, 99, 140, 145; and traffic laws,
58–59
Sheriffs' Association of Texas, 89, 132,
150, 211
*Sheriffs' Association of Texas Magazine
(Texas Lawman)*, 131–32, 135, 143,
162, 206
Sheriff's office: history of, 3–6
Shire-reeve, 4
Simmons, Lee, 31
Smith County, 60, 100, 206
Smithville, 26, 179
Somervell County, 32–33, 133, 199–200
Sonnichsen, C. L., 8–9
Spradley, J. H., 60, 68, 112, 122, 126
Springer, T. E., 62
Stanton, Tex., 163, 178
Steck, Marcus, 16, 20–21, 47, 54, 68
Stevens County, 159
Sterling, William W., 32, 159–60
Stock law, 183–84
Stout, Wesley, 73, 166
Stubblefield, C. F., 135
Strunk, Otto, 48
Surratt, Fannie Pearl, 142
Surratt, Hershal, 39, 142
Sweeten, Jess, 28–29, 34, 50, 53, 63–64,
100–101, 108, 113, 122, 126, 128,
132, 134, 156, 167–68, 191, 193, 210

Talley, J. S. ("Sid"), 177–78
Tarrant County, 45, 67, 85, 176, 208
Tarzan, Tex., 189
Teague, Delmus E., 123
Temple, Tex., 52
Terrell County, 68, 176

Texarkana, Tex., 144
Texas Commission on Law Enforce-
ment Officer Standards and
Education (TCLOS), 197, 208–209
Texas Department of Public Safety
(DPS), 205, 212–13
Texas Jail Standards Commission
(TJSC), 93, 197
Texas Liquor Control Board. *See*
Liquor Control Board (LCB)
Texas Rangers, 7, 10–13, 23, 28–29, 32,
56–57, 79, 93, 99, 101, 108, 140, 145,
158–62, 203–205, 213
Thompson, Clyde, 135–36
Thompson, John W., 157
Tindall, Nathan, 14–15, 36, 59, 69–70,
98–99
Tindall, Willie Earl, 173
Tittle, Ennis, 94
Tittle, John E., 49, 207
Titus County, 68
Traxler, Pete, 98
Trinidad, Tex., 28–29
Trinity County, 8–9, 32, 34, 57, 64–65,
102, 128–29, 141, 149, 164
Troup, Tex., 206
Tucker, Frank, 142
Turner, Ross C., 206
Tyler, Tex., 62, 100, 206
Tynes, N. J., 124

Upshur County, 192
U.S. Supreme Court: decisions
regarding law enforcement procedures, 208
Uvalde County, 94

Van Zandt County, 22
Vigilantes. *See* Sheriff, and local feuds

Waco, Tex., 204
Walbridge, Monroe, 68
Waldrip, Ben, 134

Walker County, 111
Waller County, 9
Walls, "Buck," 11
Walls, Eugene, 12–13
Walls, George, 11–13
Walls, Lopez, 13
Ward, Forrest, 16, 19
Ward County, 210–11
War On Drugs, 202–204
Washington County, 44, 123, 142–43
Wasson, Jim, 158
Wharton, Tex., 73, 163, 183, 206
Wharton County, 24, 36–37, 49, 51, 56,
    64, 67, 70–75, 85–86, 88–89, 94, 111,
    113, 115–20, 140–43, 163, 165,
    167–72, 175–76, 184, 205–206, 208,
    210
Whatley, George, 120
Wichita County, 155
Willard, Louis L., 65

Williamson County, 208
Wilson, Will, 146
Wilson County, 49, 78, 80
Winkler County, 68, 87, 159
Winsboro, Tex., 49
Wood County, 60
Wright, Bill, 159
Wright, E. A. ("Dogie"), 78, 80, 158
Wright, Glymer, 143
Wright, Harlon, 85
Wright, Michael B., 123
Wright, Will, 78, 120

Yamada, Joe, 98
Yeary, Frank, 94
Young, Roger, 33
Young County, 9

Zapalac, Lester, 144